HISTORIC BUILDINGS

Ann Arbor, Michigan

Second Edition

by
Marjorie Reade and Susan Wineberg

Acknowledgements

We warmly acknowledge the hours of volunteer time contributed by the Historic Buildings Book Committee which is made up of members of the Ann Arbor Historical Foundation, the Ann Arbor Historic District Commission, and other interested townspeople. The members are Rosemarion Blake, Barbara Carr, Mitzi Dickson, Jacquelyne Greenhut, Jean L. King, Kip Miller, David Pollock, Marjorie Reade, Stephen Rogers, Norman Tyler, and Susan Wineberg, with Louisa Pieper as project coordinator.

The revision of the first edition was written by Marjorie Reade. Susan Wineberg has done the research and writing on the buildings being added, with the exception of the Palmer House, which was written by Marjorie Reade. The book was edited by Mary Culver, Mitzi Dickson, Jean L. King, Louisa Pieper, and Grace Shackman.

Maps for this edition were created by Michael Klement. The cover illustration is taken from a painting by Brian Curtis, courtesy of the *Ann Arbor Observer*. SunGraphics has done the layout design.

Photographs and drawings for the guide book were provided by:
Ann Arbor Historic District Commission Reports: Downtown (Michael Klement), Washtenaw/Hill (Louisa Pieper), and Landmarks (Frances Wright).
Bentley Library: Ivory Collection, Sturgis Collection
Ecology Center
Lester Fader
Hobbs & Black Associates, Inc.
Balthazar Korab, Courtesy of William and Mary Palmer
Kip Miller
Robert R. Tisch
Susan Wineberg

We are grateful also for the cooperation of the staff of the Lawyer's Title Company who very kindly permitted the use of their records for research purposes, to the staff of the University of Michigan Bentley Library, and to Ray Steinbach and Terry Abrams, faculty members of the Photography Department of Washtenaw Community College, for their advice.

This project has been funded in part by grants from the Ann Arbor Area Community Foundation, the Ann Arbor Historical Foundation and with federal funds from the National Park Service, U.S. Department of the Interior as administered by the Bureau of History, Michigan Department of State. However, the contents and opinions do not necessarily reflect the views or policies of the U. S Department of the Interior or the Michigan Department of State, nor does the mention of trade names or commercial products constitute endorsement or recommendation by the U. S. Department of the Interior or the Michigan Department of State.

Table of Contents

Architecture is the most unselfish of arts, it belongs to passers-by, and every old house and garden... is a gift to the nation, to be enjoyed by future generations...

George Sitwell
On the Making of Gardens

This program received federal funds from the National Park Service. Regulations of the U.S. Department of the Interior strictly prohibit unlawful discrimination in departmental Federally Assisted Programs on the basis of race, color, national origin, age or handicap. While under Executive Directive 1979-4, the State of Michigan prohibits discrimination on the basis of race, color, creed, religion, age, sex, handicap, or national origin. Any person who believes he or she has been discriminated against in any program, activity, or facility operated by a recipient of Federal assistance should write to:
Director, Equal Opportunity Program, U.S. Department of the Interior
National Park Service, P.O. Box 37127, Washington, DC 20013-7127

Preface

The Ann Arbor Historic District Commission and the Ann Arbor Historical Foundation take pleasure in presenting this guidebook to the people of Ann Arbor. It is the second edition of *Historic Buildings, Ann Arbor, Michigan*, first published in 1977 and revised in 1986. We hope to promote greater awareness of local history by calling attention to some of the city's notable buildings.

In 1974, during the celebration of Ann Arbor's 150th birthday, the Sesquicentennial Commission and the Historic District Commission began an historic building recognition project. Incorporating the burr oak symbol from the City's seal, designed by John Morton of the Planning Department, local artists designed a marker to be placed on each recognized building.

A committee of architectural historians compiled a list of seventy-three buildings. Many of their choices had been cited in the 1973 *Ann Arbor Historic Architecture Survey, Downtown Area.* That survey graded approximately 500 pre-1940 buildings on the basis of their quality and rarity as specimens of a particular architectural style as well as their structural condition and alterations. Not wishing to ignore the rest of the city in this initial phase of the marker program, the committee selected the buildings in the Division Street Historic District (DSHD), the Liberty Street Historic District (LSHD), twelve representative buildings from the Old West Side, and a few well-known landmarks from the city's north and east sides.

Since the publication of the first edition of Historic Buildings, the Ann Arbor City Council has designated eleven additional historic districts, namely:

Ann Street Historic Block (ASHB)
Cobblestone Farm Historic District (CFHD)
East Liberty Historic Block (ELHB)
East William Historic District (EWHD)
Fourth/Ann Historic District (FAHD)
Main Street Historic District (MSHD)
Northern Brewery Historic District (NBHD)
Old Fourth Ward Historic District (OFW)
Old West Side Historic District (OWS)
State Street Historic District (SSHD)
Washtenaw Hill Historic District (WHHD)

A number of landmark buildings have also been designated as Individual Historic Properties (IHP). This edition has been expanded to include all of the landmarks, significant buildings from the new historic districts and a small selection of other notable buildings. It should be noted that buildings in historic districts are legally protected from demolition or incompatible alteration.

Additional criteria include:

> All buildings rated A in the survey of 1973. These are irreplaceable structures of outstanding value which form the nucleus of the architectural heritage of the city.
>
> All buildings listed in the National Register of Historic Places (NR), the official list of the nation's historic and architectural resources administered by the National Park Service under the Historic Sites Act of 1935 and the National Historic Preservation Act of 1966. Many of these buildings are also on the State Register of Historic Sites (SR).
>
> Buildings in the Historic American Buildings Survey (HABS), a collection of measured drawings, photographs and other data filed in the Library of Congress.
>
> University of Michigan buildings are not included in this book with the exception of three National Register sites (the President's House, the Detroit Observatory and Newberry Hall). Campus buildings form a distinct architectural community best described and documented as a whole.

Within each section of the book, buildings are grouped by geographic proximity although not in "loop" walking tours. It is important to stress that, among residences, only the Kempf House and Cobblestone Farm are open to the public. Other dwellings, described herein as components of the city's history, are recognized for the visual pleasure they afford passersby. Users of this guidebook are requested to respect the privacy of present-day owners and residents.

Building names are usually those of the original owners, following standard architectural nomenclature and the practice of the National Register. Names of later owners long associated with the buildings, or those of current occupants, are given in parentheses when helpful for identification (Kempf House, etc.).

Foreword

Ann Arbor Architecture

Like most cities, Ann Arbor is a cluster of visually distinct districts. It has a central commercial core surrounded by neighborhoods which are identifiable by the "flavor" or character of the buildings which fill them.

Most of the neighborhoods are residential, and each has a high degree of visual consistency. That is, styles of architecture are similar from building to building and block to block. This consistency results from a pattern of gradual growth outward from the center of town. In contrast to neighborhood areas surrounding it, Ann Arbor's downtown is characterized by architectural diversity as the product of years of growth and evolution. Growth has brought continual renewal of the built environment through replacement and remodeling of old buildings, producing a varied mix of building styles.

Because architecture is a cultural product, it reflects changes in its social and economic environment. Consequently, each historic period has a unique stylistic expression. The following brief summaries describe the physical characteristics and historic background of each style period important in Ann Arbor. Of course not all buildings can be readily categorized. Styles frequently overlap and there are no clear-cut starting and stopping dates for each period. One style often melts into the next.

GREEK REVIVAL (1830-60)

The earliest identifiable style in Ann Arbor is Greek Revival which was sweeping the country when the city was settled. It was therefore natural that the earliest buildings of any consequence would be built in the Greek Revival manner. The style began with a resurgence of European interest in ancient Greece during the middle of the eighteenth century. By the 1820s it had spread to America; use of classic forms was deemed particularly suited to the social and political system of the new nation. America had recently defended her independence in the War of 1812; modern Greece had cast off the yoke of Turkish rule, and citizens of both new nations felt a strong identification with the democratic ideals of ancient Greece. As the classical style spread, it was applied to every conceivable building

312 S. Division

type by adaptation from published designs. Over time, Greek Revival became a distinctly American architectural expression.

Greek Revival buildings are characterized by simple rectangular masses, low-pitched roofs, and classical details. Such detailing usually consists of squat-proportioned porch columns and pilasters (flat columns projecting from a wall surface), a pediment (triangular area above the porch), rectangular door and windows openings (no round or pointed arches), gable end returns, sidelights and transom (narrow windows on each side of the door and a horizontal window over it). The most common building materials, brick and wood, sometimes stuccoed, were used in structures ranging from pretentious porticoed mansions to small un-adorned cottages, and were almost always painted white.

Whereas Greek Revival buildings normally have gables on the front or street facade, many early examples of the style were really adaptations of the traditional eastern Colonial or Federal styles. A building of this type, while having Greek Revival features around its doorways or elsewhere, has a plan and orientation derived from the earlier periods. The street front is the broader dimension, the eave rather than the gable parallels the street, and there is a center doorway and hall.

GOTHIC REVIVAL (1845-75)

The Gothic Revival style overlapped the Greek Revival chronologically, although its peak of popularity occurred slightly later. It was in part a romantic reaction to the formalism of Greek Revival and the earlier Federal style architecture.

Based on medieval architectural forms, Gothic Revival was transplanted from England in the early 1840s. It flowered as a full-scale revival through the influence of pattern books published by important architects. Classic white forms of the Greek Revival were abandoned in favor of the picturesque forms and earth-tone colors of Gothic. Because the Gothic style was associated with ecclesiastical architecture (St. Andrews's Episcopal Church), its popularity was a manifestation of the wave of religious enthusiasm which swept this country at mid-century. Its use was deemed most appropriate for church and residential buildings.

The balanced order and formal restraint of Greek Revival were replaced by asymmetrical designs and picturesque arrangements of wings, porches, dormers, and gables. A perpendicular effect was achieved by steep roofs, tall chimneys and long pointed windows. Gable ends, dormers, roof edges, and porches were embellished with lacy decoration.

205 North Division

ITALIANATE (1855-80)

Like Gothic Revival, the Italianate style represents a search for historical precedents. The style was derived from domestic architecture of the Italian Renaissance. It was a mode which competed with Gothic and, in Ann Arbor at least, gained the greater popularity.

Italianate houses typically featured low-pitched roofs, projecting eaves with ornamental brackets, and round-arched doors and windows. Buildings of this style sometimes have Greek Revival details, especially entrances with sidelights and transoms, evidence of the reluctance of builders to completely abandon classical elements. A house of this style with a square or rectangular floor plan is often called an "Italianate cube" while an "L" or "T" shaped plan and a square tower placed in one of the inner corners is known as an Italian Villa (1115 Woodlawn). A variation of the

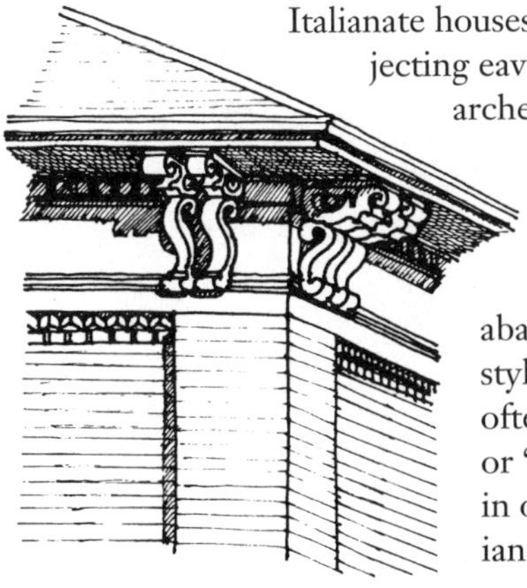

716 North Fifth Avenue

Villa style was sometimes used for non-domestic architecture (219 East Huron).

Italianate commercial facades are characterized by tall, narrow window openings with ornamental flat or arched lintels, by bracketed cornices, and by varying planes of brick in detailed corbeling. Ground floor shops usually maximized glass areas, expressing the commercialism of the period (111 South Fourth Avenue, 114-22 West Liberty).

VICTORIAN ECLECTIC (1865-95)

219 East Washington

Prior to the Civil War, individual buildings conformed to a single style — Greek, Gothic, or Italian, for example. Later, these and other styles were often combined in the same building, resulting in what has come to be called Victorian Eclectic. The term is most often applied to commercial buildings, since they were embellished in the most eclectic manner. The development of cast iron as a practical building material was an outgrowth of war technology. More flexible than carved stone, it could be cast in an endless variety of shapes and ornamental designs. Since the original molds could be used again and again, items such as columns, cornices, window arches, ornamental tracery, and even entire facades could be produced inexpensively in any quantity. The same was true of pressed sheet metal, whose dies could be reused indefinitely. Even the smallest town could afford such ornamentation, and conditions were suitable for the flowering of the lavish ornamental motifs which we associate with the Victorian era.

QUEEN ANNE (1875-1900)

Despite its name, this style recalls the building elements of Elizabethan and Jacobean England (c.1550-1625), not those of Queen Anne's time (early 1700s). The term is confusing because of the great adaptation it underwent in this country: its characteristic English articulation in tile and masonry was usually translated in America into wood frame construction with much decorative woodwork. Queen Anne was a residential style, the product of advances in household engineering in the last quarter of the nineteenth century. Heating, ventilation, lighting, and sanitary facilities were greatly improved, permitting large, flowing interior spaces and larger window areas (which were often embellished with patterns in stained glass). Pattern books and magazines with standard plans and details fostered adaptation of the style, resulting in an indigenous American expression.

The style is characterized by light wood-frame construction, irregularity in floor plan and roof line, steep-pitched roofs, projecting bays, towers, and turrets, beveled corners, and a variety of decorative ornaments, textures, and colors. Houses were painted in two or three contrasting colors: natural hues such as sumac red, olive, brown, and gold. Repetition of small decorative elements, — spindles, scroll work, fretwork, shingles, clapboards — produced effects of contrasting patterns and textures in large, sweeping areas.

1014 Cornwell Place

Foreword

RICHARDSONIAN ROMANESQUE (1880-99)

100 North State Street

Another manifestation of Victorian romanticism, as evidenced by the borrowing of Romanesque forms of the Middle Ages, this style developed as a significant expression with integrity of form and function. The original adaptation and evolution of the forms was inspired by Boston architect Henry Hobson Richardson (1838 -86). After Richardson's lifetime the style gained popularity and continued to spread, becoming widely known as "Richardsonian Romanesque." It is primarily a commercial and institutional style, characterized by massiveness and texture in the use of brickwork and rusticated stonework. Walls are thick, with window and door openings deeply recessed, creating strong contrasts of sun and shadow on exteriors. Large, articulated, round-arched window and door openings are typical.

SHINGLE STYLE (1890-1910)

Shingle style is a graceful refinement of Queen Anne design whose elements often are integrally combined with Richardsonian Romanesque. Both are characterized by large, sweeping, textured surfaces, Richardsonian Romanesque most often in rusticated stonework and the Shingle style, as the name suggests, in wood shingles. The great strength of the Shingle style is its simplicity and lack of applied decoration, qualities which were later reflected in modern designs of the Bauhaus and Frank Lloyd Wright.

730 Tappan

BEAUX ARTS CLASSIC (1900-30)

220 N. Main St.

The Beaux Arts Classic style represented a new sense of formal order. By the end of the nineteenth century, the romantic attachment to picturesque effects was waning. Architects developed a renewed interest in classical simplicity, symmetry, and well proportioned restraint. The name Beaux Arts Classic comes from the Ecole des Beaux Arts in Paris, the prestigious center of architectural education at the time. The style was by no means universally popular. It was one of several styles embraced in this period, collectively described as eclectic, meaning that they looked to history for inspiration. Beaux Arts Classic, an extreme reaction to the frenzied concoctions of the Victorian age, was best adapted to commercial and institutional structures of great size and solemn function. Beaux Arts Classic buildings possess formal symmetry, rectilinear walls and details, strong horizontal exterior lines, and elaborately decorative detail on plain backgrounds. Roof forms are submerged behind facades.

ART DECO (1910-40)

106 N. Fourth Avenue

The 1920s represented a period of optimism and growth following "the war to end wars." Technological progress, given momentum by war, was beginning to reach the consumer. A spirit of modernity prevailed; in architecture this spirit rejected the historicism of previous designs. The Exposition des Arts Decoratifs held in Paris in 1925 supplied both the impetus for a new approach to design and the name which describes it. Art Deco is also known as"Modernistic."

RICHARD NEUMANN

Main Street looking North from Liberty at the turn of the century

Hose Co. #3, September 17, 1906

Introduction

Downtown

The oldest photographs of downtown Ann Arbor show a generation of frame and brick commercial buildings from the 1830s and 1840s, with covered sidewalks giving the town a frontier look. As the town grew and prospered, the plain clapboard stores, often flimsy, with few classic details, were demolished to make way for bigger structures. Houses lined streets that are today commercial: Ashley (then called Second Street), First, Washington and Liberty. Main and Huron crossing at the Courthouse Square were the chief business streets of the town. A few downtown residences from Ann Arbor's pre-University period survive today —The George Corselius House (1830s), 317 Ann Street, and the John W. Maynard House (1838), 218 North Division, are included in this book.

The second generation of commercial buildings were the three-story Italianate brick structures with round-arched windows erected around the time of the Civil War (Dr. Chase's Steam Printing House — 1864, the Schaeberle buildings — late 1860s, the Philip Bach Building and the Bank Block — 1867, the Heinrich Building — 1868, and the Hoban Block — 1871). These were followed by later Italianate commercial buildings, similar in style but more ornate (Walker Brothers Building — 1886, Germania Hotel — 1886), that still give downtown its character today.

Ann Arbor was the main trading center for prosperous Washtenaw County. As the town's business district expanded, the side streets filled in. Houses with sizable yards were replaced by blocks of brick commercial buildings. Many of the newer buildings erected in the 1880s and 1890s varied the standard Victorian commercial architecture established earlier with decorative metal trim or pressed brick.

East of Division Street the University of Michigan campus dominated development. The first University buildings were erected in 1841 on a donated 40-acre field at the edge of town. For many decades that campus alone, the "Diag," was the University. It contained professors' homes, student dormitories, and classrooms. An expanding faculty and President Tappan's 1854 decree closing the dormitories produced a district of professors' homes and student boarding houses between the campus and Main Street. Before home delivery of mail was instituted in 1886, it had to be picked up at the post office on Main Street, so most people wanted to live near downtown. From 1843 to the 1890s distinguished residences of diverse architectural styles were erected on or near Division Street. Other prominent houses were built on Main Street, Fourth and Fifth Avenues south of

Introduction

Firemen's Hall circa 1882-1895

William Street, mostly by business people. Churches tended to build in or near prestigious residential areas while student-oriented religious organizations were built close to campus.

Compared with the frankly ostentatious showplaces of the well-to-do in Michigan lumbering towns and industrial centers, Ann Arbor's architecture was marked by restraint — possibly as a result of academic influence. Nevertheless, some splendid Victorian public buildings were erected in Ann Arbor: the second Courthouse (1878), the Beal Block Post Office (1883) and the firehouse (1882-83). Of these, only the firehouse remains today.

After 1890 development shifted eastward, stimulated by expanding University enrollment, home mail delivery, and the new Ann Arbor Street Railway which ran from Main Street up William, around the campus and out to Burns Park. State Street began to develop as a commercial area. The affluent gradually moved away from downtown, commuting to work by streetcar and automobile. Downtown dwellings became tenant housing, no longer owner-occupied; large single-family houses were divided into apartments. Student housing was built south of campus, with middle-income and working-class housing between Packard and State. The West Side, new North Side, and Northwest area became densely settled.

An increasingly complex local economy produced more agents, lawyers, and businessmen, all of whom demanded office space. New office buildings were erected, beginning in 1906 with the Glazier Building (now Society Bank) and culminating in the soaring First National Building in 1929. State Street became a prestigious shopping area, finally anchored by the Nickels Arcade which was built in 1915. Between State and Main, commercial structures were replacing old houses: the Zwerdling/Darling Block and the Michigan Bell Telephone Building exemplify this trend.

After World War I the automobile brought drastic changes to Ann Arbor. Landmark buildings were demolished for service stations and parking lots.

North

Remnants of village life in frontier Michigan abound on the North Side. In 1832 when businessman and speculator Anson Brown established a commercial center on Broadway near the river, he hoped it would rival and outshine the older settlement (1824) on the hill at Main and Huron Streets. Brown erected two substantial brick business blocks in "Lower Town." The Anson Brown building at 1001 Broadway still stands. With judicious application of political pressure, Brown succeeded in relocating the post office to Broadway, a significant coup. Frontier Ann Arborites eagerly awaited mail from distant friends and relatives, and residents had to fetch it in person from the post office. In 1834 Brown died of cholera, and the post office returned to the upper village. Lower Town's business district entered a long period of stagnation, but houses continued to be built on the hills of Broadway, Traver, and Pontiac Trail. Since they were not threatened by development pressures, most of them still remain, ranging in size from tiny Greek Revival houses to impressive residences like the Lund House at 1324 Pontiac Trail.

East

The area south and east of campus was a district of country residences, orchards, and farms until the 1890s when the street railway was extended to the Fair Grounds (now Burns Park). In 1860 Professor Frieze built a stone house in the forest at Washtenaw near Hill. Across the street was J. D. Baldwin's stuccoed villa (1848), surrounded by prize apple and peach orchards. Pharmacist Christian Eberbach erected an imposing Italianate villa (1869) on his country estate on Packard, now off Woodlawn. Dwellings on more distant farms included the Benajah Ticknor House (1844), the Anderson House (1846), and the Bell-Spaulding House (1854).

To provide housing for the growing University student body, many of the grander residences in town near campus were converted to boarding houses. As the early farms and orchards were gradually platted and developed, Washtenaw Avenue became a fashionable area of elegant homes with spacious gardens, and the east side turned into the residential area for the wealthier Ann Arbor families. Later fraternities and sororities bought up many of the large houses and converted or replaced them.

West

Old timers know the West Side as "the old Second Ward," harking back to a time when ward boundaries determined elementary school districts and social networks. The neighborhood was the center of a German settlement that began in 1830 and grew rapidly as several waves of immigrants came to this country between 1830 and 1890. Family names—Gott, Staeb, Mann, Allmendinger—reflect this ethnic background.

When town and gown differences ran deep in Ann Arbor, the West Side was the "town" side. Most breadwinners were craftsmen and tradesmen; many worked in or near the neighborhood, in workshops, at the brewery and adjacent furniture factory on Fourth Street, the mill on First Street, the vinegar works on Liberty, or the organ factory on First Street at Washington. Liberty and West Huron streets contain both the oldest and the most fashionable West Side dwellings. Most of the near West Side was developed between 1890 and 1915. Newer areas out toward Crest and Pauline consist of homes built after World War I.

The typical West Side streetscape has a special visual rhythm. Frame houses face peaked gables to the street, and airy front porches lend shaded depth to simple facades. Differences in decorative trim, size, and landscaping give a variety and interest to similar house forms. In large part these qualities still exist today, despite interruptions caused by apartment house development and porch remodeling.

The Old West Side Association emerged from a crisis in 1967 when a planned development of mixed medium- and high-density housing was proposed for an entire block of First Street between Madison and Jefferson. First Street residents met to discuss the project and began to realize how much they valued their older neighborhood's existing qualities. They ultimately opposed the project.

Soon the Old West Side Association was incorporated in order to protect the area from Pauline Street to Huron, extending from the Ann Arbor Railroad tracks out to Crest. A regular newsletter was (and is) published, and a analysis of the neighborhood structures was begun. This analysis formed the basis of an environmental survey, published in book form in 1971 (Old West Side, Ann Arbor, Michigan. A Report on the Environmental Survey of a Neighborhood).

The survey results were used in a successful application for inclusion in the National Register of Historic Places. The Old West Side (OWS) was the first neighborhood of architecturally modest houses to be entered on the Register for its total environmental qualities.

List of Buildings

Note: Buildings are numbered in alphabetical order by address. The letters following each indicates its section in the book: (D)=Downtown, (N)=North, (E)=East, (W)=West

List of Buildings

List of Buildings

ANN ARBOR HISTORIC BUILDING

DOWNTOWN

Ann Arbor

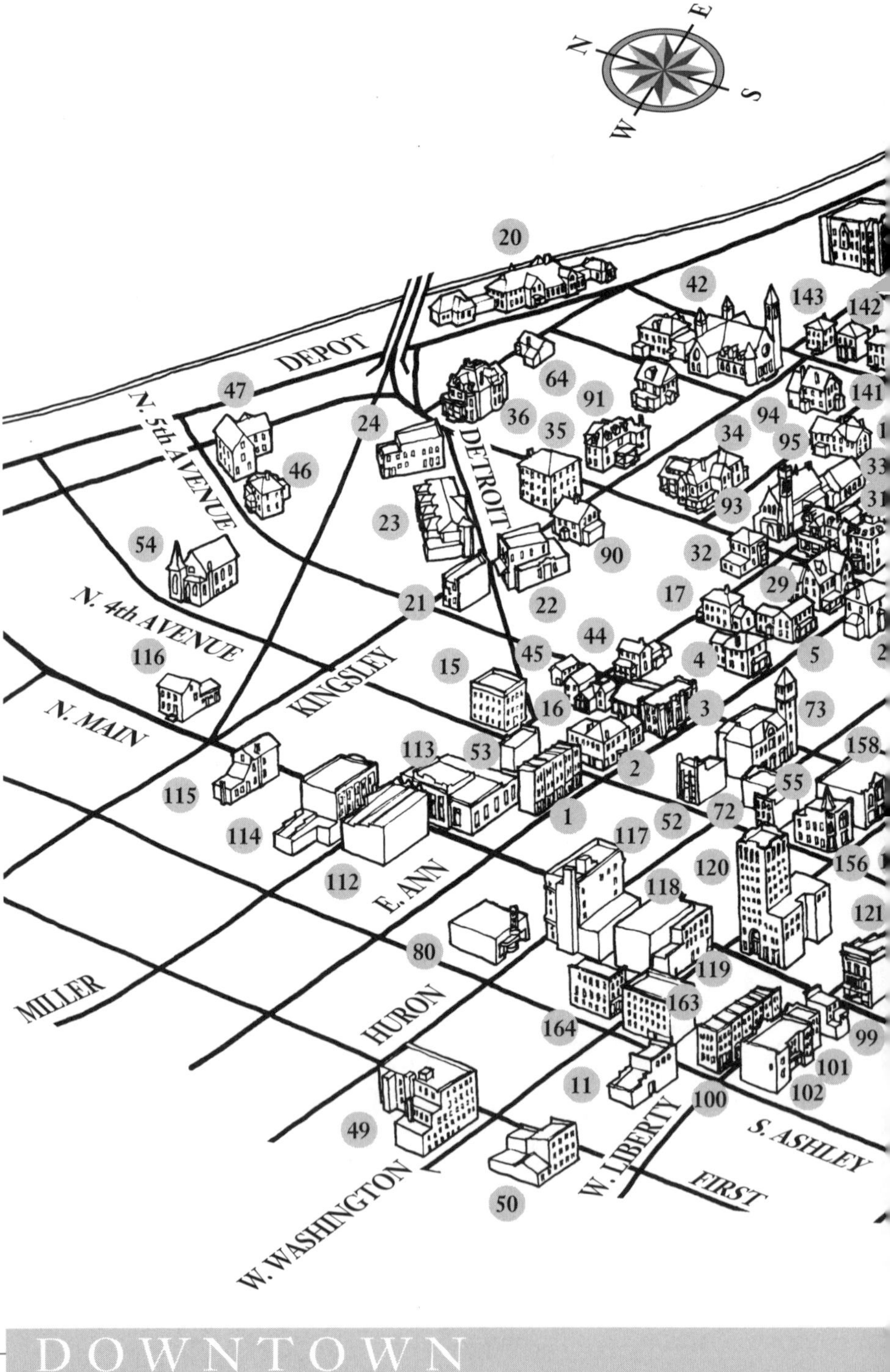

DOWNTOWN

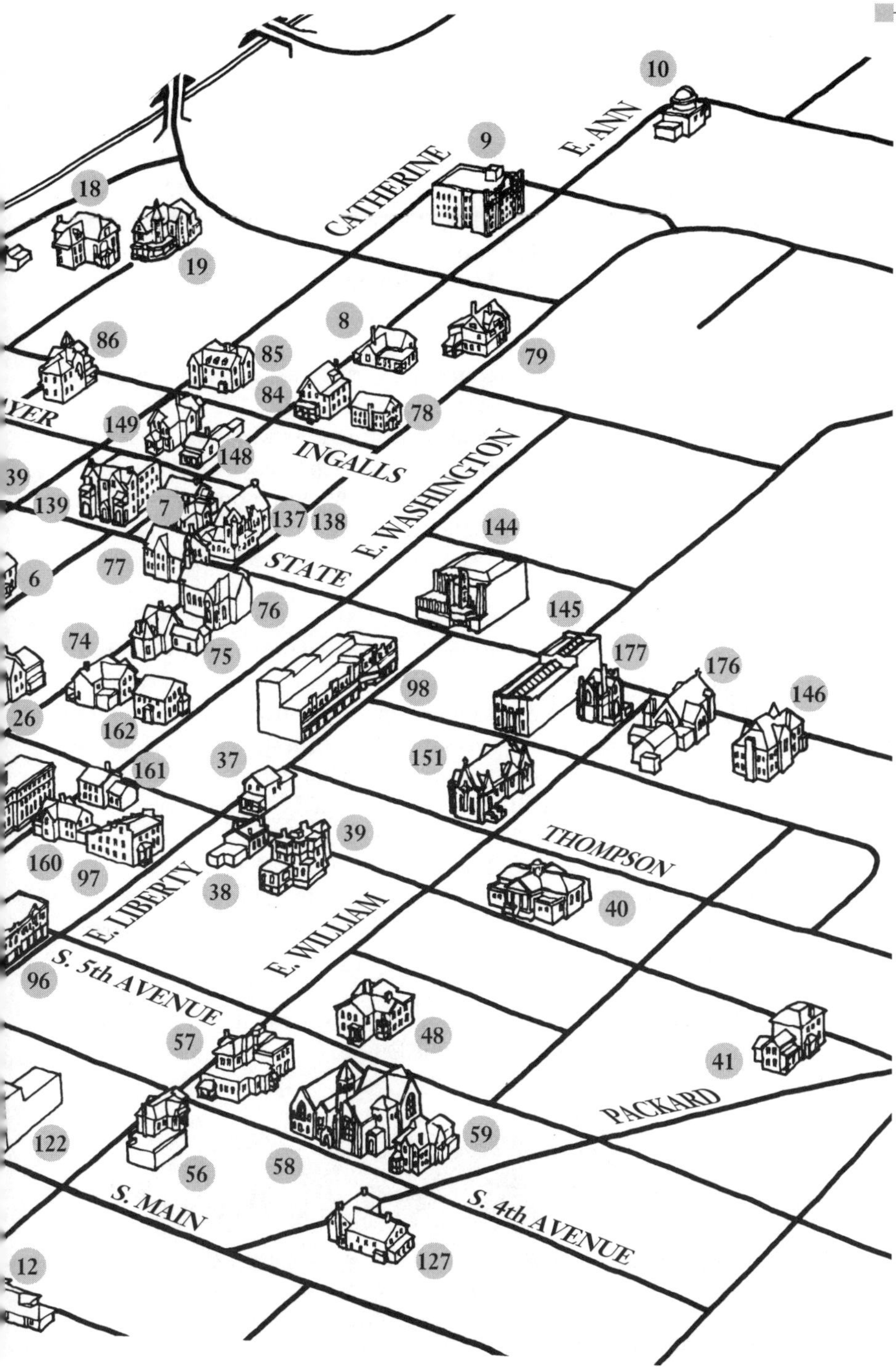
10
E. ANN
9
CATHERINE
18
19
8
86
85
84
79
78
149
148
INGALLS
E. WASHINGTON
39
139
7
137
138
144
STATE
6
77
76
145
74
75
177
176
146
98
26
162
151
37
161
39
THOMPSON
160
97
38
E. LIBERTY
E. WILLIAM
40
96
S. 5th AVENUE
57
48
41
PACKARD
122
59
56
58
S. MAIN
S. 4th AVENUE
127
12

DOWNTOWN

1

109-119 East Ann Street

Hoban Block

1871

Prior to the Civil War, tailors and grocers were located in this block, but the headline in the December 30, 1870 issue of the *Michigan Argus* "Fire on Rotten Row" reveals its true character at the time. The paper reported that the buildings, owned by Mrs. Hoban, were a total loss. By March of 1871, however, the *Peninsular Courier* reported that ground had been broken for a new building and by the summer of that year it was completed. The 1881 *History of Washtenaw County* commented that Mrs. Hoban had "built a substantial business on Ann Street in 1871 at a cost of several thousand dollars."

It was the epitome of commercial architecture at the time: a row of almost identical brick storefronts in the Italianate commercial style. Three stories high, the first floor contained storefronts with large glass windows, while the second and third floors were office and residential. Characteristic of the style are the brick arched windows with round tops on the third floor and segmental arches on the second. Except for the building at 109, brick corbeling unites the facades of all six of these storefronts. At one time a bracketed cornice united them as well.

The block contained the usual collection of businesses: restaurants, groceries, and butcher shops. But it also had more than its share of saloons and "disreputable" establishments. In 1898 a local newspaper published a map showing the saloons that were corrupting the University of Michigan students were all clustered in the block north of the courthouse. Just around the corner from the Hoban Block was "Ann Arbor's Official Bawdy House."

Though the unsavory character of the area persisted, the "Ann Street Block" was also known for its blues bars in the 1960s and 1970s. Clint's Club was a popular meeting place for African-Americans who supported the block's bars, pool halls, and barber shops.

In the mid-1980s, owner Peter Bilakos began to restore the storefronts individually and his legal offices now occupy the first floor of one of them.
FAHD

Louisa Pieper

201 East Ann Street

Washtenaw Bank

1836

Kip Miller

In the 1830s, with land sales booming the Michigan Territory needed banks. The liberal banking laws permitted banks to be founded with very little capital, so in 1835 a group of local men formed the Bank of Washtenaw and built this Greek Revival building to house their banking rooms. When the banking system of the United States collapsed in the Panic of 1837, the Bank of Washtenaw went under and the building stood empty for almost a decade. In 1847 the property was finally sold to local businessman Volney Chapin who converted it to a residence. He and his wife Chloe made it their home for over 25 years. During that time it became a genteel showplace surrounded by exotic catalpa trees and a garden whose rose-bordered paths reached all the way to Catherine Street.

The original building is stucco over brick, scored to resemble stone, a common conceit of many Greek Revival houses of this period (see 28, 37, 75, 131, and 143). Though it has been enlarged to the west, one can still spot the Greek Revival detailing in the Ann Street entryway with simple Doric columns supporting a dentillated entablature. Hinges for the once massive shutters which flanked the windows are still visible as well.

By the 1890s the area had become more commercial. The house became the Arlington Hotel, later renamed the Catalpa Hotel after those famous trees. Joe Parker's tavern occupied the corner commercial space from 1913 until 1920, when Prohibition drove it out of business. Joe Parker's and other saloons have been immortalized in a University of Michigan college song that reminisces about going "back to Joe's and the Orient (another saloon) back to all the money I spent." Shortly after the tavern closed, the Ann Arbor Chamber of Commerce bought the building, but one can still see the name "Joe" spelled out in tile in the corner of the present bookstore.

The Chamber eventually sold the property to Christ Bilakos in 1942. He renamed it the Peters Hotel after his son and the property is still owned by this family. The building now houses a variety of eclectic businesses.

FAHD

3

223 East Ann Street

Ann Arbor Armory

1911

In 1910 the passage of a new state law enabled local communities to house military units. Those interested in military affairs in Ann Arbor wasted no time in organizing a fund drive to build an armory, only the third to be built in Michigan under the new law. The city donated the lot at the corner of Ann and North Fifth Avenue. The building was built by the Koch Brothers and completed in 1911 at a total cost of $25,000.

It housed a drill room 80 feet square, a reading room, billiard room, the captain's office, orderly rooms, locker rooms, an indoor shooting range, and a kitchen in the basement. Today it is the home base for the Company D 156 Signal Battalion.

The style is often referred to as "Collegiate Gothic" but might more appropriately be called "Military Gothic" due to its common use for armories. The smooth stone foundations and stone quoins bordering the windows, the end "turrets" and the two octagonal towers which flank the entrance on Ann Street, make the whole resemble a medieval fortress.

Over the years the Armory has served as more than a military staging area. Its large drillroom has been rented for weddings, dances, and gospel revivals. In the 1930s dances with Red Ritz' Band were held here every Friday and Saturday night. In the spring of 1975 the room was the site of the election-night ballot count in Ann Arbor's famous preferential election in which Albert E.Wheeler was elected Ann Arbor's first African-American mayor.

Membership in the battalion is 500 today, down from a high of 1000 men and women. The Guard plans to move soon to the new Washtenaw Armory complex and new uses for the old Armory are now under discussion.

OFW

Louisa Pieper

311 East Ann Street

James F. Royce House

1866

James F. Royce, an early pioneer of Washtenaw County, built this pristine example of an "Italianate cube" in 1866. Royce came to Ann Arbor from Connecticut in 1830 as a skilled cabinet maker and began a chair-making business which lasted for several decades. He later operated a carriage factory and clerked for Philip Bach, his son-in-law. Royce was 61 years old when he built this house and Bach may have paid for it as a form of "social security" for his aging father-in-law.

Kip Miller

The house exhibits typical features of the Italianate Cube style: a low, hipped roof with paired brackets under the wide eaves, a symmetrical arrangement of windows and doors, and ornamental sawn woodwork or "gingerbread" on the front and side porches. Thin chamfered porch posts with no railings are also typical of this style, though the still-working pairs of French doors and louvered shutters are very unusual in Ann Arbor. What is most remarkable is that almost no changes have been made to this house since its construction. Even the windows still have their original blown glass.

Mrs. Royce's will gives us an idea of how this house was furnished in the 1880s. She left her "large lamp with glass pendants" to Philip Bach and "a small marble top stand" to his wife, while other members of the Bach family received her mahogany sofa covered with hair cloth. The wife of the minister of the Baptist Church received her "gold bowed glasses as a memento of my love and respect for her."

Following Mrs. Royce's death, the house was sold to two unmarried sisters, Harriet and Electa Knight, daughters of another Washtenaw County pioneer. They lived here and rented rooms to various relatives attending Ann Arbor High School. Later they rented rooms to doctors and nurses working at the hospitals nearby. By the 1920s many upper and middle class people moved out of the Old Fourth Ward into Burns Park and other newer subdivisions. The house remained a single-family dwelling until the 1960s. Since then it has been rented as apartments.

OFW

5

317 East Ann Street

George Corselius House

Late 1820s

"Mother told me we lived in it in 1838, and boarded the engineers who were laying out the Michigan Central Railroad," Cornelia Corselius wrote of this simple dwelling in 1909. An early deed indicates that it was occupied by a Dr. Randall in 1834, but it may actually have been built by Sylvester or Willard Mills in 1829-30.

Kip Miller

It may well be the oldest remaining home in Ann Arbor. Originally a typical "I-house," that is, with gables to the side, at least two rooms in length, one room deep, and two full stories in height (as defined in *Folk Housing*, by Fred B. Kniffen), the residence long ago became a square with an ell. The walls were built ten inches thick, and as late as 1937, the first floor joists were still bark covered. Professor Emil Lorch noted then that the triangular field of the end gables formerly had half elliptical make-believe fan lights. The pilastered casing of the entrance dates from 1938 when the house was remodeled.

What is known is that it was the home of pioneer journalist George Corselius, who arrived in 1829 to become editor of the *Western Emigrant*, the first newspaper in Washtenaw County. The *Emigrant* was owned by John Allen and Samuel W. Dexter, key figures in the early development of Washtenaw County and the Michigan Territory. While editor of the paper, Corselius joined other stockholders to start the county's first lending library, a short-lived enterprise.

Corselius married Clementia Cardell of Bennington, Vermont. An early Ann Arbor historian wrote that Corselius was descended from French barons and his wife from Norman kings, describing him as "an ungainly figure, but with a spiritual symmetry; a gentle and benevolent disposition." Later, frail in health and struggling in his profession, he was employed by the University of Michigan to catalogue its library. To better his fortune and to cure his tuberculosis, he joined the forty-niners, starting for California by the Panama route. He turned back at Panama, only to die at sea. Cornelia, the only one of his four children to remain in Ann Arbor, taught school for many years, and wrote a book of children's stories, some with local settings.

HABS, DSHD

511 East Ann Street

Willcoxson-Easton House

6

Late 1820s

This simple white clapboard house has several aspects commonly found in the Eastern U.S.: its orientation with the long side of the house facing the street, the symmetrical arrangement of windows around a center door, and the general massing.

Its exact age and origin cannot be documented since the house was moved to this location by 1866. It may be the house built by attorney Gideon Willcoxson who arrived in Ann Arbor in 1824 and purchased ten acres from John Allen — what is now the area bounded by Huron, State, Catherine, and Division Streets. Willcoxson went back East but then returned to Ann Arbor in 1827 to practice law and accept an appointment as Washtenaw County Prosecuting Attorney from Governor Cass.

Willcoxson died three years later, leaving the property to fellow attorney George Jewett to administer for his children until they came of age. Jewett occupied the house for a number of years until the heirs — John and James Willcoxson, Amelia Ormsby, Sarah Pease, and Mary Jane Maynard —sold the property to George Sedgewick who then sold it to Mary Jane's husband, John W. Maynard. Maynard platted and subdivided the property in 1858 and named this part of it Willcoxson's Addition. Dr. Ebenezer Wells and his wife Margaret purchased four of the lots to build their magnificent brick house on Division Street (see 30). The $1,700 Charles Easton paid for the lot (compared to the $325 price of the lot next door) hints that the house may have already been on the lot.

The low picket fence, designed and built by the current owners, and the small front garden of perennials, rose bushes, and peonies accentuate the simple lines and original six-over-six windows of the house. The rear addition may have been moved from a larger house of similar design that stood to the east until after 1900.

Susan Wineberg

Widdicombe and Martha Schmidt purchased the house in 1975, and have restored much of it inside and out, using great care in replacing rotted siding with poplar and in preserving the original hand-blown glass of the windows.

ASHB

7

712 East Ann Street

Moses and Jane Gunn House

1851

This handsome Greek Revival structure with its two-story pedimented portico is often overlooked because of its cramped location. When the house was completed in 1851, however, it stood on a large landscaped lot at the southeast corner of State and Ann Streets. It was purchased by Dr. Moses Gunn, a newly hired Professor of Anatomy and Surgery at the just-opened University of Michigan Medical School.

Gunn's wife Jane, in a memoir published in 1889 after his death, noted that when they "purchased a roomy house nearly completed," the long pillars in the front "suggested a style of Grecian architecture now almost obsolete." Born in East Bloomfield, New York, Moses Gunn entered Geneva Medical College in 1844. After receiving his medical degree in 1846, he travelled to Ann Arbor where he joined with Silas Douglass and Abram Sager to open a private medical school in the Washtenaw County Courthouse. In 1850 he was appointed to his positions in the University Medical School where he worked for the next 13 years. Though a bit aristocratic, he was very much respected and today two portraits of him hang in the present University Hospital. A student described him as a "...striking figure of a man with an erect military carriage, clad in a snug-fitting, carefully buttoned-up black frock coat... who frequently raised his gold-rimmed eyeglasses to note the architectural peculiarities of each house he approached... then the eyeglasses were allowed to swing from their long gold chain to be quickly readjusted should anything seem worthy of attention"

The house is a fairly unusual example of the domestic Greek Revival in the Midwest. Built entirely of wood, it has a full pediment supported by four very tall two-story columns. These columns are square, not round and fluted as are those on more high style examples (see 28). It also has "shouldered" or "eared" trim around the doors and windows, a detail that is repeated on the interior.

The residence of a former governor of Michigan, Alpheus Felch, stood just to the south of this house on State Street. The two houses were reputed to be almost identical, designed by local builder Andrew DeForest (see 32). They must have made a spectacular impression on people entering the city coming up State Street from the railroad depot on their way to campus.

Although Gunn remained a faculty member until the 1860s, he left Ann Arbor in 1854 for Detroit where he could find more patients for his private practice. The house was sold to Richard Hooper, owner of the city's oldest brewery. The Hooper sons continued to live in the house after their father's death in 1866 until the Depression of 1873 drove them and many other brewers out of business.

CONTINUED on next page

The house was then empty until William H. Payne bought it in 1883. Payne was a new professor at the University of Michigan teaching a new subject: the science and art of teaching. He pioneered what later became the University of Michigan School of Education. He lived in the house only four years, but his diaries about his life in Ann Arbor, dictated to his wife many years later in 1901, reveal his interest in this house. He noted that the house was believed by the townspeople to be haunted by the ghost of a Hooper who had committed suicide. The oldest known photograph of the house, probably from 1915, comes from Payne's papers at the Bentley Library.

By the 1890s the neighborhood was no longer fashionable and the house became a rental, though it had the same owner for many years and was never divided up into apartments. In 1898 it was moved to the rear of its original lot, its orientation was changed to face Ann Street, and three newer houses constructed where it had been. Some of the earliest tenants included the well-known librarian Nellie Loving, who lived here with her mother for a short while.

Dr. David James, a respected orthodontist, and his wife Naomi, an interior decorator, purchased the house and lovingly restored it while they raised their two children here. In 1986 Mrs. James received a preservation award from the Ann Arbor Historic District Commission but by 1987 was forced to sell the house due to illness. The new owners, Lars Bjorn and Susan Wineberg, continue to maintain this historic structure and recently added a classical "deck" above the rear kitchen wing which is very much in keeping with the classical facade.

Louisa Pieper

OFW

8

920 East Ann Street

Keating Family House

Circa 1865

This nice example of a vernacular "upright and wing" (a house form with both front and side sections) was first occupied by the Keating family around 1868, although a smaller house appears on maps as early as 1866. The property jumped in value in 1873 which may be when the home was enlarged to its current size.

Perhaps this was due to the success of the 1872 *Ann Arbor City Directory*, compiled and published by John Keating with James Cole. That directory lists John living here with his brothers Thomas J., a cigar maker, and Timothy, who was actually the owner of record by 1873. Timothy was a mason who did the stonework for the first St. Thomas School, yet he lived in an entirely wooden house with a porch of thin chamfered columns and lacy gingerbread common to houses built in the 1860s.

Of all the Keating residents, John was probably the most well known as the publisher of a professional medical journal, *The Physician and Surgeon*, from 1879-1915. This journal, under the associated editorship of Keating and several University of Michigan faculty members, had a national circulation.

Although John Keating later moved to a house of his own on Kingsley Street, the Ann Street house continued to be occupied by members of Timothy Keating's family throughout the 19th and 20th centuries. Like most of their Irish neighbors, they were members of the St. Thomas parish and are buried in a family plot in the St. Thomas cemetery. The last surviving descendant of Thomas Keating lived in the house until 1971. It is now a rental property but still maintains its quiet dignity on its large, well-landscaped site.

OFW

Kip Miller

1127 East Ann Street

Planada Apartments

9

1929

After World War I, student enrollments at the University of Michigan increased dramatically, putting a strain on available rental housing. In addition, with the completion of the new University Hospital in 1925, more housing units were needed nearby for the personnel associated with this huge enterprise. As a result, a type of apartment building more commonly associated with larger urban areas such as Detroit and Chicago was constructed in Ann Arbor.

Kip Miller

Like the others in the area, the Planada is in one of the revival styles popular in the 1920s. As the name suggests, the yellow-brick building has a Spanish Revival flavor, from the red clay roof tiles decorating the front roof line with a shaped stone pediment in the center, the wrought iron balconies, twisted stone columns and various pointed window arches, to the small colored tiles in the entry foyer and the charming set of murals on the ceiling depicting various rustic scenes in pastels of pinks and greens. It is almost a pastiche of its period, with every window having a different hood shape, material and form. Like all apartment buildings of this era, it used steel casement windows with many panes of glass. Similarities between this building and buildings in Detroit's Palmer Park suggest it might have been designed by a Detroit architect.

The first occupants were predictably professionals associated with the hospital: teachers, nurses and bacteriologists. Others were students, insurance agents and small business managers. All were taking advantage of the latest in interior design, which usually included Pullman or Murphy kitchens and sometimes Murphy beds.

Many fondly remember this building and make an effort to drive by it on their visits to Ann Arbor. It was one of the many buildings owned by the Lueck family (see 153) which meant it was kept in good repair and rented at a reasonable price.

1308 East Ann Street

10

Detroit Observatory

1854

Frances Wright

Built in 1854, and called, until 1931, the Detroit Observatory, this building housed the first large telescope constructed in the United States, for years the third largest refractor in the world. The twelve and one-half inch telescope was made by Henry Fitz of New York, who held it as a matter of both personal and patriotic pride that he, an American locksmith and inventor untrained in optics, had invented his own process for making the complex and difficult achromatic lens, and that he was able to manufacture telescopes to compete with those of European make. The meridian circle, still intact, was used to compute time from observations of stars crossing the meridian. A special telegraph wire connected the Observatory with the Ann Arbor depot of the Michigan Central Railroad, which bought time readings to set its schedules.

The Observatory itself is a monument to the broad vision and indefatigable fund raising efforts of University President Henry Philip Tappan, who suggested the project to Henry Nelson Walker, a prominent Detroit lawyer with iron mine and railroad interests. Walker, who initiated and guaranteed construction, took an active part in fund raising and in choosing the site. He engaged George Bird to plan and superintend the building. A brass plate on the meridian circle, for which Walker was the major contributor, indicates that it was named in his honor.

"I cannot speak of the Observatory without emotion," Tappan wrote. "No one will deny that it was a creation of my own." Tappan, eager to advance the science of astronomy at the University of Michigan, spent weeks in Europe purchasing scientific equipment, and engaged Dr. Franz Brunnow to come from the Berlin Royal Observatory to direct the work here.

The center section of this Italianate building is thirty-three feet square, surmounted by a revolving dome twenty-one feet in diameter. The side wings are each twelve by twenty-nine feet. Later classroom and office additions were razed in1954 and 1976, leaving the original edifice intact.

NR, IHP

210 South Ashley Street

Hertler Brothers

1899/1912

Back when the horse was king of the road, Ashley Street was lined with blacksmith shops, feed barns, and livery stables. Farmers drove into town on Saturdays and took their hungry horses to barns like Hertler's where horses were fed for ten cents a day. The old drive-through barn, built in 1912 of rock-faced brick and covered with brick veneer in the 1920s, still stands today as does the original store next door. With its creaking wooden floors, its ladders sliding along the shelving, and its barrels full of bird seed, Hertler's has the atmosphere of a turn-of-the century country store. Emma, the house cat, completes the scene.

Hertler Brothers was organized in 1906 when brothers Gottlob, George, and Herman Hertler purchased George Mann's horse barn. They set up their sister, Emma, as bookkeeper (older customers can remember her pecking away at her manual typewriter well into the 1970s). In addition to handling horses and boarding livestock, Hertler's also sold farm machinery, feed, and seed.

An elaborate system of chutes from the basement to the second floor simplified the sale of bulk seed. "An endless elevator of cups mounted on a pair of chains moved the seed up to the second floor where it was directed into a bin. The sales person on the first floor had only to pull a string to the appropriate bin and fill a bag."

Since the 1970s the store has successfully managed to make the transition from farm to garden and from rural to urban. Seed now takes precedence over feed and the former horse barn now accommodates lawn furniture and wood stoves as well as an impressive selection of flower bulbs and gardening supplies.

In 1976 Hertler's received an award from the Ann Arbor Bicentennial Commission as "an excellent example of intelligence and taste in successfully preserving not only a building but a business that continues a tradition of earlier merchandising methods."

MSHD

Kip Miller

12

416 South Ashley Street

Toledo, Ann Arbor and Northern Michigan Railway Depot

1889

Kip Miller

The passenger depot for the Toledo, Ann Arbor and Northern Michigan Railway, affectionately known as "Annie," is one of the few reminders of Ann Arbor's "second" railroad. Second because it could never compete with the glamorous passenger trains of the Michigan Central Railroad, whose station on Depot Street now houses the Gandy Dancer Restaurant (see 20).

Annie was always the "people's railroad." It took families from town to picnics at nearby Zukey or Whitmore lakes, or further north to resorts in Traverse City. Lela Duff wrote: "It's true that the Ann Arbor station never had about it the glamour for townspeople that attached to the Michigan Central. One seldom saw expensive luggage bearing foreign labels piled up on the platform. But the place was not without drama. Patients who had to be lifted on stretchers... on their ways to the local hospitals were no rarity. In the resort season too there was a special gaiety about the place... "

Annie was the brainchild of James M. Ashley, an energetic man who had been governor of the Montana territory, a United States congressman from Ohio, and a personal friend of Abraham Lincoln. In a eulogy at the Unitarian Church in Ann Arbor in 1897, he was described as a large man, "intellectually, physically, and morally. There was nothing petty, small or mean about him." The name of the street upon which this station stands was changed to Ashley to honor him.

James Ashley built the railroad to connect his home town of Toledo, Ohio to the wheat and lumbering industry in northern Michigan. Always struggling financially, the line managed to open in 1877 and reached Ann Arbor in June

CONTINUED on next page

of 1878, in time for the commencement at the University of Michigan. The present depot, built in 1889, replaced an earlier depot that was moved across the tracks. The railroad eventually made most of its money by connecting Toledo with Frankfort, Michigan, where car ferries took passengers and freight across Lake Michigan to Wisconsin.

Passenger service fell victim to competition from the automobile and air travel and it ceased on July 19, 1950. Although freight service continued, the depot was boarded up for several years, after which it had a succession of uses as a beer warehouse, a night club, a restaurant, a boutique, and a kitchen-counter business. It has been the Law Montessori School since the mid-1980s.

The building is a clapboard structure with a long hipped roof and a wide overhang supported by ornamental wooden brackets. The side facing the tracks is actually the principal facade although the Ashley Street entrance is now the main entrance. The interior spaces of the original waiting room are remarkably well preserved, despite the many previous tenants. The room retains its aura of elegance created by 15-foot ceilings and three tiers of wall paneling. Deeply incised mantel brackets accent the fireplace and in the area just beyond the entry is a 15-foot wide wooden archway with columns capped by carved floral designs.

The depot was beautifully restored to its current condition in 1985 by the Law Montessori School.

SR, IHP

Ann Arbor Sesquicentennial Collection

15

201 Catherine Street

Davis Block-Agricultural Hall

1856

Kip Miller

"The excavation is being made at the junction of Detroit and Fourth Streets preparatory to the erection of a fine brick block to be used as an agricultural implements warehouse. It will be a fine improvement." This small announcement appeared in the September 19, 1856 *Michigan Gazeteer*. The undertaking must have been too much for the builders, Davis and Greenman, as they dissolved their partnership a year later. Three years later, in March of 1860, the *Michigan Argus* noted: "Moses Rogers has sold out on Washington Street and purchased the Davis Block and will soon have an extensive agricultural implement manufactory in his new quarters."

Rogers arrived in Ann Arbor from New York State in 1831 and operated agricultural implement factories from several locations prior to this purchase. While he owned the Davis Block, Rogers was also instrumental in establishing the Soldiers' Aid Society for Civil War Relief. As one local historian noted "...The Society sponsored a continuous flow of socials and contests, both as money-making projects to finance their work and as a means of bolstering the morale of the home folk.... Moses Rogers repeatedly gave the use of his large hall." In the spring of 1865, a "glorious" party was planned for the celebration

CONTINUED on next page

of the end of the war, at which Miss Flora Jewett would be crowned May Queen. "Though the war had ended... the pageant was held... with grief mixed with joy due to the assassination of President Lincoln."

Rogers sold this building to John Finnegan in 1867 and bought the building at 417 Detroit Street which now houses the Ecology Center (see 21). From then on, the Davis Block was commonly referred to as Agricultural Hall. Dealing in agricultural implements and seeds, Finnegan's establishment carried "...the latest and most approved styles of agricultural machinery, mowers, reapers and binders, of which the men of fifty years ago knew nothing."

Finnegan operated this business until around 1892 when he sold the building to the Hay and Todd Manufacturing Company of Ypsilanti. This was their Mill No. 2, specializing in underwear. In the 1920s Horace Prettyman bought it for his White Swan Laundry. That name for the building persisted even after the University of Michigan purchased it in the 1950s. Today the unadorned straightforward brick structure is the second oldest commercial building in the city. Along with the Anson Brown Building on Broadway (see 14), it is the only commercial building remaining from the era before the Civil War and before the Italianate style began to dominate commercial architecture. Its rectangular, rather than round-topped, windows are one of the clues to its age.

The building was extensively rehabilitated in 1988 by Michael Vlasic and a post-modern addition, designed by Frederick H. Herrmann Associates Inc., was added and designed to complement the older structure. The Davis Block now serves as the home of the *Ann Arbor Observer* and other professional offices.

16

216 Catherine Street

Anton Eisele House

1869

Atlas of Washtenaw County, 1874, page 59

The unusual carved stone lintels above the windows of this house are a clue to the profession of its builder. Anton Eisele, an immigrant from Germany, owned a stone-cutting business specializing in American and Italian marbles. Originally in partnership with his brother John W. in a business organized in 1868, he was prosperous enough to build this house in 1869. By the time the 1874 *Atlas of Washtenaw County* published an engraving of the house and Marble Works at the southeast corner of Catherine and Detroit Streets, Eisele was in business for himself.

Using stone and marble cutting skills learned in Germany, Eisele supplied both the marble and the carving for tombstones and other cemetery work. Recent renovations to a nearby building at 216 North Fourth Avenue yielded discarded fragments of his carving art.

After Eisele died in 1887, his stepson John Baumgardner continued to live in the house and run the business for which he built a two-story brick building across the street. It too exhibited the fine carving which characterized the family home but it was demolished in the 1930s for a gas station (now Argiero's Restaurant). Baumgardner expanded the business from tombstones to building stone, used primarily for sidewalks. Some of these still line the east side of Main Street between Washington and Liberty Streets. The house remains as a testament to the stone carving skills brought to Ann Arbor by Eisele and other Germans. It is now the home and office of attorney Pauline Rothmeyer.

OFW

324 Catherine Street

William G. and Mary Foster House

1870

This two-and-a-half story brick building is an austere version of the Italianate style, lacking the more exuberant arched window hoods, bay windows and belvederes commonly found in this style. Only a few of the characteristic elements can be found such as the paired carved brackets under the eaves and the half-size "eyebrow" windows on the third floor. Although the porch is not original and the windows have been replaced, the exterior is basically little changed, including the classical doorway with transom and sidelights.

The house was built for attorney William G. Foster and his wife Mary. When Foster died suddenly in 1873, his widow entered the University of Michigan Law School and, in 1876 at the age of 51, obtained her law degree with high honors. She opened her practice in this house as Ann Arbor's first female lawyer.

Mary Lowry Foster was a native of New York State who had come to Michigan at the age of one and grown up in Lodi Township. Hers is the only portrait of a woman in her own right (and not as a wife) in the 1881 *History of Washtenaw County*. Described in this history as ranking "high among the profession," Foster wrote the next year that she "ignores the base, pities the ignorant & commits all to the great Law Giver" and that her home was "a place the very atmosphere of which is freedom to think, act, and plan wisely."

Mary Foster was active in the Women's Christian Temperance Union and a member of several pioneer societies. In 1879 she read a paper in Lansing entitled "Echoes of the Past," that was reprinted in 1880 by the Pioneer Society of Michigan. Since 1988 the Women Lawyers Association has presented an annual "Mary Foster Award" in memory of this remarkable woman. Today her home is a rental property with most of the tenants being students at the University of Michigan.

OFW

Kip Miller

18

1009 Cornwell Place

Wirt Cornwell House

1886

In the 1880s when Wirt Cornwell constructed this brick mansion overlooking the Huron River, he had a magnificent view of an unspoiled countryside. An old photograph shows Cornwell's house with a large fieldstone porch and the new "clipped" or jerkin-head gable which still characterizes this Queen Anne structure today. Although the fieldstone porch was altered in the early 20th century, the house retains much of its original grandeur.

Kip Miller

Like many Queen Anne houses from the 1880s, the building is fairly symmetrical with windows and doors of more or less the same size and configuration. Variation occurs in the numerous roof gables and complicated roof lines and in a less boxy floor plan than the earlier Italianate or Greek Revival styles. This house today is one of only two survivors on a street which originally contained 10 spectacular mansions built by Ann Arbor's late 19th century elite.

The Cornwell family owned paper mills in Ann Arbor and Ypsilanti and had large real estate holdings in both towns. Harvey Cornwell, Wirt's father, lived nearby on Ingalls Street in a large house demolished for St. Joseph's Hospital in the early 20th century. He platted his land into Cornwell Place, which he obviously named for himself.

Wirt and Mary Cornwell and their descendants owned the property at 1009 Cornwell Place for nearly 40 years, after which their large house was divided into apartments. The Cornwell name has been perpetuated by the Wirt and Mary Cornwell Prize in Pure Science which is awarded each year by the University of Michigan College of LS&A to students who show "great intellectual curiosity and creative work in pure science." It was established by Irene and Alice M. Cornwell, both University of Michigan graduates, in honor of their parents.

OFW

1014 Cornwell Place

George Dock House

19

1894

Perched on a steep bluff overlooking the Huron River valley, this elaborate house was built in 1894 for George Dock, Professor of Clinical Medicine and Pathology at the University of Michigan. The irregular massing of forms, the polygonal tower with tent roof, the wrap-around porch, the use of cross gables, windows in varying shapes and sizes, and the combination of various materials including clapboard, board and batten, and unusual cut shingles are all features of the late Queen Anne style of the 1890s. They combine to give the house a complicated, eclectic look — the essence of this style.

Dr. Dock no doubt wanted to be close to the Medical School and University Hospitals which were then located at Catherine and Glen Streets, but after 14 years he sold the house to another professor, Dr. Albert Barrett. Barrett, who was also Director of the State Psychopathic Hospital, lived in the house for a decade, after which it served a number of owners including the Gamma Alpha fraternity from 1925 to 1950. By 1970 it was known as Clark's Tourist Home. It remained a rooming house until 1986 when it was purchased by the University of Michigan to house its "Med Inns" program. Today the University rents its rooms to foreign students.

The house is remarkably intact despite its many changes of ownership. It had an almost identical twin, the Jacob Laubengayer House formerly at 416 South Main Street, which was moved several years ago to 2345 Huron Parkway. Together with another transplanted Queen Anne, it now houses a medical clinic. Since Laubengayer's house was designed by the noted Detroit architectural firm of Spier and Rohns, it is possible that the George Dock house may have been designed by them as well.

OFW

Kip Miller

401 Depot Street

Michigan Central Depot

20

1886

Kip Miller

Built in 1886, this elegant structure was considered to be the finest station on the Michigan Central line. The first depot, built when the Michigan Central Railroad came to Ann Arbor in 1839, was located further west on the other side of Broadway. A two-story section of that structure was later moved to the southeast corner of Beakes Street and North Fifth Avenue, where it still stands in use as a residence.

Architects Spier and Rohns designed the new building in 1886 in the popular Richardsonian Romanesque style. The heavy stone walls, deep-set, round-arched openings, the asymmetry of the composition with its square squat tower and tall chimney, all expressed the strength, solidity, and prestige of the railroad, then at the zenith of its power. Stained glass windows and two large terra cotta fireplaces further embellished the interior.The contractors took special care in the choice and fitting of the stone, which was quarried a short distance up the Huron River at Foster's Station on Maple Road. The two smaller buildings, a Railway Express office and a baggage station, were connected to the central structure by a low metal canopy running along the track side.

In 1969, the C. A. Muer Corporation purchased the property from the Penn Central Railroad. Muer's renovation of the main building turned it into a distinguished restaurant, the Gandy Dancer, with a new balcony in the interior and a service wing added to the west end. In 1976, an expansion of the kitchen and dining area filled the space between the main structure and the east baggage building. A glassed-in dining area was created under the metal canopy on the track side.

NR, SR, DSHD

417 Detroit Street

David Henning Cooper Shop

1864

Barrel and stave manufacturer David Henning built this commercial Italianate building with its round topped windows in 1864 during the midst of the Civil War. Born in Ireland, he came to Ann Arbor in 1836. Enriched by lucrative contracts with the Union Army, Henning became one of Ann Arbor's wealthiest citizens.

In 1871 another business pioneer Moses Rogers bought the building. Rogers had operated a large and successful agricultural implements business at 201 Catherine (see 15) throughout the 1860s. Feeling the need to slow down, he went into partnership with John Treadwell in 1867, expecting that Treadwell would be the proprietor and he would provide "aid and experience."

Milton Kemnitz

After a disastrous fire destroyed their inventory, Rogers purchased the Henning building and started in business all over again at the age of 61. Rogers banked on his good reputation and his well known civic activities, especially for Civil War Relief. He continued here in business until his death in 1888, after which his daughter Katie continued to run the store, giving up her own career as a well-known artist and portrait painter. She sold the business in 1895 and died six years later.

The building's condition declined, along with the rest of the neighborhood, throughout the 20th century. Over the years it served as a warehouse, a creamery, a machine shop, a pattern works, and an art gallery. Yet despite its many changes of ownership it was never seriously altered and still retains its original wavy, hand-blown glass in the windows.

In the 1960s Travis and Demaris Cash purchased the building and began to rehabilitate it, preserving its fine original details. The Cashes salvaged the wrought iron fence from the old Rominger property on South Fifth Avenue when that house was torn down for the Ann Arbor Public Library parking lot. Their long-time tenant has been the Ann Arbor Ecology Center whose flagship office has been here since 1970. In 1976 the preservation efforts of the Cashes were cited with an award from the Ann Arbor Bicentennial Commission.

OFW

22

422 Detroit Street

Desderide Grocery Store

1902

Italian immigrant Rocco Desderide constructed this brick-veneered building to house his grocery and confectionery business in 1902. The round arches above the windows, with their bands of corbelled bricks fanning out, have been filled in, no doubt in the 1920s when steel casement windows became popular. A carved stone near the cornice gives the date of construction.

Desderide's was a central meeting place in the neighborhood, according to Ann Arbor native Milo Ryan. In his book, *View of a Universe*, Ryan remembers that Desderide's was second only to St. Thomas in regulating his universe.

Kip Miller

"Desderide's was known even to other neighborhoods as a paragon of corner grocery stores. His friends were legion and his store was famous for its huge pickle barrels, coffee, and Bull Durham tobacco for our dads." Though Rocco was the owner, it was clear that his wife was in charge. "We were in luck when Rocco was tending store, for into our grubby hands along with the change would go a piece of candy, a gum ball, or something equally choice." Desderide lived to be over 105 years old and a newspaper interview on his 100th birthday quoted his philosophy of longevity: "Don't work very hard and smoke a cigar every day."

In 1921, Desderide sold the grocery store to the Diroff family who operated a similar kind of "Mom and Pop" store until 1980. Illness forced the Diroffs to sell their building to attorney Arthur Carpenter, founder of Kerrytown, whose attempt to operate a delicatessen was not successful. The proprietors of Zingerman's, however, who followed him in the deli business at this location, now have a million-dollar business specializing in huge sandwiches, unusual foods, and catering. They are one of Ann Arbor's major tourist attractions and the hustle and bustle of the shop is evidence of their success. They opened for business in March of 1982 and have recently expanded to operate a cafe in the house next door.

OFW

501-507 Detroit Street

Stofflet Block

1900

This handsome corner structure with its symmetrical end towers and projecting porches is Ann Arbor's first apartment building. Built by news and book dealer Francis Stofflet for his children, the building originally contained four two-story apartments. Francis proudly inserted the name "Stofflet" at the center of the Detroit Street facade. Two of his children, Harvey and Elmer Stofflet, lived in the end apartments until the mid-1920s, when Mary Stofflet, Francis' widow, moved into the first unit and divided the four original apartments into eight one-story flats. In 1934 the mortgage was foreclosed and the building began to fall into disrepair. Taylor Collins, who walked by daily, admired the unique structure and vowed to purchase it someday "with hardly a quarter in my pocket to call my own." He realized his dream in 1938 and lived there with his wife until 1973.

Stofflet was a businessman, who had moved here to attend the University. He obtained a law degree in 1871 and taught in Rochester, Michigan, until 1877. When he returned to Ann Arbor in 1878 he published a news sheet, the *Ann Arbor Daily Times*, which never amounted to much. In 1881 he began a business which distributed newspapers and magazines, including monthlies from London and Paris. His son Harvey and grandson Ross carried on the business as the Stofflet News Service until 1970.

When Taylor Collins sold the building in 1973, it was renovated and renamed the Olde Town Apartments. By the mid-1980's, the building was divided into the Brownstone Condominiums, eight two-story units created by accessing the previously unused space in the basements and attics.

OFW

Kip Miller

529 Detroit Street

John G. Miller Planing Mill

1869

Kip Miller

This Italianate brick building with its heavy triple-arched brick trim over the windows was built by John G. Miller as a planing mill specializing in "sash, doors, blinds [shutters], molding and scroll work." It replaced an earlier wooden mill built in 1853 which, when it burned in July of 1869, the *Michigan Argus* lamented as "a public as well as private loss." The earlier mill had made carriages and sleighs using a new steam process for bending wood. When Miller began rebuilding three months after the fire, the *Michigan Argus* reported he was again building a "steam bending shop on the site of the one that burned."

Miller's new shop concentrated on the more lucrative business of providing millwork for the boom in house construction that followed the Civil War. Throughout the 19th century, Detroit Street hummed with industrial activity as other planing mills and carriage manufactories plied their trade nearby.

In 1878, Miller sold the mill to Herman Krapf who renamed it the Detroit Planing Mill and kept it operating until his death around 1906. By the 1920s this part of town was no longer a business center and the building was frequently vacant or used as a warehouse. In 1960 it was leased by Mrs. Demaris Cash who had dreamed of opening a retail consignment shop. She named her store the Treasure Mart, and today it ranks as one of Ann Arbor's most cherished institutions.

In 1983 Mrs. Cash purchased the building and the miller's house next door. Though now in her eighties, she still works behind the counter, having passed the management of the business on to her daughter, Elaine Johns.

OFW

120 North Division Street

1894

George and Emma Wahr House

This exuberant Queen Anne style house is one of several built and occupied by book dealer and stationer George Wahr. After purchasing the Wilson house at 126 North Division (see 28) at a tax auction in 1892, Wahr built this house on the side lot in the current style of the day. Projecting gables, varying sized windows, an almost circular porch with spindle work at both the top and bottom, and a general asymmetrical organization of the various spaces are typical features of the Queen Anne style.

George Wahr was the son of pioneers from Germany who arrived in the area in 1835. He clerked at a local bookstore from the age of 14 and eventually bought that store with two other partners. Five years later, in 1887, he bought out his partners and became sole owner. Wahr specialized in student supplies, books, and stationery, but he also had a lucrative publishing business which printed tracts on various subjects. By 1892 he was successful enough to open a second store on State Street — obviously to be closer to his main customers. It seems odd today that for over 40 years students had to shop on Main Street for supplies.

Wahr's ultimate accomplishment was building this house on North Division Street, a true symbol of success as this was then the most prosperous part of town. Today, Wahr's grandson, George Wahr Sallade, rents out its luxury apartments. Carefully tended, both the buildings and the grounds still exhibit the grandeur that once was North Division Street.

OFW

Kip Miller

27

121 North Division Street

Moses Rogers House

1861

This is one of the few nineteenth century homes in the Division Street Historic District that has been modernized and maintained as a single family home. Although originally surrounded by larger and more elegant homes, the simple lines of this Italianate house with its finely detailed brackets have long been admired. The original porch has been removed and a dormer added on the third floor, but the house has otherwise changed little in its outward appearance.

The house was built about 1861 for Moses and Letitia Sweetland Rogers and their daughters, Ellen and Katie. Moses and his more famous brother Randolph were sons of an Ann Arbor baker. Randolph left Ann Arbor to become world renowned as a sculptor; among his works are the bronze doors of the Capitol in Washington, D. C. A full-sized version of his popular genre statue "Nydia" (the blind heroine of Bulwer-Lytton's novel *The Last Days of Pompeii*) is in a collection of the University of Michigan Museum of Art, purchased for the University by the Randolph Rogers Art Association of Ann Arbor. Moses was also a talented artist but had little time to devote to his painting. He owned the Ann Arbor Agricultural Works, (see 15), which grew from a downtown store to a sprawling factory on Broadway by the river, producing Advance sulke rakes, chilled plows, and hay tedders. Moses also held a number of local political offices and was a trustee of the First Unitarian Society of Ann Arbor.

Kip Miller

Rogers' daughter Katie born in 1849, achieved considerable fame as an artist, particularly as a painter of portraits. Professor Gookins, her tutor at the Chicago Academy, was impressed by her work and wished to show one of her paintings at the great Centennial Exhibition in Philadelphia, a rare opportunity for any artist. Katie modestly declined. The 1881 *History of Washtenaw County* describes her portraiture as "lifelike and striking. Whether painting the soft dimple upon the cheek of an innocent babe, or the harder lines of the aged pioneer, there seems to be a reality about the work which makes one feel that he is in a living presence." When her father died in 1888, Katie forsook her home studio for seven years to run his farm machine business. She herself died in 1901. Some of her surviving paintings are in the possession of the Washtenaw County Historical Society.

DSHD

126 North Division Street

28

1835, 1843

Judge Robert S. Wilson House
(Wilson-Wahr House)

Lester Fader

Often described and pictured in books on architectural history, this is Ann Arbor's most famous house. Rexford Newcomb, in his *Architecture of the Old Northwest Territory*, 1950, praised its perfect proportions, and Fiske Kimball traced the model for its "four sturdy Ionic columns, rising through two stories, with graceful flutes and capitals," to the original Temple of the Wingless Victory at Athens (*American Architecture*, 1928).

An Historic American Buildings Survey in 1934 noted that the original kitchen was located "in the basement under the dining room ... the hearth and Dutch oven being still intact. A stair led from the old kitchen at the rear of the present library, which was evidently the original serving room, and the main hall extended back to that point." The house probably was erected in three stages with the middle section the first to be built, possibly as early as 1835. The kitchen and servant quarters at the rear were probably added in 1850.

CONTINUED on next page

Probate Judge Robert S. Wilson built the famous temple portion in 1843 in a setting of extensive grounds and gardens. His career took him to Chicago and in 1850 he sold the estate to John A. Welles, a newcomer from the East. Welles' son Henry joined in the merchandising and land speculation enterprises of his father, moving into the house with his four daughters after the death of his wife in 1855. Henry was city recorder in 1851-52 and treasurer of the University from 1858 until his death in 1860. The Welles girls, Clarissa, Sarah, Mary Fiske, and Susan Holly, and their cousins, the children of Silas and Helen Welles Douglass, were active in society in Ann Arbor and Detroit and made frequent trips to the East Coast and Europe. A Welles wedding was the occasion for installing the unusual wood-paneled ceilings of the first floor of the mansion.

Times change, and in 1892 the house with a smaller garden was auctioned in a tax sale on the courthouse steps with bookseller and publisher George Wahr making the high bid. He and his wife, Emma (Staebler) Wahr moved into the home but they disliked the inside well, thinking it unhealthful. The Wahrs excavated in the garden a few feet to the south to begin a new house at 120 North Division (see 26), and while construction was under way, Emma took a trip east where she visited the Lee mansion in Virginia. As she approached the Lee house, she was struck by the realization that the visual effect of their Greek Temple mansion in Ann Arbor would be destroyed by building the new house so near to it. Although she telegraphed her husband to stop construction, for perhaps the only time in their lives together he failed to accede to her wishes. The Wahrs moved into the new house, leasing the mansion next door to sororities and fraternities. After twenty years, they filled the noisome well and returned to the mansion where Emma Wahr, an avid collector of antiques, displayed her treasures. Much of her notable collection was sold at auction in 1974 after the death of her daughter, Natalie Wahr Sallade. The Sallade family still occupies this mansion.

NR, DSHD

205 North Division Street

1855

Alonzo Palmer House (Laubengayer-Ryan House)

One of the finest Gothic Revival houses remaining in the city, this home was built in stages. Dr. Alonzo Palmer, an early member of the University Medical School faculty, came from New York before 1850 to teach and practice in Ann Arbor. With his young wife he purchased a small square brick house on Ann Street. His wife lived only a few years, and in the mid-1860s Dr. Palmer went back east to marry Miss Love Root of Pittsfield, Massachusetts. In 1867, as a new bride wealthy in her own right, Love Root Palmer added the larger and more elaborate portion of the house facing Division Street.

Lester Fader

Love Palmer survived her husband by many years. Upon her death in 1901 the house was purchased by Tobias and Sarah (Staebler) Laubengayer to be used as their residence. Their daughter and son-in-law, Wanda and Mack Ryan, lived in the house until Mr. Ryan died in 1970. Since then the ownership has changed several times.

In 1957, the *Ann Arbor News* was effusive in describing the interior: "a myriad of oak doors, suspended from huge hand-carved hinges, swing open to all sorts of interesting rooms and closets, large and small. The walls are like those of a fortress while the fireplaces are small and adorned by ornate marble hearths. Elaborate chandeliers, their crystals clustered in serried ranks, hang from high paneled ceilings ... Wide, winding stairs, built of solid walnut and at least one other small, tunnel-like stairway join the first and second floors which include an estimated thirteen rooms. A mural in the hallway and up the stairs, painted by an Italian artist in the early 1930s, depicts the history of the Staebler family in Germany and the United States."

The attractive carriage house has been converted for residential use and the house itself is now a multi-family conversion.

DSHD

208 North Division Street

30

Ebenezer Wells House (Wells-Babcock House)

1858

Lester Fader

This house was built for Dr. Ebenezer Wells, a physician, and his family. The mayor of Ann Arbor in 1863-64, Wells also became the president of the First National Bank, the first bank chartered in Michigan under the National Bank Act of 1863. He held that position until his death in 1882.

James L. Babcock bought the house in 1890 when he moved to Ann Arbor to manage the wool business of his uncle, Luther James. *Past and Present of Washtenaw County* (1906) states that Babcock paid some $10,000 for the property "which was surrounded by beautiful and extensive grounds, richly adorned with flowers and ornamental trees and situated in one of the most delightful portions of the town."

Luther James left a fortune to his nephew on the condition that he marry within five years. James Babcock met the deadline and proceeded to remodel the house throughout. Embossed leather wall coverings were imported from Europe for the reception rooms, as were carvings, mirrors and marble. The Babcock coat of arms was done in stained glass for the windows on the north side of a rear addition. Elegant beveled and etched glass still remains in other windows and doors.

In 1910, after the death of James Babcock, a third story was added, and the mansion and carriage house were converted to multifamily use.
DSHD

218 North Division Street

John W. Maynard House

1838

When John W. Maynard constructed his center-entry side gabled brick house in 1838, this was in the middle of a large, undeveloped block. Catherine Street would not extend between Division and State Streets until 1898. Maynard, a successful grocer with a store on Ann Street, had come to Ann Arbor as a child only months after John Allen and Elisha Rumsey founded the town in 1824. In a letter dated June of that year, John's father Ezra, a farmer in Pittsfield Township, wrote the first eyewitness account of the emerging village.

A *Michigan Argus* account in 1849 entitled "Notes on Our Village, No. 4," included his house among those that exhibited "the style of architecture which is an ornament to our village, and evinces the taste, judgment and liberality of their owners." Today John's house is one of a row of important buildings on large lots with deep setbacks lining the east side of Division Street that exemplify the mid-19th century look and feel of the town.

Maynard family members occupied the house for over half a century. In 1908, Russell T. Dobson, publisher of the *Ann Arbor Times*, purchased it and in 1910 added the large porch, roof dormers, and two-story center portico in the popular Colonial Revival style. The main entry was then shifted from the center of the house to the south side, where it remains today.

After pneumonia took Dobson's life in 1938, the house was sold to the Christian Reformed Church for a student center. Around 1950 the Episcopal Student Foundation of St. Andrew's Church purchased the house and named it "Canterbury House" to use as a center for their outreach program. In 1992, Trailblazers, Inc., a group working with those recovering from mental illness, bought the property for a clubhouse for their members.

OFW

Lester Fader

32

303 North Division Street

Andrew DeForest House

1845

Andrew DeForest was only 17 years old when he arrived in Ann Arbor in 1836 from Montgomery County, New York. According to the 1881 *History of Washtenaw County*, DeForest worked as a contractor and builder for the next 15 years, "erecting many of the substantial buildings that now stand in the city." His financial successes undoubtedly allowed him to build his own house in 1845 on fashionable Division Street, opposite the Episcopal Church.

Kip Miller

DeForest's house is said to have been a Greek Revival house with a colonnaded portico across the front much like other houses he built (see 7). Old bird's eye maps show some kind of porch structure on the Division Street side of the house as well as a "widow's walk" on the roof. According to Lela Duff, a local historian, DeForest later removed the pillared porch and changed the roof line to make the square house pattern. The house retains some Greek Revival features in its corner engaged columns, its white color, and its many-paned windows.

DeForest sold the house in 1888 to Henry Brown, a druggist, who lived here until his death in 1918. His wife Jane continued to live in the house until about 1933. During their tenure, according to Lela Duff, Louis H. Boynton,Professor of Architecture, oversaw the remodelling into the Colonial Revival house it is today. These colonial aspects were emphasized by the next owners when the house served as the Colonial Inn in 1936.

Following Mrs. Brown's death, Mrs. Sue Horner operated an antique business here in the 1940s and 1950s and lived in the house until the late 1970s.

After 1981 it became a student house dubbed the Colonial Inn. In 1979 the asbestos siding and wooden arbor over the front entry were removed to reveal the earlier structure. It was handsomely rehabilitated at this time and in 1988 the house once again became a single family residence.

OFW

306 North Division Street

St. Andrew's Episcopal Church

1868-69

St. Andrew's Church in Ann Arbor was organized in 1828. As the church grew in numbers and wealth, its history was filled with names that are familiar as well in the progress of the town. The early congregation included the Dexter, Kingsley, Clark and Chapin families. George Corselius, popular editor of Ann Arbor's early *Western Emigrant*, conveyed one acre of land to the church in 1835, upon which a church building was constructed in 1839 and enlarged in 1856 to provide "free sittings" (in contrast to pew rents) for University students. This building stood just north of the present structure at some elevation from the street, and was approached by a flight of twenty steps — an interesting topographical note.

When the congregation needed a larger church building, it was decided to start with only the nave, and to accept the plans and specifications of Detroit architect Gordon W. Lloyd, who, the *Michigan Argus* stated, "is doing so much for church architecture in the west." The cornerstone was laid in June of 1868, consecration of the finished building taking place on November 10, 1869. In 1879 a chapel and rectory, also designed by architect Lloyd, were added and in the 1890s the recessed chancel and choir stalls were built. Finally, in 1903, a gift from Mrs. Love Palmer in memory of her husband Alonzo made it possible to complete Lloyd's design by constructing the tower, which added to the long, low church "just the culmination and decision which it has always needed." (Arthur Lyon Cross, *History of St. Andrew's Church*, 1906).

The style is English Gothic, after the style of the parish churches of Lloyd's native land. The construction material, selected field boulders, generally granite and beautifully varied in hue, were split and laid in courses, each course varying from ten to fourteen inches wide. The gable is surmounted by a stone Greek cross. The roof is laid in diamonds of different colored slate, finished with ornamental cresting of cast iron on its ridge. Lloyd incorporated unusual long clerestory windows along each side wall under the patterned roof, with quatrefoil windows to let more light into the nave. The stained glass in these windows was furnished by Friedrichs of Brooklyn, New York. The interior plan follows the typical basilica form of a central long nave flanked by side aisles. The tower, topped by battlements and conical pinnacles, is over eighty feet high. In an attached turret on the front of the tower are stairs to the second story and belfry. A pleasant enclosed cloister to the north of the sanctuary was finished in the 1960s.

CONTINUED on next page

Memorial gifts over the years have further embellished the interior. Of special note are the walnut eagle lectern (circa 1875) and a brilliantly colored central south window by the renowned Louis Comfort Tiffany. Two stained glass windows were installed behind the organ chancel by Willet & Company of Philadelphia in the late 1970s as a memorial to George Hunschey, organist and choir master in the church for many years.

St. Andrew's was included in the Division Street Historic District at the request of the vestry or governing board, which is mindful of the treasure in its custody. New front doors, careful copies of the deteriorated originals, were installed in 1975.

DSHD

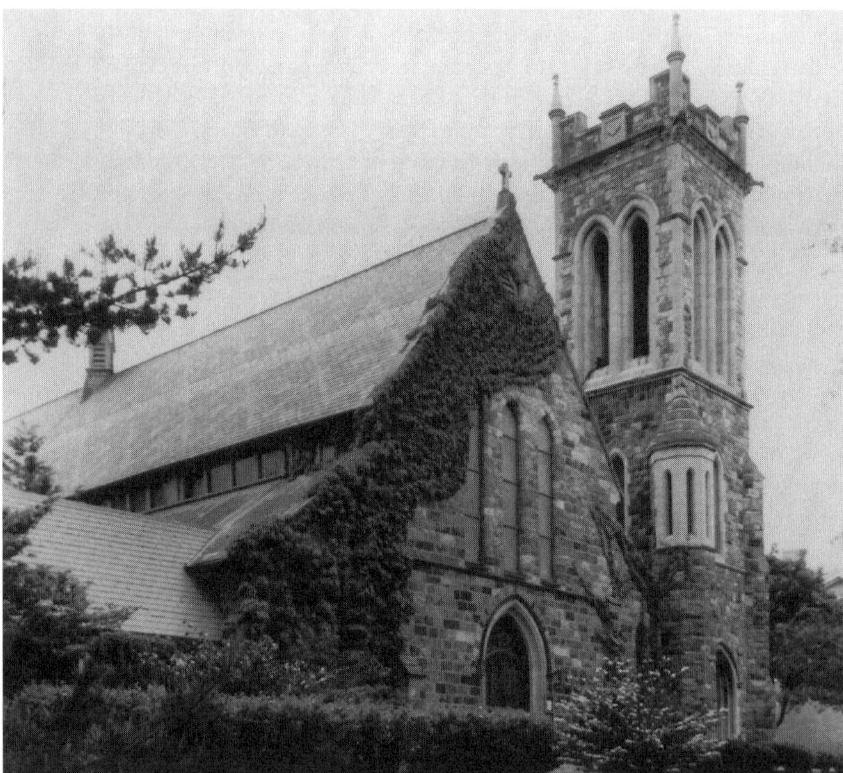

Kip Miller

406 North Division Street

George Rinsey House

34

1915

Kip Miller

After the death of his father David Rinsey, George Rinsey and his wife Ina constructed a bungalow for themselves on part of the north lawn of the David Rinsey estate, so that they might live next door to his mother and sisters (see 93). George's career was in insurance. After his death in the 1940s, his widow continued to live here until the mid-1970s.

Nestled behind an ancient oak, this house with its intact pergola on the south side forms an interesting contrast to the original Queen Anne family home. Where the 19th century emphasized verticality and monumentality, the early 20th century encouraged simplicity, craftsmanship, and a back-to-nature ideal, of which this house with its horizontal emphasis is a good example. Its original interior has been preserved to a large degree though the house now serves as a rental property.

OFW

505 North Division Street

35

Clark Girls School

1865

The most famous and most permanent of the private schools in 19th-century Ann Arbor was the Misses Clark's Seminary for Young Ladies. This simple brick building, now converted to apartments, was the sixth and final location of that school.

Mary Clark came to Washtenaw County in the 1830s with her family and established the school in Ann Arbor in 1839 with her sisters Chloe and Roby. All three were graduates of the famous finishing school of Mrs. Emma Willard of Troy, New York, and brought the Willard philosophy of education into the wilderness. According to the 1881 *History of Washtenaw County*, "many prominent women owe their high culture to the facilities enjoyed in [the Clark] seminary."

Kip Miller

So famous was this school in the 1840s and 50s that one-third of its pupils came from outside Ann Arbor, some from as far away as New York. The education philosophy was heavy in moral tone and stressed observations of nature as Mary Clark was an avid botanist. Boarders were not allowed to receive callers except on Friday or Saturday evenings with the principal present. Shopping was allowed only on Wednesday or Saturday afternoons as the Misses Clark did not want to "promote an undue love of society, but an acquaintance of the courtesies of life."

When Mary Clark died in 1875, the school closed, never to be re-opened. Chloe died shortly thereafter in 1880 and an era of old-fashioned gentility died with them.

By 1900 the building had been converted into apartments. Called the Oakwood Apartments in the 1910s, it was further subdivided in the 1920s into eight units and renamed the McLean Apartments by its owner and resident Donald McLean. McLean family members still own and reside in it today.

OFW

538 North Division Street

Henry Cornwell House

1894

The exterior of this impressive brick structure belies its owner's renown as a self-made lumber baron. Only the lavish use of wood in the 17-room interior provides a clue to his occupation. In 1840 Henry and his brother Harvey established a paper mill on the Huron River west of Ann Arbor. By the 1860s they were already wealthy men, owning lumber mills in Ypsilanti as well. When Henry built this Queen Anne /Colonial Revival house, he was replacing his earlier Italianate house which had stood on the same site. The new house was one of several highlighted in the 1896 *Ann Arbor Headlight*.

Kip Miller

Henry's son Frank and his family remained in the home after Henry's death but moved out after World War I when the house became too big for them. In December 1927 the house was sold to the Beth Israel Congregation and served as its synagogue for nearly 20 years. In 1946 it was sold to Mrs. Ruth Farley Pack, a local realtor, and in April of 1949, to the Pentecostal Church of God.

In 1951 St. Thomas Church bought it for a youth center. It was used in this capacity until the late 1970s when it was sold to William DeBrooke who began a restoration of the house as a residential property. In 1983, Deucalion Resources Group, a computer software company, completed the restoration of the house, this time for offices. Deucalion preserved the 15 black walnut trees on the front lawn as well and in 1984 received a Preservation Award from the Ann Arbor Historic District Commission. The house today is the home of Baseview-Macintosh Publishing Systems for Newspapers.

OFW

37

303 South Division Street

Emanuel Mann House

1853

Emanuel E. Mann came to Ann Arbor in 1830 with his parents, Jonathan and Louise Mann, at the age of 16. He learned the tanner's trade under his father's direction and opened the first steam tannery in Ann Arbor. After the tannery was destroyed by fire, Mann went into business with Christian Eberbach under the firm name of Eberbach and Company, manufacturing pharmaceuticals and medical apparatus. Some years later he purchased a drug store on Main Street. His sons, Albert and Eugene, were proprietors of the Mann Brothers Drug Store well knto the 1900s.

Kip Miller

A successful and much esteemed man, active in politics, Emanuel was vice president of the organizational meeting of the Republican Party "under the oaks" at Jackson, Michigan, on July 6, 1854. His office at Eberbach and Company was a meeting place for politicians of his day and a rendezvous for prominent early settlers. His sister, Louise, became the wife of Frederick Schmid, the first Lutheran minister in Michigan and the organizer of many German Lutheran churches in the state. Emanuel served on the school board and as an alderman, and for a time represented his district in the state senate.

In 1850 he purchased this lot on the corner of Liberty and Division to build a home for his wife Anna (Niethamer) and their children. Mann sold the house in 1868 when he moved to a nearby farm.

Although its appearance has suffered from use and neglect, the structure is notable for its clean Greek Revival silhouette, the classical doorway with sidelights, and the stucco veneer over its brick surface, scored to resemble large blocks of stone. This aesthetic device, which was practical as it made a dry, snug house, and was characteristic of early local building, once earned Ann Arbor the nickname "little stucco village." Ownership has changed frequently and the house has been adapted for many different residential and commercial uses.

312 South Division Street

1853

Henry DeWitt Bennett House (Kempf House)

38

Thousands of people breathed a sigh of relief when this house was purchased by the City of Ann Arbor in 1969 in one of our earliest efforts to preserve our architectural heritage. The Ann Arbor Historic District Commission was created by city ordinance in 1971 and has had its offices in the house since 1975.

The Kempf house was built in 1853 for Henry DeWitt Bennett, an active citizen who served some years as postmaster and, from 1869 to 1886, as secretary and steward of the University of Michigan. Long renowned for its graceful simplicity, the temple-style Greek Revival architecture of the Kempf House has been described in books, magazines, and newspaper articles, and won entry in the National Register of Historic Places in 1973.

A classic story-and-a-half of the front gabled temple form, the home was described in 1919 by architectural historian Fiske Kimball as an illustration of the "simplification often introduced in the Old Northwest to adapt the ambitious temple type to less pretentious uses. Square piers are substituted for the costly circular columns; the 'anti-capital,' simplest of Greek Doric forms, is used to crown them. Instead of two full stories below the cornice, the house has its upper story in the roof, with small 'frieze windows... screened by delicate iron gratings designed on the motif of the Greek anthemion."

Compared to the exterior, the interior is quite plain. The most elaborately decorated room is the studio, designed originally as a parlor for special occasions and the reception of important guests. An interesting feature here is the tapering of door and window frames.

When Bennett retired and left Ann Arbor, he sold the house to his wealthy neighbor, A. L. Noble, who owned the Star Clothing House on Main Street. Noble removed some interior walls and rented the house first to James M. Stafford, a merchant tailor and then, in 1890, to musicians Reuben H. and Pauline Widenmann Kempf. After Noble's death, the Kempfs purchased the house from his widow in 1894.

Born in Pittsfield Township in 1859 into one of the county's earliest families, Reuben Kempf graduated from the Royal Conservatory in Stuttgart, Germany, and returned to Ann Arbor to pursue a long career as a musician and teacher. Kempf organized and directed concert series which attracted artists from a wide area. At the suggestion of University of Michigan President James B. Angell, Kempf assembled a singing society, the Beethoven Gesangverein (later the Lyra Male Chorus), to foster better understanding between town and gown through the universal language of music. He served for 33 years (1895-1928) as

CONTINUED on next page

organist and choir director of St. Andrew's Episcopal Church. Mrs. Kempf, the former Pauline Widenmann, was a graduate of the Cincinnati Conservatory and a pupil of the celebrated voice coach Oscar Saenger. An accomplished contralto, she taught her voice pupils to sing while facing two large mirrors, reminding them that proper posture is an essential foundation of sweet song. Mr. Kempf trained future Paderewskis on his Steinway, the first concert grand piano in Ann Arbor, which remains in the Kempf House and is often used at social events. Paderewski himself played on this instrument when it was borrowed by the University for one of his concerts.

Mr. Kempf died in 1945 at the age of 86. When Mrs. Kempf died eight years later, the house was acquired by neighbors, Mr. and Mrs. Earl V. Parker. After Earl's death in 1968, Mrs. Parker sold the house to the city to protect it from potential demolition.

With assistance from the Parks Department, the Kempf House Society, a volunteer organization, is refurbishing the interior of the house and maintaining it as a Center for Local History. The Society provides open houses, tours and special events.

NR, HABS, DSHD

Kip Miller

320-322 South Division Street

1882 and 1892

A. L. Noble House and Carriage House

Adelbert L. Noble came to Ann Arbor in 1869 to study at the University of Michigan. "Difficulty with his eyes would not permit of his continuing his studies and he turned his mind toward business" wrote the county history of 1881. After six years in the clothing business with Joe T. Jacobs (see 57), Noble sold his interest and opened the Star Clothing Store at the corner of Main and Washington Streets. Star specialized in "Men's, Boys' and Children's" clothing, advertising "Plain Figures and One Price."

Kip Miller

By 1883 Noble was successful enough to buy this piece of land from Henry Bennett who had built the Kempf House next door in 1853 (see 38). Noble erected a large and imposing brick house, transitional in style from the Italianate to Queen Anne. The slate roof, decorative chimneys, pressed brick, arched windows, and carved wood details on porches, gable corners, and brackets show the influence of both styles. The fine stonework over the windows illustrates the craftsmanship of Anton Eisele (see 16).

In 1892 Noble became the first president of the State Savings Bank. He erected the carriage house in the rear of the property and the two buildings form a unique grouping, now very rare in central Ann Arbor.

After Noble's death in 1894, followed by his wife in 1902, the house had a succession of owners until 1920 when Dr. David M. Cowie purchased it. Dr. Cowie, a physician and Professor of Pediatrics and Infectious Diseases at the University of Michigan, turned the home into a private hospital. One of Cowie's major achievements was the adoption on a statewide basis of the use of iodized salt to prevent goiter. After Cowie's death in 1940, the house and carriage house were both converted to apartments and remain as such today.

EWHD

40

409 South Division Street

First Church of Christ, Scientist

1913

Kip Miller

This building was originally the home of the First Church of Christ, Scientist. Its members first organized as a society in 1900, and re-organized into a church in 1901. Services were held in a rented home on this site which the church eventually bought. They removed the house and laid the cornerstone for this church building in 1912. It was opened to the public in 1913 and officially dedicated in June of 1926, free from debt.

The church is designed in a neo-classical style, somewhat reminiscent of Monticello, the home of Thomas Jefferson, whose models for classicism came from the Romans rather than the Greeks. The architect was Spencer Solon Beman, son of Chicago architect Solon Spencer Beman, who is famous for his design of Pullman, a planned community in Chicago.

Spencer was the successor to his father's business and after training at Oxford, returned to Chicago. His commissions were mainly residential buildings and churches, the latter primarily for the Christian Scientists in the Georgian and Neo-Classical styles popular at that time. He designed over 100 churches in more than 20 states. The builders were a local firm, Koch Brothers, who built many of Ann Arbor's public structures in the early 20th century.

Though the Christian Scientists moved to Washtenaw in the late 1940's, the building continued to serve as a church for over 75 years. It has recently been converted into a residence by an owner who plans to make it a showplace for downtown living.

EWHD

530 South Division

John George Koch House

41

1874

Showcased by its high-profile location next to Hanover Square at the intersection of Division, Packard, and Madison Streets, this brick Italianate "cube" was built in 1874 for John George Koch. Koch was a local furniture maker who had originally apprenticed in Germany. Like many other Germans in Ann Arbor, Koch immigrated from Wurttemberg in 1866. Also like many men of this era, he worked and traveled through many parts of the country including New Haven, Connecticut; Columbus, Ohio; and Dexter, Michigan before finally settling in Ann Arbor in 1872. For seven years he was a stockholder and assistant superintendent of the Keck Furniture Company. In 1880 Koch attempted to go into business on his own but soon teamed up with Jacob Haller in the firm of Koch and Haller, furniture dealers.

Koch sold the house in 1888 to Sarah and William Rice, a wealthy farmer descended from pioneer families of Washtenaw County, who had retired to Ann Arbor that year. A 1906 biography of him states that "he removed to the city of Ann Arbor and there his wife purchased a residence which he made his home until the time of his death, enjoying in well earned ease the fruits of his former toil." The house remained in the Rice family until about the time of World War I, after which it was rented and its tenants changed every decade.

In the late 1940s, it was purchased by the present owner who has maintained the seven room house in pristine condition, preserving original brackets and the heavy brick arches over the windows. The woodwork in the two downstairs parlors has been refinished after seven layers of paint were removed. Recognizing that these efforts were a contribution to the entire community of Ann Arbor, the Ann Arbor Historic District Commission awarded the owner a Preservation Award in 1988 for keeping this "gem" in top-notch condition.

Kip Miller

42

517, 520, 530-540 Elizabeth Street

Complex of St. Thomas the Apostle

1899, 1902, 1911, 1929

Kip Miller

The history of St. Thomas the Apostle Church is intimately connected with Irish immigration to Washtenaw County and their eventual concentration in Ann Arbor in the area bounded roughly by Huron, Glen, North Main Street, and the Huron River. The Irish first congregated in Northfield Township, but in the 1830s they slowly began to move into Ann Arbor. Louis W. Doll's *History of St. Thomas Parish, Ann Arbor*, reports of a momentous meeting in 1835 that resulted in the first concentrated effort to construct a Roman Catholic church in Ann Arbor. It took another ten years before the first church was built on East Kingsley Street in 1845. In 1868 the parish purchased the former public school at 324-326 East Kingsley Street (see 90) for their first parochial school. By 1886 the school had grown so much that the parish built a new building in the middle of the block between State and Elizabeth Streets and sold the old one.

By the time Father Edward Kelly arrived in 1891, the parish was badly in need of a new church. The ranks of church members had swollen not only from an influx of more Irish but with many prominent German Catholics, including grocer David Rinsey (see 93) and his partner Moses Seabolt. Fueled by the energy and determination of Father Kelly, the drive for money to build the church was successful.

The Detroit firm of Spier and Rohns designed a handsome Romanesque building, reminiscent of Italian hill churches. This firm also designed the Michigan Central Railroad Station (see 20) and Tappan Hall on the central campus. The local firm of Koch Brothers constructed the church of granite fieldstone and Bailey bluestone and proudly showcased it in their advertisements. The corner

CONTINUED on next page

Louisa Pieper

stone was laid in 1897 and the building dedicated in 1899. A large stained-glass rose window dominates the entry above marble pillars flanking wooden doors with quatrefoil carving.

Soon after, in 1902, the yellow brick rectory was constructed behind the church at 530 Elizabeth (actually facing State Street). This Georgian Colonial Revival building is a long rectangle with a projecting center capped by a highly decorated full pediment. The large center porch has a fieldstone base topped by slender Ionic columns supporting a graceful balustrade. Two small pedimented dormers add to the impression of a country estate. The Georgian style contrasts sharply with the Italian style of the church, despite the use of clay roof tiles on both buildings.

The last building constructed under Father Kelly's tenure was the convent for the Sisters of the Immaculate Heart of Mary at 517 Elizabeth Street. It resembles the rectory in general form and materials and in fact Doll noted that the convent "was built of the same substantial brick as was used in the rectory." More pronounced than on the rectory are the pedimented dormers embellished on the sides with fish-tail shingles and finished off with the same unusual green clay tile as the main roof. Built by parishioner and contractor Henry G. Pipp, the total cost of the convent was $8,600. The Sisters moved in by October 1911.

Kip Miller

This eclectic complex of buildings remains today as a monument to Father Kelly's tireless efforts. The second decade of the 20th century saw the razing of the old school behind the church and its replacement by several school buildings for both elementary and high school students.

SR (church), OFW

44

220 North Fifth Avenue

Jacob Vandawarker House

1844

Jacob Vandawarker came to Ann Arbor from Herkimer County, New York in 1834 and wasted no time in getting married and setting up a shoemaking business. After a decade he was able to purchase two large lots and construct this fine brick "Philadelphia townhouse." The elaborate front door surround, with its transom and sidelights, was a common design feature in the 1840s but had almost disappeared by the 1850s when the Greek Revival style was at its height in Ann Arbor. In addition to the door, the house has other features reflecting the mingling of the Federal and Greek Revival styles. These include the simple stone lintels over the windows, the six-over-six window pane arrangement, the long side of the house facing the street, and the modillion detailing under the eaves. One interesting feature is the "blind"or fake window placed on the north wall for the sake of symmetry. The full front porch dates to the 1860s when porches, particularly with Italianate gingerbread and thin chamfered columns, were the height of fashion.

Kip Miller

The *Ann Arbor Courier* lamented Vandawarker's death in 1881: "Soon none will be left to tell the tale of the early settlement of Michigan." Local artist Charles Ciccarelli recently immortalized in a print, the shoemaking enterprise Vandawarker operated on the west side of Main Street between Huron and Washington for almost 50 years.

Sons Edwin and Frank Vandawarker took over their father's business and continued to live in this house until World War I. Occupied as a single family house until the 1930s, it became a rental property during the Depression and was somewhat neglected. In 1978 it was restored inside and out by local realtors Casey and Myra Jones, who received a preservation award in 1984 from the Ann Arbor Historic District Commission for their efforts.

OFW

301 North Fifth Avenue

Baumgardner's Barn

1887

This plain brick barn with an 1887 date stone under the eaves is the last surviving building of a complex that once dominated this small triangle of land. The buildings were all part of John Baumgardner's stone and marble business that specialized in sidewalks, tombstones, and sills and lintels for buildings. His business was the successor to that of his stepfather Anton Eisele and examples of their work can be seen on the Eisele house across the street at 216 Catherine Street (see 16). The entire complex later became the Wurster Dairy and the barn was used to stable the horses that pulled the milk wagons.

By the Depression of the 1930s, the other buildings in the complex were razed for a gas station. In the 1950s both gas station and barn served as a used car lot and paint and bump shop and were almost demolished by urban renewal. Today the barn is a rare survivor of another era in the heart of a thriving revitalized commercial district.

Though the hayloft door remains intact, the large garage door below was replaced by a window and entry door after a car smashed into the southeast corner of the building in 1978. The original windows were replaced during a renovation in the 1980s. The building recently housed an Italian grocery store run by the Argiero family who operate a restaurant in the former gas station next door.

OFW

Kip Miller

716 North Fifth Avenue

John Adam Volz House

1873

This exceptionally handsome and symmetrical Italianate house, with its bracketed eaves, segmental arched windows and brick detailing, was built for John Adam Volz in 1873. The intricate carving of the wood entry porch is still in fine condition. A summer kitchen to the rear was converted to a dining room and a new kitchen added in two stages in 1880 and 1890.

Volz had been the proprietor of the Ann Arbor Central Brewery next door at the corner of Fifth and Summit, since its opening in 1858. Water for the brewing operation was obtained from a spring behind the house. Volz sold the brewery the same year he built the house and two years later he sold the house as well to Jacob F. Beck, one of the new owners of the brewery. John Volz' daughter, Amelia, married John Jacob Muehlig. The second of their five children was Ann Arbor dry goods merchant and philanthropist, Bertha Muehlig, born in 1874.

In 1885, another young German emigrant, Frederick Walther, a miller by trade, purchased the house. His family and its descendants occupied it for more than eighty years. The Walther family took cuttings from a garden of lilac varietals in the Nichols Arboretum. The arboretum lilac garden is gone but the large old lilac shrubs which shelter the garden of this house grew from those cuttings.

DSHD

Lester Fader

724 North Fifth Avenue

Central Brewery

47

1858, 1898

The first specific mention of a brewery here is in the 1860 City Directory which lists Lawrence Trube, brewer, "on fifth." By 1868 brewer John Adam Volz is listed as proprietor of the Ann Arbor Central Brewery.

The larger of the building's two wings is a fairly simple example of the Commercial Italianate style with arched windows and projecting brick window hoods. The gable roof is unusual for this type of building as is the foundation of square-cut fieldstone.

Although Volz ran this large brewery successfully enough to build an elaborate Italianate home next door in 1873 (see 46), the Panic of 1873 forced him out of business. The brewery business, which expanded rapidly after the Civil War, was beginning to decline, not only because of the 1873 depression but also because local prohibition laws were beginning to squeeze many local brewers out of business. This brewery ceased operations sometime in the late 1870s. By 1883 the building had been converted to Bert Stoll's "Ann Arbor Pop Works," specializing in bottled ginger ale, root beer, and excelsior water. By 1886 it was Ross and Welch's Bottling Works and remained as such throughout the early 1890s. It was converted in 1899 from commercial to residential use, a year after the construction of the brick veneer wing along Summit Street.

Kip Miller

It first housed various German families then, during the 1920s, so many Italians that it was known as "Little Italy." From 1921 to 1956 the building was owned by Italian clothier Daniel Camelet. After World War II, it housed Japanese-Americans released from detainment camps. In the late 1970s, John Hollowell and Robert Harrington renovated the building into six contemporary apartments renamed "The Brewery Apartments."

IHP

48

415 South Fifth Avenue

Gaskell-Beakes House

1838, 1859

Kip Miller

Probably built by Clayton Gaskell around 1838, this house then passed through inheritance to the Beakes family who enlarged it in 1859. With its pedimented gable-front orientation, attic lunette, elaborate cornice, pilasters and classical entry, the house resembles many Greek Revival houses in upstate New York.

The house was the residence for two Ann Arbor mayors: Hiram Beakes, mayor from 1873-75, and Samuel Beakes, mayor from 1888-1890. Hiram lived in the house from 1860 until the late 1880s and also served as Probate Judge of Washtenaw County in the 1870s. His daughter Annie Beakes married Samuel Beakes (no relation).

It is Samuel Beakes after whom Beakes Street is named and it is he who authored the voluminous history of Washtenaw County in 1906 known as *Past and Present of Washtenaw County*. Samuel Beakes was also a major figure in local politics as chair of the county Democratic party, city treasurer, and editor of the *Ann Arbor Argus*, a local newspaper with a Democratic orientation.

In 1909 local historian Cornelia Corselius wrote of the house: "Mrs. Hiram Beakes spent over sixty years under that roof as maiden, wife and widow. It has been modified and modernized, but the low, spacious rooms are still charming and old fashioned. A spirit of kindly hospitality always pervaded this home as Mrs. Beakes enjoyed having her friends around her."

Although the house underwent considerable interior alteration in the 1920s when it was converted to apartments, its exterior remains largely intact. An addition on the south elevation includes a bracketed Italianate bay window. In 1936 it was photographed and studied as a candidate for the Historic American Buildings Survey (HABS) by Emil Lorch, former Director of the University of Michigan College of Architecture.
IHP

120-130 South First Street

1888, 1895, 1906, 1911

Allmendinger Organ Factory

This block-long group of brick buildings was built in four stages as a factory for the Allmendinger Organ Company. The company was founded in 1872 by David F. Allmendinger, who first worked from his frame house which stood on this site. A descendant of one of Ann Arbor's earliest pioneers, Allmendinger was apprenticed to master organ builder Gottlieb Gaertner in 1867. When Gaertner left for Ohio in 1871 to manage another factory, Allmendinger bought his equipment and married his daughter.

Allmendinger began modestly in the back rooms of his home where he hand-carved his earliest organs, sometimes using soup bones for the keys when ivory was unavailable. A conservative businessman, he preferred to peddle his finished organs personally by wagon, often trading them for flour, wood, and farm products. His earliest commissions were for church organs, but eventually he began to specialize in lightweight, affordable reed organs which many farmers proudly displayed (and played) in their parlors.

By 1888 he was successful enough to establish a stock company and build a four-story brick building (later reduced to two stories after a fire) on Washington Street. In 1895 the company began manufacturing Henderson Pianos as well as Ann Arbor Organs. They built a four-story brick building at the corner of Washington and First Streets, moving Allmendinger's house to a lot just beyond the railroad tracks. The company name was changed to the Ann Arbor Organ Company and a salesroom opened on South Main Street (see 121). In 1906 another two story brick section was added along First Street, and in 1911 the final two stories were added.

In 1915 competition from low-cost suppliers such as Sears Roebuck & Co had driven this company and many other small factories out of business. From 1916 to 1926 the buildings housed the Motor Products Company which made windshields for automobiles. By 1930 the buildings were empty and deteriorating.

CONTINUED on next page

Kip Miller

Mr. Carroll Benz, a local real estate agent, purchased them around 1935 and remodeled various spaces for rent. In 1947 Benz moved his own real estate office into one of the buildings and for almost 40 years this complex was known simply as the "Benz Building," despite the fact that Benz sold the buildings to the University of Michigan in 1969. The University housed several research institutes here until budget cuts in the recession of the 1980s forced the sale of the buildings in 1984. The purchaser, William Martin, with the expertise of Architects 4, completely renovated the building, replacing original windows and creating a modern entry for the 1895 structure.

Except for these changes, the exterior remains much as it was at the height of its days as an organ factory, a time when 5,000 organs and 600 pianos a year were produced and shipped to every state in the Union and to England, Scotland, Australia, the West Indies, and South Africa. These simple brick structures, imposing in size, remain a fine example of utilitarian factory design, reminding us of the days when workers lived in nearby neighborhoods and walked to and from work. In the new lobby, a visitor will find an original Allmendinger Organ and display panels telling the story of the factory, its owner, and the organs he built.

206-222 South First Street — *text on next page*

Sturgis Collection

206-222 South First Street

1853-1905

City Brewery-
Ann Arbor Central Mills

Due to its proximity to Allen Creek and to the main roads leading out of central Ann Arbor, this was an ideal location for a brewery. The 1853 map of Ann Arbor indicates "brewery" on this site. By 1860 the first City Directory lists it as G.F. Hauser's City Brewery; in 1868 it is John Reyer's City Brewery and in 1872 the Ekhardt Bros. Brewery. This German proprietorship has left its mark to this day: arched brick vaults in the basement are where beer "lagered" (lay) in barrels to age to the German taste for lighter beer.

The Panic of 1873 bankrupted many breweries, including this one. The Ann Arbor Central Mills acquired the property in 1882 and became the nucleus for a major flour mill operation lasting well into the 20th century. In the 1880s Washtenaw County was a highly profitable wheat growing area due to the increased use of the thresher. The beer industry still involved part of the property, however, as shown by an advertisement in the University of Michigan Yearbook, *The Palladium*, for 1886: "— W. Fred Schlanderer, Ann Arbor City Bottling Works, west side First, between Liberty and Washington, Schlitz Export, Pilsener, and Detroit Peninsular Brewery Co.'s Beer, delivered to any part of the city, daytime or evening."

The first building housing the mill was clapboard. The brick building here today was probably built around 1900. Since its windows are identical to those visible in photographs of the earlier wooden mill, it is likely that they were re-used in the new brick building. This gives the building an older feeling, as does the faded sign on the south wall advertising "KING AND WHITE LOAF FLOUR".

Other sections to the north of the mill include a two-story brick structure (probably from the 1860s) which originally had a pitched roof and rounded windows with thick brick arches. The northernmost part, built in 1905 for the mill offices, now houses the Blind Pig Saloon. It still contains the Central Mills' original walk-in safe, now used as a wine cooler by the restaurant.

In 1921, Ernest ("Ernie") F. Lohr bought the mill buildings and used them as a feed store until 1939 when he moved his own farm implement store into the structures. Today Ann Arbor Implement is still operating under the guidance of his son and son-in-law. Lawn and garden equipment have replaced farm machinery but the friendly atmosphere harks back to an earlier era, including the willingness of the owners to give tours of the lagering vaults when not too busy. In 1976 the Ann Arbor Bicentennial Commission awarded Lohr and the new owners of the Blind Pig a certificate for their preservation efforts.

IHP

106 North Fourth Avenue

Land Title Building

1927

Frances Wright

The Art Deco front of this building was designed by Albert J. Rousseau, graduate of the Ecole Nationale et Speciale des Beaux Arts in Paris and a distinguished professor of architecture and design at the University of Michigan. Professor Rousseau was well known for his designs for public architectural monuments. St Mary's Student Chapel on Thompson Street (see 151) is also his design.

In 1909 attorney Arthur Brown, a former mayor of Ann Arbor, and his wife, Cora, purchased this lot to construct a building for the Washtenaw Abstract Company, which he founded in 1893. The original small building was known for years as Brown's Little Old Office. Additions have been made several times and the building now extends to the alley at the back. As in many of the older buildings downtown, the partial basement is below the city sewer system and requires a pump.

Gertrude Norris, who joined the firm in 1900, succeeded Brown as its president in 1917. It was a matter of community interest that Miss Norris employed only women until Brown's daughter, Ruth, and her husband, George Wyman, joined the firm in the 1930s.

Gertrude Norris' tenure as president ended in 1956 when the Abstract and Title Guarantee Company absorbed the original company. In 1960, the Lawyers Title Insurance Corporation, a nationwide organization, purchased both the company and the building. The local office has been generously cooperative in opening their early files for researchers on Ann Arbor historic buildings.

IHP

Kip Miller

209-211 North Fourth Avenue — *text on next page*

209-211 North Fourth Avenue

1899

Kayser Block

53

This simple commercial structure, built in 1899 for office and retail use, was originally known as the Kayser Block. The sunburst brick patterns fanning out from the windows on the upper floors stand out as an exuberant display of the bricklayer's art. It was made possible by the new popularity of brick veneer over cinder block. By 1905, the building was known as Forester's Hotel and, according to City Directories, had "colored" managers throughout the early decades of the 20th century.

In 1921 the Colored Welfare League, a benevolent organization dedicated to helping African-Americans find jobs and housing in the community, purchased the building. The Welfare League had been the brainchild of Reverend Ralph Gilbert, Pastor of Second Baptist Church, who helped construction workers temporarily housed at the Dunbar Center at Fourth and Kingsley find permanent housing.

John Ragland, a 1938 University of Michigan Law School graduate who was active in the NAACP and who was the League's lawyer, described the building's transition from hotel to community center in a 1978 newspaper interview. Mr. Ragland, whose papers are housed at the Bentley Library, recalled that the League used money left over to help African-Americans after World War I to purchase the building. As new owners, the League evicted the Huron Club, a local gambling den and house of prostitution, and gradually turned the building into an African-American community center. This was especially important because the nearby YMCA refused to let their children use its facilities.

The many uses of this building by African-Americans for commercial and recreational purposes speaks to their commitment to help each other, especially considering the low wages and de facto segregation that existed at the time. By 1930, businesses that rented the ground floor space included a barbershop and beauty salon. African-American fraternal groups used meeting rooms upstairs and other rooms were rented to produce income. A tea room even occupied part of the upstairs from 1939 to 1943.

In 1966 J. D. Hall, a young barber, purchased the building. Though the costs of repairs were daunting, Hall persevered. He still owns the building today and maintains his barbershop there. The third floor has six reasonably priced rooms for rent while the second floor is still used by community groups. It is the only downtown commercial building owned and operated by an African-American businessman.

IHP

632 North Fourth Avenue

54

Bethel AME Church

1891-96

Kip Miller

Before the Civil War, African-Americans in Ann Arbor worshipped in a small Greek Revival church which still stands today at 504 High Street (see 64). Then it was simply known as the "Union" church or the "Colored" church.

Eventually two denominations developed: the African Methodist Episcopal (AME), organized in 1855, and the Second Baptist. The date of the first AME church building is unclear. All sources agree, however, that the present church building was begun in 1891 after the older structure was moved to the rear of the property. Bishop Henry McNeal Turner, an important figure in the AME church who had served President Lincoln as the first black chaplain in the United State Army, laid the cornerstone. Due to financial problems, however, the building was not dedicated until 1896.

During the Depression of the 1890s a trustee mortgaged his own home so the church would be saved. In the ensuing decades Ann Arbor's African-American population grew and so did this congregation. Racial discrimination was endemic, neighborhoods were segregated, low-paying jobs were the norm. But the church was a refuge in these hard times. As one member recalled: "— Our lives revolved around the church. We socialized there, did our homework there. If you were passing by and saw the light on, you went in to see what was going on."

The congregation eventually prospered and built a new church on Plum Street selling the old one to the New Grace Apostolic congregation in 1971. New Grace Apostolic belongs to the Pentecostal Assemblies of the World of Apostolic Faith, an interracial group of fundamentalists.

111 South Fourth Avenue

Heinrich Building

1870

There was a saloon at this location from the time the first courthouse was built in the 1830s until Prohibition days. With Solon Cook's Temperance Hotel across the street, the saloon was probably a popular refuge. It survived a reform period in the 1870s when the number of saloons in Ann Arbor was cut from 80 to 32.

John D. Heinrich, proprietor of the Kossuth House Saloon at the corner of Pontiac (Beakes) and Summit, acquired this property on South Fourth Avenue in the early 1860s. Before the decade closed he replaced the old saloon with this commercial Italianate brick structure, which Heinrich and his son-in-law George Stein operated as a saloon-hotel-residence until his death in 1890.

Number 111 South Fourth continued to be a saloon, changing management several times, until 1918 and the coming of the prohibition era. Thereafter it housed a succession of small businesses. The adjoining building at No. 113, which originally housed a blacksmith shop, was erected in the early 1900s.

The Heinrich Building is in good condition with its Italianate cornice and most of the ground floor facade intact. The facade is unusual, having pilasters at the corners and between the windows. The upper levels now make up a condominium and the first floor awaits an occupant. The original wooden basement steps, worn away through the years by beer barrels rolled to cellar storage, were used as a sculpture on an exposed interior brick wall by attorney Peter DeLoof during his tenure as owner and occupant.

IHP

Frances Wright

402 South Fourth Avenue

56

Ottmar Eberbach House

1875

Ottmar Eberbach, like his pharmacist father, Christian, received his professional education in Germany. Returning to Ann Arbor, he joined the firm of Eberbach and Sons, manufacturers of pharmaceuticals and scientific equipment.

When Ottmar married Katherine Haller in 1870, he began to build this red brick Queen Anne house. Cherry panels were used for the interior trim and the house was furnished with six handsomely decorated fireplaces. The finest of these, the parlor mantel, was removed with the permission of the Eberbach family when the house was occupied by the Harris Tire Company many years later. Efforts to locate it have been unsuccessful.

The original lot is still defined by two "rustic" iron hitching posts, one at the corner and the other at the far side of an adjacent house which occupies what was the Eberbach garden area.

At the turn of the century, the intersection of Fourth and William was a distinguished residential area, with a fine home on each corner. By 1908, however, the DeFries home on the northwest corner had been converted to the Alpha Hotel-Boarding; the southeast corner home had become the Ann Arbor Sanitarium (now Muehlig's Funeral Home); the Bach house was on the lot now occupied by the Ann Arbor Y. Although the tire company began use of the house in 1928, the Eberbach family retained ownership until 1974. The beer depot addition was made in 1938. The house is now a multifamily conversion.

EWHD

403 South Fourth Avenue

1874, 1928

Joe T. Jacobs House (Muehlig Funeral Chapel)

This brick house was originally constructed by local builder John Gates as a private residence for Joe T. Jacobs, a clothier. The house features pairs of curved brackets supporting the roof, tall windows capped by stone keystones, and small attic windows—all hallmarks of the late Italianate style. Although partially obscured by the funeral parlor's additions, these original features are still quite visible. It was one of four high-style buildings which graced this intersection. Today, only this house and the Eberbach house across the street (see 56), remind us of this era of gentility.

Jacobs came to Ann Arbor from Ohio and started his clothing business in 1867. In 1880 he was nominated by the Republicans for State Senator from Washtenaw County. He was also a major benefactor of the Toledo, Ann Arbor and Northern Michigan Railway (see 12) and helped it to succeed.

Jacobs sold his house to Dr. J. B. Lynds, who used it as a private hospital until he died in the 1918 influenza epidemic. In 1928 Muehlig's Funeral Chapel purchased the property and added the porte-cochere (covered driveway) and a large garage accessible from two directions. More remodeling occurred in 1951 and again in 1964 when the front portion was added and the parking lot expanded.

Muehlig Funeral Chapel itself has a long history. Florian Muehlig began a coffin and cabinetry business in 1852 in the upper floors of the 200 block of South Main Street. Today it is the oldest funeral parlor in the state and the oldest continuously operating business in Ann Arbor.

EWHD

Kip Miller

58

423 South Fourth Avenue

Bethlehem Church

1895-96

Kip Miller

The history of Bethlehem Church is closely tied to that of German immigration to Ann Arbor and Washtenaw County and to the subsequent divisions within that community. In 1833 Reverend Frederich Schmid arrived from Basel, Switzerland, responding to a call for the gospel to be preached in German. A zealous missionary, Schmid organized many churches in Michigan but Bethlehem appears to have been the first. Schmid and his congregants built a small frame church in what is today Bethlehem Cemetery. A large stone now marks the location. In 1849 the congregation completed a new church in town on the northeast corner of Washington and First Streets.

In 1874, Schmid and some members broke away and formed what is now Zion Lutheran Church. The conflict arose over whether to expel members who did not pay their pledges for a new building, the old one having become too small. "For a time, there were strong feelings between Bethlehem and Zion, not known as love" said Reverend Orval Willimann in a talk before the Washtenaw County Historical Society in 1983. But today the two churches enjoy warm relations and share a common descent from Ann Arbor's pioneer German families.

Because of the split, the members of Bethlehem had to wait until 1895 to build their new edifice. It was designed by architect Richard Rasemann of Detroit,who was selected by a committee led by their energetic Pastor John Neumann. Built of native fieldstone in the Richardsonian Romanesque Style and incorporating Gothic features, it was constructed by Clanfield Contractors of Ypsilanti for $20,000. When it was dedicated in January of 1896, it was considered "Gothic with just enough variation to suit the modern eye." In 1935 an annex was added in a style similar to that of the original buildings.

No fewer than four congregations claim to be the oldest German church in Michigan but the State of Michigan has recognized Bethlehem as the oldest and placed it on the State Register of Historic Places in 1982. A State Marker was erected in front of the church in 1983 in honor of the church's Sesquicentennial.

IHP

445 South Fourth Avenue

George and Emma Wahr House

59

1890

Four years before George Wahr constructed a similar high-style Queen Anne house on North Division Street (see 26) next to the Wilson-Wahr House (see 28), he built this house on South Fourth Avenue near the intersection with Packard Street. Embellished with an elaborate display of the woodworker's craft, the house is detailed with carved barge boards, sunbursts, dormers, bays and gables, all blending together in a wonderful example of Victorian excess. It is rumored that Wahr had a feud with his neighbor who hung the wash out on a line to dry. This apparently upset him enough to move to the other side of town! (His increasing prosperity might also have prompted the move to a more exclusive part of town.)

Wahr's bookstore on Main Street became quite successful by the late 1880s when his name appears in bold letters in the City Directory. Four years after he built this house, he opened his second bookstore on State Street. It outlasted his Main Street store by many years, remaining in business until the 1970s. The first occupant after that was Border's Books, then a used and rare book shop.

Wahr sold the property to the Schaffer family who lived here for close to a century, which helps explain its intact condition today. George D. and Elizabeth Schaffer moved into the house in 1894 and by 1900 they had seven children: Anna, Bertha, Carrie, Elizabeth, Ella, George Jr. and William H. By 1915 only Carrie, Anna, and Bertha were still living with their parents and by the mid-1930s only Anna and Bertha were still here. In 1935, their mother Elizabeth, a widow, married the man next door, Mr. Frank Ohlinger, and moved into 451 South Fourth Avenue. In 1965 she was again widowed. In the late 1970s, probably after her mother's death, Bertha moved into 451 and rented out 445.

Kip Miller

After Bertha's death, both properties were sold and the house at 445 was purchased by the William Johnson family in 1981. They did a major overhaul of the house, restoring it to its original splendor. They were recognized by the Historic District Commission in 1988 for their splendid efforts at reviving this glorious structure.

916 Fuller Road

61

Washtenaw Light and Power Building

1902

Kip Miller

Passers-by have always been intrigued by this unusual structure. The two-story tower portion was erected in 1902 as a relay station by the Washtenaw Light and Power Company, eventually becoming a sub-station for the Detroit Edison Company until 1949. When architect David Osler bought the empty building in 1961, his lively adaptation of the interior for his office and library maximized the space offered by the brick shell with hip roof. An addition, constructed as a separate building to the rear, is connected by a passage, creating a small atrium between.

504 High Street

Union Church

64

1853-1857

This small brick structure appears on the 1853 map of Ann Arbor labeled simply as "Union Church." It apparently was not finished until 1857, for the *Michigan Argus* of December 25th of that year reported: "The Union Church has been completed by the Colored People of the City and is to be dedicated Sunday by Reverend J. M. Gregory. S. H. Estabrook will officiate." Although its simple classical lines are obscured by a later porch, the building serves as a fine example of the vernacular use of the Greek Revival idiom for non-residential purposes.

It continued to be used as a church into the 1870s, though by 1871 a split had occurred within the local African-American religious community. This resulted in the formation of two congregations: the African Baptist (later known as Second Baptist) and the African Methodist Episcopal (AME) Church. Both continue in operation today and trace their roots to this building on what was then known as Fuller Street.

By 1872, the AME congregation had begun to worship on the east side of Fourth Avenue between Summit Street and what is now Beakes Street. Although the Baptists continued to use the High Street Church until 1881, from 1883 until 1888 they have no listing in City Directories. In 1890 they reappear as the Second Baptist Church, worshipping in a building on the southwest corner of Fifth Avenue and Beakes Street.

In 1884 the High Street property was sold to Michael Kearns who converted it into a residence. When his widow Mary sold the property in 1907, more than 20 years later, it was still referred to in the deed as "the church lot," perpetuating the memory of its first use. It continues to be used as a residential property today.

OFW

Kip Miller

72

206 East Huron Street

Ann Arbor Tribune Building
(Kleinschmidt Insurance Company)

1931

Frances Wright

The distinctive Art Deco facade was added to this brick building in the early 1930s when the *Ann Arbor Tribune* occupied this building, on the old site of what had been Fred and Mary Heusel's City Bakery since the 1890s. The Tribune was the outgrowth of a series of German language newspapers, most directly *Die Neue Post*, published by Eugene J. Helber. Helber was outspokenly pro-German during the initial years of World War I, before the United States joined the conflict. After some difficulties with the federal authorities, he deemed it wise to change the paper to the English language and to design a new masthead. In the late 1930s the paper became the weekly *Washtenaw Post-Tribune* and moved its offices a few doors away. In 1937 the Tribune lost its young reporter-editor, Arthur Gallagher, to the *Ann Arbor Daily News* (now the *Ann Arbor News*), where he remained until he retired as Editor-in-Chief in 1976.

The Springer family bought the building in 1939 for its insurance offices, which later became the Springer-Kleinschmidt Agency. The Springer name is now gone and the Kleinschmidt Agency owns and occupies the building.

Although changes were made to the interior when it was converted to offices, the old molded metal walls and ceilings of the 1890s remain in place under new paneling and tile.

IHP

219 East Huron Street

Firemen's Hall

1882

For more than ninety years Ann Arbor's elegant, multi-arched firehouse has borne witness to the civic pride of our forebears. Built in 1882-83, the firehouse was designed by the Detroit architect William Scott. Under the watchful eye of the Council and its building committee, the new firehouse was completed by contractors Tessmer and Ross of Ann Arbor, at almost the exact cost authorized by the voters: $10,000. The building is constructed largely of brick, some of which is projected so as to form arches or rows of corbeling. For many years the building was painted red with much of the decorative brick work painted white to suggest stone. This was a common method of emphasizing high-style features when builders were faced with a shortage of stone or of funds. In the late 1970s, the paint was removed to reveal the soft tones of the original brick as well as the delicacy of the original stone detailing.

When the new fire station was erected in the 1970's, the people of Ann Arbor were determined to save their beloved landmark. Cynthia Yao proposed to City Council in 1978 that the building be converted to a special kind of museum for children, dedicated to education through a hands-on approach to the sciences. In 1979 permission for this use was conditioned on raising funds for the renovation. Due to the inspiration of Cynthia Yao and the financial and technical support of many townspeople, it is now the successful Hands-On Museum.

Kip Miller

The City of Ann Arbor has restored the exterior of the building with little change. A weather vane, typical for fire houses in the 19th century, has been added to the tower. The interior has been rehabilitated in two stages to house the museum exhibits. The old firehouse kitchen was converted to a "discovery room" and a greenhouse has been added on the west side.

NR, OFW

74

412 East Huron Street

Asahel Parkhurst House

Circa 1848

This side-entry, New England style, clapboard house was probably constructed around 1848, shortly after Asahel Parkhurst purchased the land on which it is built. In 1850 he sold it to Martha Seeley and she in turn sold it to the Wilmots who sold it to Tracy Root in 1855. The Root family occupied it for over half a century, adding the Italianate double brackets under the eaves as well as a large, two-story addition on the east which was removed after the turn of the century.

Tracy Root was the son of early Ann Arbor pioneer Erastus Root, who came to Ann Arbor from the East in 1832 and operated a dry goods store for a number of years. Tracy grew up on Spring Street, became a lawyer, and practiced for many years in his home on West Huron Street. He was also Washtenaw County Clerk in 1862 and Circuit Court Commissioner in 1872. Root was one of many professionals, including lawyers, doctors, and University of Michigan professors, who made their homes along then-fashionable Huron Street. When the advent of the automobile made living on the outskirts of the city more attractive, many of these houses were demolished for gas stations and parking lots. Root's house and two others on this block are our only remnants of the gentility of this thoroughfare in the 19th century.

Kip Miller

One reason this house survived was that it had thoughtful owners throughout the 20th century. One was University of Michigan Professor of Art Richard L. Sears who lived in the house in the 1950s and 60s. He cared for the house and even maintained the illusion of a center window on the second story using shutters, which unfortunately were removed in a later renovation.

Except for the porch and the pairs of brackets under the eaves which would indicate an 1860s date, the house probably looks now as it did when it was constructed. Its century of service as a residential property ended, however, when it was converted to office use in the 1980s. It is now owned by the Suburban Communication Corporation.

OFW

502 East Huron Street

Silas Douglass House

1848

Sturgis Collection

The Silas Douglass home is the first in Ann Arbor to be designed by an architect, Arthur Marshall. Begun in 1848, it is a splendid example of Gothic Revival residential architecture, with steeply sloped roofs, gingerbread carving under the eaves, stucco walls scored to resemble masonry, and the use of Gothic motifs such as quatrefoils and trefoils. The east wing was added in 1855, the west wing in 1856, and a bay window, gas piping and marble mantel in 1858. They added a well and cellar in 1863 and the dining room bay window in 1864. The water for the bathroom came from a six barrel tank anchored in the attic and filled with rain water. A small picturesque porch along the east front and a picket fence were removed years ago after they fell into disrepair.

Douglass, a brilliant and energetic man, came from Chautauqua, New York, to study medicine with Drs. Rice and Pitcher of Detroit. In 1844, he joined the University of Michigan faculty as professor of chemistry, where he was a leader in establishing Michigan's pioneer chemical laboratory and library. Twice mayor of Ann Arbor, dean of the University's medical faculty, head of the chemical laboratory, Douglass led a full and varied life and was often at the center of controversy. In his spare time he supervised the construction of the University water mains, a classroom building, and the Observatory. "Believing the city to have groped in darkness long enough," Douglass urged the founding in 1858 of the Ann Arbor Gas Company. While mayor in 1871-72, he reorganized the city's tiny police force and introduced a licensing system to regulate liquor traffic.

Helen and Silas Douglass raised their seven children and lived out their lives in this house. In 1902 the local Baptist Guild acquired the property for student activities. A few years later it was turned over to the Baptist Church, where it has been used as church offices and housing for the sexton. The *Ann Arbor Observer* had its birth in this house when Don and Mary Hunt were serving as sextons of the church. The Douglass estate is now filled in with church structures and a parking area, but one can still imagine the fine old trees and extensive garden beds that once were there.

OFW

76

512 East Huron Street

First Baptist Church

1880

So important was the construction of this church building, the third in the history of the First Baptist Church since its organization in 1828, that members monitored its construction and personally selected and arranged the square-cut fieldstones into pleasing designs. Parishioner John Nowland provided the black walnut for the interior from his farm and Edward Olney, a nationally-known Professor of Mathematics at the University of Michigan, mortgaged his own home to raise funds to build the church.

Historically Baptists have been champions of individualism and this freedom has often been translated architecturally into non-standard church forms. In this church, however, the reigning Gothic style, with its hammer beams reminiscent of medieval English churches, was adapted to Baptist sensibilities and rituals. Accustomed to a semicircular arrangement around a preacher with parishioners close to the pulpit, the Baptists manipulated the cruciform plan to suit their purposes.

The result is a blending of the shape of the cross with a spread-out seating arrangement that produces in the onlooker a pleasant sensation as one enters the church. Prominent balconies sweep down to meet the front altar on each side and the hammer beams further accentuate the sensation. Although the altar and front entrance were remodelled and the steeple replaced some years ago, the church remains remarkably the same as it was over 100 years ago. "Shaded by magnificent oak trees, its sharply rising roof line and slender central spire and its capping front ornament of 'Cross and Crown' the church is still the pride of the congregation." These words, written by Lela Duff in 1961, still hold true today.

The First Baptist church was organized in 1828 in a farmhouse three miles west of Ann Arbor. Four years later services were held in town above Anson Brown's store on Broadway and construction of a church building began on Wall Street in 1835. In 1849 the congregation erected a brick church on Catherine Street between Division and Fifth Avenue in order to be closer to the university students. In 1880 they commenced building the present church and the old brick church was demolished shortly after the new one was completed.

OFW

Kip Miller

Harris Hall *(see next page)*

Kip Miller

617 East Huron Street

Harris Hall

77

1886

Bishop Samuel Harris and members of the St. Andrews's Episcopal Parish began planning in 1883 for a student center and parish hall on a site which would provide the students with an alternative to the worldly recreations offered downtown. It was a time of vigorous religious activity on the campus and the more traditional churches were disturbed by the numbers of students crowding in to the popular lectures at the new Unitarian church and social center at State and Huron.

Architect Gordon W. Lloyd was asked to design a two-story brick building "economically and of sober design." Although Lloyd was a Gothicist, the building was designed in the Richardsonian Romanesque vogue of the time. The red brick building is trimmed with stone string courses. While the arches of the upper windows have colored glass transom lights, the recessed arches over the lower windows are finished with red terra cotta in a checkered pattern. The arched and gabled entrance portal covers the steps, and the broad arch flanked by buttressed walls is crowned by a stone drip molding and carved capitals of a Gothic character.

The Hall was finished in 1886 with funds raised throughout the Diocese and other parts of the country. J. P. Morgan contributed $l,389.50. The project required $28,000 for the building and additional funds to endow a lectureship. Originally named Hobart Hall (after the Reverend John Henry Hobart, the first Bishop to officiate in what is now the state of Michigan), the building was renamed to honor the memory of Bishop Harris when he died in 1888.

In 1943, parish and student activities were removed from Harris Hall to Canterbury House on North Division Street, and the building was leased to the USO for its work with servicemen being trained on the U-M campus. At the end of the war Harris Hall was leased to the University of Michigan and served for many years as headquarters for band activities, particularly as offices for the Michigan Marching Band and its director, William D. Revelli.

The non-denominational Word of God Community, which started in Ann Arbor in the late 1960s and became a leader in the charismatic renewal movement, purchased the building from the Episcopal Student Foundation in June of 1974. The firm of Buckheim and Rowland acquired the building in 1980 and thoroughly rehabilitated it for office space. While the interior has been somewhat altered in the conversion, the mantel piece, the staircase, and other fine appointments have been retained.

NR, OFW

78

903 East Huron Street

Harvey Bannister House

1858

This simple brick house, with a pediment suggested only by its roof-pitch and cornice returns, is typical of the late Greek Revival houses built in Ann Arbor just before the Civil War. The building was constructed by local mason Harvey Bannister, who built it as a rooming house for University of Michigan students.

Kip Miller

Until 1852 students lived in the University dormitories. That year they were notified by newly appointed President Henry Philip Tappan that they would have to find lodging and board within the community since their former living quarters were needed for classroom space. Howard H. Peckham noted in his history of the University of Michigan, Tappan "no doubt was aware that his friend President Wayland of Brown [University] blamed dormitories for most of the evils of college life: temptations to vice from evil student leaders, the costs of building that should go into libraries and laboratories, danger of epidemics from contagious diseases, and imposition on the college of responsibilities it could not carry out effectively." Tappan also wanted to end the institutional isolation of students and make them community citizens. His new policy set off a building frenzy in many areas near the university, particularly in the area just north of the campus.

Bannister's is one of many boarding houses that sprang up in this area, historically the city's Fourth Ward. It continued to be a boarding house throughout the 19th and into the 20th centuries. In the mid-1920s, it was purchased by Catherine Meier who, with her daughter Joy Meier, occupied it as a family residence for over 50 years. In the 1970s it became an owner-occupied duplex, and in the late 1980s it again became rental apartments. Its classical proportions and details have been carefully maintained through all these years and it still retains its original six-over-six windows.

OFW

1007 East Huron Street

Charles Whitman House

79

1891

With its broad expanse of roof, the overall use of saw-tooth shingles and the multi-paned and curved glass windows on the first floor, this handsome house is an example of the Shingle Style rare in Ann Arbor. It was built by railroad tycoon and State Commissioner of Railroads, Charles Whitman, in 1891 in an eclectic style which combined features of the Dutch and Colonial Revival styles with a shingle overcoat. The simpler design and balanced proportions signal the waning appeal of the Queen Anne style, though it would be a decade before newer styles really took hold.

The house still retains most of its original character including its round bowed windows on the first floor which is built almost entirely of cut-fieldstone, its multi-paned windows, and the unusual shingle pattern. The attached porte cochere on the west is also unusually distinctive. Emily Hollister, a visiting, nurse, commented in the July, 1891, entry in her diary that "lawyer Whitman is building a new place up the street to cost $1,000." Hollister also noted that Mrs. Whitman was very haughty and status conscious — indicating their choice of house site was quite high class in 1891. So outstanding was the house at the time that it was featured in the 1896 *Ann Arbor Headlight* as one of the prominent homes in the city.

Technological innovations, especially the invention of the automobile and the telephone, led to this neighborhood rapidly losing its appeal to the upper classes. In 1898 Whitman sold his home to the Chi Psi Fraternity. In the 1920s it became the Psi Omega Fraternity and in 1936 it was purchased for $75,000 by the Rackham Trustees of the University of Michigan to establish the Institute for Human Adjustment's Speech Clinic.

Still owned by the University of Michigan, it has served since the 1930s in some capacity for the Institute. It was the Counseling Center in the 1970s and 80s and currently is the Center for the Child and the Family. Long recognized as an almost pristine example of the Shingle Style, the building received an award in 1976 from the Ann Arbor Bicentennial Commission.

Kip Miller

OFW

116 West Huron Street

Ann Arbor Bus Depot

1940

Kip Miller

Shortly after opening with a ribbon-cutting ceremony by Mayor Walter Sadler on September 5, 1940, the Ann Arbor Bus Depot was featured in an book entitled *Modern Bus Terminals and Post Houses*. New bus terminals, the authors noted, were being designed not only to meet new demands by travelers but also in a modern and more aesthetically pleasing style. Designed by the architecture firm of Banfield and Cumming of Cleveland, Ohio (which also designed similar bus depots in Kalamazoo and Windsor, Ontario), in association with Ann Arbor architect Douglas Loree, the Ann Arbor Depot was one of a small number of new bus stations designed in the streamlined Art Deco style popular in the 1930s and 40s.

The depot represents a simple yet eye-catching example of this style with its wide expanse of curved glass, smooth-sawn Indiana limestone, and black granite base. The vertical porcelain enamel sign, trimmed in stainless steel, enhances the effect as it plays off the horizontal sweep of the window which ends in a semi-circle at the west end of the facade.

Older residents remember the elegant interior with its stainless steel stairways and birchwood cabinetry that matched the sleekness of the exterior. Although the interior no longer exists in its original form, the exterior is intact and remains a popular photographic subject in town. It has appeared in many guide books about Ann Arbor and other promotional materials and was cited in 1986 as a 'favorite building' by a majority of a panel selected by the *Ann Arbor Observer*.

A national journal recently commented that the "— old Greyhound Bus Depot, once the soul of modernity, is now often the only Art Deco component in many small towns." In its bus depot, Ann Arbor preserves its only Art Deco public structure and joins a handful of other towns which still possess these rare jewels.

IHP

114 North Ingalls Street

John and Electa Carman House

84

1880

This transitional Italianate brick structure, built by retired farmer John Carman in 1880, shows traces of Gothic influence in the steeply pitched roof and elaborately pierced and cut wood trim under the front gable. A careful observer can see the outline of the arched windows that were squared off sometime in the 20th century when arches were no longer fashionable. The current porch was constructed in the early decades of the 20th century.

Carman and his wife Electa raised several children here. The most memorable in the community was their daughter Georgianna who was principal of the Fourth Ward School in 1883 and later became principal of the Perry School. Georgianna and her husband Hartwig Herbst lived first with her parents at this address and later in the house next door at 110 North Ingalls Street. The Carman family continued to occupy the house at 114 until 1909, when daughter Mary sold it to Charles and Anna Rankin. The house then served as a nurses' home until the late 1920s when Mrs. Bertha Edwards lived here with a succession of changing tenants in the other half of the house.

Despite many changes and additions, the house retains the flavor of the late 19th century and is well maintained despite its heavy use as a student rental.

OFW

Kip Miller

85

220 North Ingalls Street

Phi Rho Sigma Fraternity

1929

Kip Miller

In 1949 the directors of St. Joseph Mercy Hospital notified the local chapter of Phi Rho Sigma, a medical fraternity, that it "coveted their land for a hospital expansion." The chapter agreed to move to a new site and, according to a 1981 article in the fraternity's journal, "The entire house was lifted off its foundation and moved, intact, across Catherine Street to rest on a new foundation at 220 North Ingalls. Here it stands today, sturdy as ever. Word has it that the transition was so smooth that chinaware left in the cupboards during the move was not broken."

Organized in June of 1897 at the home of Roy Bishop Canfield, the fraternity has always been located close to the hospitals and other medical buildings of the university. It occupied various buildings on Cornwell and Huron Streets until it was able to purchase the Stevens property at the northeast corner of Catherine and Ingalls Streets. After remodelling the house they had purchased, the fraternity moved into it in 1911.

By 1929 enough money had been saved to build a new house and the fraternity hired architect Myron E. Pugh to design their new home in the English Tudor style. The 84-foot long building is mostly of sandstone laid in a random ashlar pattern. Gables are faced with wood half-timbers and tapestry brick and the roof is of rough slate. Other features of the Tudor style include leaded glass, oriel windows and quatrefoil designs. With joists of steel and walls of stone, brick and hollow tile, this structure was built to last.

With the admission of women into the formerly all-male fraternity in 1975, the Phi Rho Sigmas made the transition from a medical fraternity to a medical society. Their coed living arrangement continues to be satisfactory to all parties.

OFW

321 North Ingalls Street

Reuben Kempf House

86

1889

Although most people are familiar with Reuben Kempf's Greek Revival house on Division Street (see 38), few are aware that there was another Reuben Kempf in Ann Arbor. This Reuben Kempf was originally from Chelsea, Michigan, and made his fortune as a banker. He built this muscular Queen Anne style house in 1889 and a few years later it was featured as one of the premier local residences in the Ann Arbor Headlight of 1896.

The house is the epitome of what one would call "Victorian." Built of brick on a high foundation, it has the asymmetrical arrangement of space and the use of various materials so characteristic of the Queen Anne style. These contrasting materials have long been hidden by a uniform coat of grey paint, however. The octagonal tower features a combination weather vane/finial with a crown and banner motif, while the two-story porch facing Ingalls Street has very unusual detailing with double balustrades, turned porch posts, and lattice spindle work on the upper section. Original porches on Queen Anne houses are extremely rare in most towns, and these are truly unique survivors of Ann Arbor's architectural heritage.

In 1883, Reuben Kempf organized the Farmers and Mechanics Bank, at the southeast corner of Main and Huron Streets, serving as its President until his death around 1916. His widow occupied the house only a short while afterwards, selling it to fruit merchant Albert Basso in 1918. Following World War II, Edith Hagerman purchased the house for her husband, Dr. George Hagerman, to use as his office since St. Joseph Hospital was then conveniently across the street. Eventually the Hagerman's moved into the house. After the Doctor's death, Mrs. Hagerman remained there until the early 1990s. In 1992, the house was purchased by a long-time neighbor who is now in the process of remodelling the house for commercial and residential use.

OFW

Kip Miller

90

324-326 East Kingsley Street

North District Public School

1846

Numerous private academies flourished in Ann Arbor from the 1830s, but it was not until the 1840s that any effort was made by the citizens to tax themselves and construct public schools. This building, the first public school for the North District in the Upper Village, was erected in 1846 in the austere Greek Revival style which matched so well the prevailing sensibilities about the role of education in securing the morality of youth. This building also has the distinction of being the site of the formation of the Washtenaw County Agricultural Society in 1848. A second public school for the South District was located in the "Old Academy" at Fourth Avenue and William Street (now the site of a parking garage).

It was not until after Ann Arbor officially became a city in 1851, that the public school system began in earnest. The 1881 *History of Washtenaw County* laments that "it is a matter of regret that during these years, up to the reunion of the two districts in 1853, the materials for a school history of Ann Arbor are so meager that not even the names of the teachers have been preserved."

By 1869 the rapid growth of the school population required the building of a larger school which was constructed on Division Street on the site of what is now Community High School. When the new school opened, St. Thomas Parish bought the old building and opened their first parochial school (see 42). In 1886 the parish, having built a new larger building on Elizabeth Street, sold the old school to John Pfisterer.

Kip Miller

Pfisterer apparently used the old school as a residence. Some years later, around World War I, it was converted into its present duplex arrangement. The most notable tenants during the 20th century were the Pastorino family who lived both here and next door for over 35 years. Rosa Pastorino was the daughter of Rocco Desderide, first owner of the building now housing Zingerman's (see 22). Desderide lived here with his daughter until the age of 104, making model ships in the little potting shed that still stands in the backyard.

OFW

407 East Kingsley

John Lawrence House

1903

Kip Miller

This large Colonial Revival house with its symmetrical facade and Georgian detailing, still reveals a few traces of the Queen Anne style in its asymmetrical floor plan and varied windows. The house was reputedly designed by the well-known Detroit architect Albert Kahn, who was responsible for many University of Michigan buildings including the Clements Library, the Natural Resources Building and Hill Auditorium. Kahn designed only a few residential structures in Ann Arbor, including the Delta Upsilon Fraternity house (see 68), and the Edward Campbell House (see 169).

The house was built for attorney John Lawrence, who became a United States District Attorney and Circuit Court Commissioner. He was the son of Edwin Lawrence, a respected judge for whom Lawrence Street was named. The Lawrence family were active in developing Ann Arbor and platted the area south of Packard Street and east of Division, naming the streets Edwin, Sybil, Benjamin, and Mary after family members.

John's father's house, which he tore down to build a more stylish and modern one, was a large 1840s structure. It was one of a number singled out by the *Michigan Argus* in 1849 as showing the good taste of its citizens. Edwin's home had also been a center of social activity in the mid-19th century and was where Ralph Waldo Emerson gave his "manners and morals" address in 1860.

After John died in 1921, his wife Marie lived in the house until her death a few years later. The house was then sold to Professor William Butts. In the 1940s it was home to the Edward Conlin family, also members of the legal profession and parishioners of nearby St. Thomas Church. It has thus sheltered many of Ann Arbor's most notable judges and lawyers. Like most of the large houses in this neighborhood, however, it was converted to apartments after World War II.

OFW

92

809 East Kingsley Street

Kingsley Apartments

1929

Kip Miller

"One of the largest of the many which sprang up in Ann Arbor last summer. It overlooks — from the rear — the Michigan Central tracks. It is on Kingsley Street near St. Joseph's Hospital." So wrote the *Michigan Alumnus* in December of 1929 when this Mediterranean Revival apartment building was built. With Moorish overtones in the multi-colored stone entry reminding one of the Alhambra, and long tapering window recesses topped by Islamic arches, the building resembles many built in Detroit in the Palmer Park area at this time. Only a few apartment buildings were built in this style in Ann Arbor (see 9, 139 and 153).

The building was designed by Ypsilanti architect R. S. Gerganoff who later designed many of Ypsilanti's public buildings, primarily schools, as well as the Washtenaw County Courthouse built in 1954. Gerganoff's use here of orange brick, terra cotta panels, diamond-shaped accents in green-and blue-glazed tile, tapestry brick panels, and black wrought-iron railings, epitomizes the Spanish influences characteristic of this style.

This 37-unit building has always housed many nurses and medical students due to its proximity to the nearby hospitals and continues to afford its tenants magnificent views of the Huron River Valley.

OFW

401 Lawrence Street

David Rinsey House

93

1890

When grocer David Rinsey built his house on the corner of Division and Lawrence Streets in 1890, Division was still a very fashionable place to live. The intricately detailed Queen Anne house was intended as a symbol of both the owner's prosperity and good taste. The house still retains its "Victorian" look with its many gables, variety of surface patterns, and cutaway corners.

Rinsey was a true American success story. He came to America at the age of 16 as an indentured servant and was able to establish his own grocery and bakery in 1867. His partner, Moses Seabolt, was also from Baden, and their German firm of Rinsey and Seabolt served Ann Arbor for over 40 years. Rinsey also became director of the Ann Arbor Savings Bank and the Ann Arbor Fruit and Vinegar Company.

When Rinsey purchased this property in 1890 there was a house on the site, the former home of James Kingsley, pioneer, judge and University of Michigan Regent. Rinsey moved Judge Kingsley's house to the north part of the original lot — immense by today's standards — to what is now 412 North Division Street. He built his new house on the corner, leaving a large lawn to the north where his son later built another home (See 34).

Rinsey died in 1914 and his widow Jennett and their unmarried daughters continued to occupy the big house. When Jennett died in 1938, her daughters converted the house into apartments while continuing to live there themselves. The porch was altered slightly to accomodate the front door and address facing Lawrence Street. The cherry and maple parquet floors, the oak-panelled ceilings, the wainscoting, the tiled fireplaces, and even the lincrusta wall coverings (a linoleum derived material which simulated embossed leather) remain today, making this house a showpiece both inside and out.

OFW

Kip Miller

94

601-603 Lawrence Street

Margaret Kearney House

Circa 1880

Kip Miller

In 1879, when Miss Margaret Kearney purchased this lot, it may still have contained the older house that appears on maps from 1853-1870. Since the bird's eye view for 1880 indicates no building here, it is likely that she built this fine brick Italianate soon afterward. Although its window sash have been replaced, the Italianate features, including the porch with its chamfered columns, the star cutouts in the front gable, and the long narrow windows with their arched tops remain intact.

The Kearney family began a long association with this part of town in late 1877 when Ambrose Kearney, a local grocer, purchased the property around the corner at 411 North State Street. Two years later, Ambrose's sister Margaret purchased the Lawrence Street property, which abuts the State Street property on the rear, from William Parker who had bought it at a sheriff's sale. The first tenant listed in the 1883 City Directory was Reverend Russell Pope, pastor of the Methodist Church. By 1886 Margaret Kearney lived here along with her brother Ambrose who moved back to his State Street property the following year. In the 1890s their father, Thomas D. Kearney, a farmer from Northfield Township, moved in with Margaret.

The Kearney family remained associated with the house for many years. Although the house stood vacant for part of the 1920s and 1930s, Ambrose N. Kearney, an insurance salesman with Tuomy and Tuomy, was living here as late as the 1960s. His family moved in to Ann Arbor from Webster Township in the mid-20th century. The house was converted to a duplex about 1952.

OFW

602 Lawrence Street

1848 Thomas and Margaret Mitchell House (Gregory House)

Nestled amidst some of Ann Arbor's finest landmark oak trees, this structure was part of a group of stucco-over-brick houses built in this part of town in the 1840s (see 28 and 143). An unusual feature of this particular house is that the brick is adobe, an unlikely building material for our cold, wet climate. A few adobes exist in Washtenaw County, most notably those built by Stephen Mills, but only one other adobe is known to exist in Ann Arbor (see 143). It is thus a rare structure within the local Greek Revival architectural tradition.

After Henry Bower platted the east end of the block in 1844, naming the street "Bowery," Thomas and Margaret Mitchell purchased this lot in 1848. They probably built the gable-front structure with its triangular window and dentils under the eaves that same year. The Mitchells passed the house on to their daughter and her husband, Hubbell Gregory, who had come to Ann Arbor from New York in 1853. The house remained in the Gregory family until the death of their daughter, Jennie Gregory, in 1914.

Kip Miller

Following Jennie's death, Horace Prettyman and his wife made their home here. They bought a small parcel to the west of the house and added the porte cochere. They also "bungalowed" the house in the then-current style by rounding off the corners of the window trim and adding porches with tapering pylon-like columns. Prettyman was a successful businessman who owned the White Swan Laundry (see 15) and the Ann Arbor Press. He lived here until around 1945 after which Abbie Schaefer ran it as a rooming house called Abby House.

In 1961 the house was sold to the Intercooperative Council (ICC), the organization of University of Michigan student co-ops. They renamed the house Vail Co-op to honor their former President, Stephen Vail (Stephanos Valavanis). In 1991 Vail House became the only all-female co-op in the ICC system. Co-opers are proud of their historically significant house and have recently repainted it after extensive repairs to the stucco.

OFW

213-293 East Liberty Street

Zwerdling-Darling Block

1915

Kip Miller

These two buildings, one built by Osias Zwerdling and the other for Dr. Cyrenus G. Darling, were united to form the East Liberty Plaza in the late 1970s and now house shops at the street level with offices above. The combined buildings are a part of the Main Street Historic District.

The cornice of the Darling Block on the corner is embellished with delightful terra cotta ornamentation, an example of a typical Art Deco repetitive design motif. The brick "fireproof" structure was begun in 1915 for Dr. Darling with Malcomson, Higginbotham, and Palmer as its architect. L. D. Wines superintended construction. In 1917 Dr. Darling and Dr. Charles L. Washburne opened offices on the second floor for their private medical practices.

Dr. Darling had earlier built a private hospital on Fifth Avenue where the Federal Building now stands, which he sold in 1915 to John Gates. A leader in the building of the first St. Joseph's Mercy Hospital, he also served there as chief of staff. He was on the faculty of the University of Michigan Medical School and served as dean of the School of Dentistry. Active in public affairs, he filled a term as mayor of Ann Arbor.

Osias Zwerdling came to Ann Arbor in 1903 and worked for the Mack and Company Department Store for a year before opening his own business on Main Street. Three years later he bought the old Koch residence on East Liberty, and in 1915 he moved the house to Fourth Avenue and built the present building adjoining the Darling Block.

Zwerdling was a "ladies' tailor" and furrier who was successful enough to buy the Darling Block. He retired in 1943. A well-known philanthropist and leader in Ann Arbor's Jewish community, he was an organizer of the Beth Israel Con-

CONTINUED on next page

Kip Miller

gregation, and was responsible for organizing the Hillel Foundation for university students here in Ann Arbor, the second Hillel in the United States. When interviewed in 1974 at the age of 96, he still maintained an active interest in the building and kept his own accounts. Mr. Zwerdling died in 1977.

The Zwerdling Furs sign on the west wall of 241 East Liberty, done in very early Art Deco style, depicts a wolf baying at the moon amidst a forest of trees. It was painted in 1915, not by an ordinary sign painter but "by an artist." Zwerdling had always remained proud of that sign, and spoke with the developers of the building about it after citizens became concerned over the sign's fate in the summer of 1977. Recognizing that the sign was both a work of art and a historic artifact, the developers wisely left it untouched. Today it remains the only artist-designed advertisement in the city dating prior to World War I.

MSHD, IHP(sign only)

Kip Miller

321 East Liberty

Enoch James House

1847-1849

"A two-and-one-half story Eastern City row type, rare in Michigan," was how University of Michigan Professor of Architecture Emil Lorch described this house in his 1936 survey of Ann Arbor's older buildings. In form it resembles what some today call a "Philadelphia townhouse." The tall, narrow facade has three bays with the entrance at the left. The stepped gables on the sides are also found on the Anson Brown Building at 1001 Broadway, (see 14).

Frances Wright

In 1847 Olney Hawkins began to build a house on this site for "Governor" George D. Hill. In a few months, however, Hill was in financial trouble and, in 1849, assigned his properties to William S. Maynard. After some fancy mortgage footwork, Enoch James purchased the property and completed the house which was one of a pair of brick houses built back to back. The other house, which faced Washington Street, was demolished in the 1960s. When the James house was completed in the late 1840s, it was in the midst of a residential neighborhood, halfway between the commercial district on Main Street and the University of Michigan campus on State. Its simple yet elegant doorway, surrounded by sidelights and topped by a transom, is still fronted by the porch which was photographed by local historian Lucy Chapin in 1909. Although the porch is later in date, its rounded Tuscan columns blend beautifully with the original design.

Cornelia Corselius, another local historian, described the James family in her 1909 manuscript as "prominent society people here during the 1850's and part of the 60's." After Enoch James' death in 1867, his widow Amarilla and his son Lyman inherited the house. From the latter part of the 19th century on, the house was rented as rooms and as many as seven apartments. In 1980, the Copi family converted the house into two flats but retained the gold lettered sign on the front door advertising the law offices of previous owner, William R. Kelley.

IHP

519-609 East Liberty Street

Michigan Theater Building

1927

98

The Michigan Theater Building was constructed in 1927 to house shops, offices, and a lavish theater with dressing rooms for performers. A red and gold Barton organ was installed to amplify the drama of silent films. Designed by architect Maurice Finkel of Detroit and built by Angelo Poulos of Ann Arbor in a Lombard Romanesque style, the complex consists of an 1800-seat auditorium and an office block of seven stores. When it opened January 5, 1928, the theater was the finest in Ann Arbor.

The facade's main section, a three-bay wide entry to the theater flanked by stores on either side, is complemented by the seven store fronts which are more simply constructed with a band of square-head double-hung windows topped by a continuous concrete lintel on the second floor. The stores immediately flanking the theater retain the arched window hoods of the theater itself. The original ornate marquee was replaced in 1945. An unfortunate remodeling in 1956 "modernized" the interior. The facade was refaced with black marble and imitation fieldstone trim. The Barton organ was restored in the early 70's by the Motor City Theater Organ Society, which sponsored occasional silent film and organ performances.

While celebrating its 50th anniversary, the owners announced they would no longer lease the theater. Plans to convert the interior to a shopping mall alerted citizens to the danger of losing the marvelous theater as well as the organ. After citizens voted support, the City of Ann Arbor purchased the theater in 1979. Six years later, a campaign to restore the Michigan Theater raised almost two million dollars. The entire lobby and auditorium portions of the theater were returned to their original glory. The theater is now a cultural and performing arts center, used by theater and other groups, the Ann Arbor Symphony, and for movies.

NR, IHP

Frances Wright

99

111 West Liberty Street

Ludwig Walz Grocery

1880

This late commercial Italianate structure was built in 1880 as the grocery and saloon of Ludwig Walz. Born in Germany in 1843, Walz came to Ann Arbor when he was two years old. He apprenticed to confectioner Herman Schlotterbeck and then entered business himself. Walz remained here until 1892 when his son-in-law, Sid Millard, converted the building to a printing shop.

Louisa Pieper

Until the 1970s the Millard Press was run from this address and from a small addition built to the east in the 1890s. One of Millard's biggest customers was the University of Michigan's Athletic Department. A wall of autographed photographs attested to his popularity with the home teams and Millard painted both buildings bright blue to show where his sympathies were. Upon Millard's retirement, neighbors Carolyn and Joseph Arcure bought the building and sensitively restored it, even retaining an old bake oven in the basement. In 1991 the Ann Arbor Historic District Commission presented the Arcures with a Special Merit Award for restoring the cornice using ornamental brackets from the demolished home of William S. Maynard at Main and William Streets.

The building with its fine restoration, is one of the best downtown examples of the late Italianate commercial style. It is characterized by tall narrow windows with segmental arches and keystones, a bracketed cornice and varying planes of brick corbelling under the cornice. The original storefront is one of very few remaining examples from this period. Attractive flats with flower-filled rear decks occupy the two upper floors.

IHP

112-122 West Liberty Street

The Adam and Anton Schaeberle Buildings

1866

100

The uniform architecture of this row of buildings belies the variety of the shops over its more than a century of use. Prior to 1865, small scattered buildings existed on these lots, owned by Adam and Anton Schaeberle. In 1868 the Schaeberles sold lots 114, 116, 120 and 122, retaining 118 for their own harness shop. Construction of the five buildings was begun by the Schaeberles and the new owners, George Huss, John Laubengayer, and probably Conrad Wetzel. By 1872 Jacob Binder had his meat market at 114, George Huss owned 116 which later became the Gauss Boot and Shoe Store, and John Laubengayer had a flour and feed shop at 120 and 122. Upper floors were used as residences.

By 1883 the building at 112 had been remodeled to conform to the other five, with the space between filled in (note the narrow windows on this section). An elaborate cornice with carved brackets once capped the unified structure of commercial Italianate style. The buildings had stone basements, exterior brick walls one foot thick, and pressed metal ceilings. Later the buildings were extended 22 feet into a former alley.

The five buildings are still individually owned. Ehnis & Son, originally a harness maker, now a work clothes store, has been at 116 since 1913. The Round Table Restaurant, a popular dining spot for businessmen, bankers and lawyers, moved from West Huron Street to 114 in the early 1960s. While one regrets the removal (a few decades ago) of the fine cornice, recent cleaning of the brick and rehabilitation of the store fronts have restored a handsome aspect to this row of buildings.

MSHD

Kip Miller

113 West Liberty Street

101

John Haarer Building

1888

In the 1870s photographer John Haarer operated a "Daguerrean Salon" on this site. Like most photographers of his day, he promoted himself as something of an artist. Photographs were the first portraits the general public could afford, and the typical photographer's studio was likely to carry ornamental frames and "art prints" or reproductions, as Haarer's did.

When Haarer replaced his frame house and studio with the present structure in 1888, he sought a stylish look. Many decorative touches embellish this handsome brick building: patterns of pressed brick, fancy brass hardware, and ancient-looking numerals recording the date of its construction. The round-arched windows and rounded bricks are characteristic of Richardsonian Romanesque architecture. The plate glass storefront was one of the first in town, and an impressive fireplace of marbleized slate graced the parlor of the spacious family apartment upstairs.

The Haarer family soon added a book and stationery shop to the studio. A later generation founded a general insurance company, and by 1940 Julius F. Haarer was not only the proprietor of the Haarer Book Company and the Haarer Insurance Company, but was also active in the management of the Buhr Machine Tool Company.

In 1964 the city bought the land, planning to demolish the building to provide additional downtown parking. Fortunately a later city council scrapped those plans. The building served in 1974 as headquarters for the Ann Arbor Sesquicentennial Commission.

Joseph and Carolyn Arcure purchased the building and remodeled it for their residence in the late 1970s. A bookstore again occupies the ground floor. The fine features of the building have been preserved and restored, and an imaginative renovation of the upper two floors has produced an unusual and inviting home.

LSHD

115, 117-119 West Liberty Street

1886, 1893

Walker Brothers Buildings

102

Writers in the 1881 *History of Washtenaw County* informed us that "C. Walker and Brother, carriage and wagon manufacturers of Ann Arbor, commenced in business only a few years ago and their present prosperity is an index of what may be accomplished by steady perseverance and skillful workmanship. They began the manufacture of carriages in 1868 and two years later Christian Walker began the erection of their present commodious structure, where a large force of skillful mechanics find constant employment."

Grown even larger by 1886, the firm could justify the expense of a distinguished brick building at 117-119 West Liberty, a remarkable example of commercial Italianate style, with unusual brick pilasters between the windows, and an elegant cornice.

In 1893 the carriage showroom and storage area was expanded by new construction at 115 West Liberty that was designed, curiously, as a modified copy of the adjacent Haarer building rather than of the original Walker building. In 1894 the main building was sold to Henne and Stanger Furniture Company. C. Walker and Brother, also known as the Ann Arbor Carriage Works, had display rooms in the building at 115 Liberty (now Rider's Hobby Shop) until 1921, when the firm surrendered to the automobile.

Purchased by the city and slated for demolition in the early 1970s, the buildings were spared by a later city council decree, sparked by renewed public interest in Ann Arbor's downtown architectural heritage. The Ann Arbor Art Association now occupies the corner building, where it mounts exhibits and holds classes. The Association has done a very successful rehabilitation of the store fronts. The two Walker buildings and the Haarer building next door make up the Liberty Street Historic District.

Kip Miller

LSHD

219-223 North Main Street

112

Pardon Blocks

1894/1899

An Ann Arbor booster publication entitled *Ann Arbor Industrial Edition* wrote in September of 1900: "Charles F. Pardon, Dealer in meats, provisions and groceries, 221-223 North Main Street. This business was established 7 years ago as a meat market and in 1898 Mr. Pardon bought the grocery stock of J. H. Miller and added it to this business. He afterwards bought the Eberhart Bakery, which he sold to his brother [Frank]. He also conducted a meat market at South Lyons for 6 years which has given him ample experience in his line. His stock embraces both staple and fancy groceries, meats and provisions, which he sells at prices which cannot be undersold in the city." It appears the family were quite active in the grocery business, for the same publication lists W. E. Pardon as a dealer in groceries and meats at 123 East Liberty.

Charles built his block in three stages, although the casual observer would think it one building. The first and northernmost part, at 223 North Main Street, has a date stone of 1894 in the pediment. The second portion, his brother Frank's bakery at 219 North Main Street, has a date stone of 1899 in the pediment, while the center portion of the building has a slightly higher pediment and a stone which simply reads, "Pardon Block." Though this section is rumored to have been finished last, the Sanborn Insurance Map from 1899 labels the central and southern sections "to be bakery" and "to be grocery," so perhaps they were built simultaneously. By 1916, after Charles Pardon had retired, G. W. Wagner's Meats was located in the corner store.

Charles Pardon was born in Ann Arbor in 1862 to parents who had emigrated from Germany a few years earlier. A 1906 biographer claimed: "no event of special importance occurred to vary the routine of life for Charles F. Pardon who like most boys of the middle class divided his time between play and work." Pardon apprenticed to a butcher and, after working in South Lyon for six years, eventually opened a market in his new building. His addition of groceries to his line of meats allowed him to expand to the second storefront in 1899. "As he has prospered in his undertakings he has wisely placed his savings in property and now owns considerable real estate in Ann Arbor — the safest of all investments," wrote the same biographer.

The Pardon Block (or Blocks) were built of red brick and stone in a Queen Anne commercial style with arcades of round-topped windows on the second floor, square windows on the third floor, and iron cresting on the roof. Remodelings in the past had covered the stone detailing and brick walls with red paint and altered the original shop windows to suit the commercial styles of the 1950s and 60s.

CONTINUED on next page

In 1988, new owners Quinn/Evans Architects, specialists in historic preservation, rehabilitated the southernmost building demonstrating proper preservation on this highly visible street. Evans noted that when the building was painted the contrast between the brick and the stone disappeared. "We removed the paint and the stone popped right out." The Historic District Commission presented a restoration award to Quinn/Evans that year for their fine work.

One year later, Duane Renken of Renken and Co., a real estate and development firm which now makes this building its headquarters began rehabilitating the northern two sections. When the renovation was completed, the company invited Frank Pardon Jr., who was born 86 years earlier above his father's bakery, to come and have a look. "It looks real nice," he said. The Historic District Commission agreed and awarded Renken a preservation award in 1989.

Bakeries and groceries have operated out of these storefronts for most of the 20th century, but today the two northern sections support a restaurant while the southern section is for rent. With the recent restoration of the Old Post Office across the street, and the new Johnson, Johnson and Roy building around the corner, this edge of town is beginning to enjoy a renaissance. The Pardon Block has been one of the major catalysts for the revival of this area.

Kip Miller

113

220 North Main Street

United States Post Office

1909, 1926

Ivory Collection

The Polhemus Livery Stable occupied this site from 1874 until 1909, when it was demolished to provide space for a post office. Architect Fremont Ward directed construction work which followed plans drawn by the architecture staff of the Treasury Department. Built in the popular Beaux Arts style, the building was a handsome adaptation of a classic Italian Renaissance palace, with its symmetrical formality, rectilinear characters, absence of roof form and strong horizontal lines and elaborate decorative detailing. As the building began to take shape, photographs and reports were sent monthly to the regional headquarters in Chicago.

Initially the building formed a square with entrances on all four sides. Although the building was extended on the east side in 1926-27, and enlarged again in 1933, the additions were so carefully crafted to match the original design that today it is impossible to detect the changes. Everything was done to maintain the same external appearance: the smooth-cut gray limestone, the neo-classical revival features, including the sculpted garland architraves and the scroll work on the frieze about the windows, were all matched to the original. In addition, the interior retained many original finishes, such as marble wainscoting, terrazzo floors, ornate plaster moldings on the sixteen foot ceilings, and the wonderful wood trim.

The building served as Ann Arbor's main post office until 1959 when its replacement on West Stadium Boulevard was completed. In 1977 the downtown post office was moved to the new Federal Building on East Liberty. Washtenaw County then purchased the building and restored it for its administrative offices.

NR, IHP

301-305 North Main Street

Dr. Chase's Steam Printing House

1864/1868

This commercial brick building in the popular Italianate style originally housed the printing plant of Dr. Alvan Wood Chase. It was built in two stages by W. H. Mallory during and after the Civil War. Dr. Chase published the local Republican newspaper, the *Peninsular Courier and Family Visitant* later shortened to the *Ann Arbor Courier* after which the building became known as the Courier Block.

Dr. Chase is much more famous for another publication—his book entitled *Dr. Chase's Recipes, or Information for Everybody*. Jan Longone, a nationally known culinary historian based in Ann Arbor, writes that "from a humble first edition of one thousand pamphlets— there grew a major publishing industry which issued uncounted numbers of Dr. Chase's work, perhaps Michigan's single greatest contribution to American cookbook history." Although originally only sixteen pages, by 1865 the pamphlet was in its 26th edition. Its gilt-embossed, leather-bound edition of 384 pages was outsold in America only by the Bible. It listed medical remedies and cooking recipes as well as numerous other household hints. It even explained how to keep bees and detect counterfeit money. An indispensable tool for westward bound pioneers, it was translated into several languages. It soon made Dr. Chase a very wealthy man.

In 1869 Chase retired and sold his building and the rights to his publications to Rice A. Beal. This was a decision he later regretted when he saw how rich Beal became reprinting Dr. Chase's Recipes. Beal died in 1875 and his son Junius, later a Regent of the University of Michigan, continued to publish both the Courier and the Recipes until 1906.

In the 20th century the building was used for a succession of businesses including a rug factory, wholesale grocery, and Montgomery Ward warehouse. Eventually abandoned, it was purchased and renovated in 1968 by the planning firm of Johnson, Johnson and Roy. The firm had been founded in 1957 by brothers Carl and William Johnson, landscape architects. In the early 1960s they were hired to create a master plan for the University of Michigan campus and by the late 1960s they had developed a reputation as a progressive and innovative firm. An example of this was their renovation of this building for their offices, the first investment in a historic building in downtown Ann Arbor. In 1976 Johnson, Johnson and Roy received a Bicentennial Award for "their special contribution to the quality of life in Ann Arbor through the renovation of 301-305 N. Main."

During the 20th century the building lost a good deal of its most distinctive ornamental detailing including the projecting wood cornice with carved eave

CONTINUED on next page

brackets and an arched centerpiece. Corbelled arcading, typical round and segmental window hoods, and the dentate brickwork within the central portion survive.

Although no longer a pristine example of the architectural style, the Courier Block dominates an important corner in the original central business district and marks the location of important events in publishing history. A marked increase in the restoration of other downtown buildings in the 1970s and 80s has proven that Johnson, Johnson and Roy's vision of the value of older downtown buildings was not misplaced. They started a trend which continues to this day.

IHP

Sturgis Collection

415 North Main Street

Thomas Earl House

1860

Louisa Pieper

Thomas Earl, born in Ireland in 1810, emigrated to Ann Arbor in 1833. He immediately purchased 200 acres of land in Northfield Township, and in a few months he married Mary Duncan. An ambitious man, he rapidly accumulated a fortune and began to take an active part in the political life of the township. In 1849, saddened by the death of their young daughter, the Earls moved to Ann Arbor and opened a grocery store. They lived above the store until 1857 when they purchased two lots at this location, building this house on one and planting his orchard on the other. Earl served for some time as Alderman in Ann Arbor. Mary Earl survived her husband by many years, living to be a very old woman and providing her own subsistence by raising fowl and keeping a good garden. It is said that she sheltered her geese on the third floor of the house. At her death in 1899, she bequeathed the house to St. Thomas Catholic Church.

The quality of the classic details in this Greek Revival house make it quite distinctive. Many of the six-over-six double hung windows still retain their old glass panes. The bricks of an unusually small size reputed to have been made in Ann Arbor at the time, are very evenly laid, demonstrating the mason's skill. The front porch was added about 1908. The lintels appear to be of cut stone painted white and shaped to match the interior window and door trim, a bold and unusual design.

Fred Schaible bought the house at auction in 1900 for $1,300. In 1910 he borrowed $500 to renovate the badly run-down house. With a family of four children and a wife, and at a wage of $6 a week, this was a major loan. But with it, he was able to install a bathroom, a new furnace, hardwood floors, gas pipes, electric wiring, and new chandeliers, which could be used with either gas or electricity. The Schaible daughter, Lucille, married Harry Schmid, and they lived in the house until very recent years. Mrs. Schmid kept the pewter numbers "57" which identified the house before the street numbering system was changed in 1897.

In 1990-91 businessman Peter Fink purchased the house and renovated it for office use.
NR, IHP

500 North Main Street

Kellogg-Warden House

1835-1839

The building that now houses the Washtenaw County Historical Society's Museum on Main Street (MOMs) was once a private residence on Wall Street, in the section of Ann Arbor across the Huron River known as "Lower Town." It is a rare survivor of the first decades of life in Ann Arbor.

The house exhibits interesting construction features that disappeared from use shortly after the 1830s including the accordion or split lathe backing for the plaster walls, very wide plank floors, and brick "nogging" in the walls—an early form of insulation. Fancy detailing on the exterior includes the front entrance, which is a complex unit of sidelights and transom, and the returns on the side gables. Channel and corner block trim grace the front parlor and the beautiful curving staircase in the front hallway is reminiscent of New England. A small ivory knob on top of the newel post, called an "amity button" or "mortgage button," was an indication that the house was free and clear of debt.

The house was built by members of the Kellogg and Ethan Warden families (Warden's wife was a Kellogg), pioneers from Cayuga County, New York. The house was constructed in various stages in the 1830s, the last being in 1839 when the patriarch of the family, the Honorable Charles Kellogg, moved to Ann Arbor. The Kelloggs had been millers and merchants in New York and ran similar businesses here.

The Kelloggs did not "strike it rich" and only one member of the family remained in Ann Arbor (the others either died here or went back to New York). The house stood empty after Charles' death in 1843 until the Ruthruff family purchased it in 1853 and occupied it for three decades. In the 1890s it became the property of Charles Greiner, a gardener, whose descendants remained in the house for nearly a century. In 1989 the Washtenaw County Historical Society intervened to save the house from demolition, and moved it to its present site. The City of Ann Arbor provided the land for the new location while the University of Michigan donated the building and some funds for moving it.

Michael Klement

100 South Main Street

Glazier Building

117

1906

In the 1890s the development of the steel frame building coupled with the perfection of the passenger elevator by Elisha Otis changed the skyline of many American cities. Impressive office buildings of 10 or 15 floors were erected, and even medium-sized cities strove for the cosmopolitan image they gave. Ann Arbor was not a burgeoning commercial center, however, but a quiet university town whose business interests were dominated by Germans who seldom affected a grand style. Ann Arbor did not have a tall office building until 1906 and then only because of the ambitions of an out of town businessman, Frank P. Glazier.

His building is a grand seven-story structure in the classical Beaux Arts style popularized by the Columbia Exposition in Chicago in 1893. Constructed of red brick with fluted limestone columns, rosettes, and garlands over the windows, it once had an elaborate cornice that was removed in the 1960s. By the time it was completed in 1908, however, its builder had declared bankruptcy.

Frank P. Glazier had developed his father's iron foundry in Chelsea into a prosperous stove factory. Glazier also owned the Chelsea Savings Bank, and had held every local political office. But Chelsea, a small town 13 miles west of Ann Arbor, was too small for Glazier. As his biographer Louis Doll notes, Glazier had a "lust for power" that eventually corrupted him and caused his downfall.

Glazier had established a wider power base by becoming State Treasurer in 1906, but his dream was to be Governor. In order to influence and control area Republicans he started *The Ann Arbor News*. He won the election of 1906 in spite of Democrats' complaints that he had deposited state funds in his own bank. The Panic of 1907 caused the collapse of Glazier's financial empire and revealed, among other offenses, that he had used state funds to build the Glazier Building. In 1910 he was convicted of embezzling state funds and sent to Jackson Prison.

After Glazier was jailed the First National Bank moved into the building and stayed until 1929, when it built Ann Arbor's second skyscraper at 201 South Main Street (see 120). From 1929 to the 1970s the Glazier Building was occupied by another venerable local institution, the Ann Arbor Trust Company, and the building took their name. Started in 1925 by Russell Dobson, the trust company was purchased in 1928 by Earl Cress and William Brown, future mayor of Ann Arbor. They dealt in securities, mortgages, insurance, real estate, and property management. In 1939 they divided the business, with Cress operating the trust company and Brown taking over the insurance portion.

CONTINUED on next page

Glazier Building *CONTINUED*

After a series of mergers and acquisitions in the 1970s and 80s, Ann Arbor Trust became part of Society Bank, headquartered in Cleveland. The Ann Arbor part of the business is run by George Cress, Earl's son. The building was renamed the Glazier Building in the late 1980s when the Ann Arbor Trust sign was removed revealing the original name carved in stone over the main entrance.

IHP

Frances Wright

120-124 South Main Street

1867

Bank Block (Goodyear's)

118

Shortly after it opened as the "Bank Building" in 1867, this structure was described as having "a freestone front, in which are large and elegant stores, and the First National Bank." The First National Bank was the first federally chartered bank in Michigan and only the twenty-second such bank in the United States.

As one of the new buildings in town, it showed "— the magnitude and growing importance of this inland city" according to the 1872 City Directory. An 1867 photograph graphically illustrates this importance. It shows the building's elaborate central Gothic facade, intended to draw attention to the bank, its primary tenant. The pointed-arch windows and doorways in this portion contrast with those of the flanking buildings that have round-topped windows in the more common Italianate style of the period. An elaborate pinnacled cornice topped the bank portion of the building, increasing its visual domination on Main Street.

The building was known throughout most of its history, however, as the Goodyear Building or simply as Goodyear's. In 1888 William Goodyear and Bruno St. James founded a retail clothing business at 120 South Main Street. This business was to stay and expand into the flanking buildings until 1983, only five years short of its centennial. Initially known as Goodyear and St. James, it became Goodyear's in 1895. From the 1950s through the early 1980s, Goodyear's was the primary retail anchor for the central business district.

The closing of Goodyear's in 1983 for non-payment of taxes was a severe blow to downtown retail trade. Yet in 1984, spurred by tax credits for historic preservation and the goodwill of the community, developers undertook an authentic restoration of the building based on the 1867 photograph.

NR, IHP

Sturgis Collection

119

126 South Main Street

Philip Bach Building

1867

A photograph taken in 1867 pictures this impressive Italianate block built at a cost of $20,000, and newly opened for Philip Bach's dry goods business. "Prices were quite high at the time and a single stair-case cost $500," a later historian recalled. The photo shows the original wide flat cornice supported by ornate Italianate brackets. The name, Philip Bach, is over the awning, and a large "Business College" sign above the cornice indicates the use of the third floor.

Bach formed a partnership with Peter H. Abel in 1867. Some years later the firm became Bach and Roath. Around the turn of the century, Bruno St. James, Jr., left the firm of Goodyear and St. James to purchase the store, hiring Miss Bertha E. Muehlig as the bookkeeper for the new firm. She took over management of the business in 1911 and in 1924 she became the owner of the building as well as the business, continuing to do the bookkeeping as before.

Bertha's paternal grandparents emigrated from Germany in 1840. A devoutly religious family, they were part of the early Lutheran congregation led by the Reverend Frederick Schmid. Bertha was certainly a successful business woman, but she was even better known for her readiness to provide food and clothing for those struck by misfortune. She became a special patron of the Patrick Donovan School on Wall Street, where the pupils did not have the normal advantages. When the Donovan School was replaced by the new Northside School, she donated the dining room furniture, a silver tea service, and an aquarium. Each year she sent the children candy at Christmas time and pencils on Valentine's Day. A friend of the ladies at the Anna Botsford Bach Home on Liberty Street, she remembered their birthdays and provided many necessities.

Bertha Muehlig received many honors in recognition of her services to the people of Ann Arbor. After her death, several local businessmen invested in the store, continuing the business as before and perpetuating the name of the kind and generous woman until the late 1970s. The store retained the interior decor and services of the beginning of the century, including a spring operated cash carrier system which was probably the last of its kind in the state.

The law firm of Hooper, Hathaway, Price, Beuche and Wallace purchased the building in 1981 for their offices. A thorough and elegant renovation was done, for which the owners received a Bicentennial award. Windows were unblocked and the original appearance was restored as much as possible, with an iron entry created to mimic the original store front. They have also kept the old elevator and the oak staircase inside. (*See previous photograph*)

IHP

201-203 South Main Street

First National Bank Building

1929

A special edition of the *Ann Arbor Daily News* on February 10, 1929, honored the opening of this proud symbol of the prosperous city of the 1920s. Most of the eighty-five original stockholders were residents of Washtenaw County. When the building was occupied, sixteen floodlights of 1000 watts each illuminated the tower, making it a focal point of the city, day and night, and the subject of a widely circulated picture postcard.

Ann Arbor's First National Bank was the first bank chartered in Michigan under the National Bank Act of 1863. The bank's first elegant building in 1867 became Goodyear's Department Store; (see 118). Later the bank occupied the Glazier building (see 117). When the bank moved to the first floor of this building in 1929, the safety of its vaults and the security of its system were advertised far and wide. The crash came in October of that year, and in 1933 all four of Ann Arbor's banks closed during the great banking crisis. The State Savings Bank was solvent and reopened immediately. The other three, the Ann Arbor Savings Bank, the First National Bank, and the Farmers and Mechanics Bank had sufficient assets to form one strong bank, namely the Ann Arbor Bank located at Main and Huron.

Kip Miller

When it opened, the bank's customer lobby occupied the corner. One entered through "an arched entrance with elaborately grilled glass— through a marble vestibule, protected by massive iron grilles of Romanesque design, into the banking room two full stories in height." The lobby entrance for the remaining offices was also sumptuously appointed, "finished with black terrazzo floor, black and gold marble base and trim, Italian travertine walls, bronze doorways and richly decorated coffered ceiling."(National Register nomination, 1982). Architect Paul Kasurin (of the firm Fry and Kasurin of Ann Arbor, designers of the building) described the exterior in 1929. "The richness of the terra cotta is

CONTINUED on next page

accentuated by the polychrome ornament about the main entrance, in the spandrels between the windows of the third and fourth floors and again in the upper part of the building." The broad vertical bands of terra cotta and the banks of narrow windows separated by thin terra cotta mullions give the building strong vertical lines. Gargoyles are mounted immediately below a decorative roof cornice.

After 1935 the former banking space was subdivided horizontally creating retail space on the first floor with offices above. The massive bronze door frame and bronze grilles were removed leaving only the huge arch on Main Street. After some years of decline, the first floor facade was restored to its original appearance in 1982 by First Martin Corporation, which purchased the building in 1981. First Martin has subsequently renovated the entire structure. They removed the dropped ceiling in the lobby and revealed and restored the painted coffered ceiling.

NR, IHP

Henry Binder's Hall — *text on next page*

Kip Miller

301 South Main

Henry Binder's Hall

1871, 1908

In the light of the success of other commercial "blocks" on this side of Main Street, Henry Binder decided in 1871 to replace his old home on this corner with a three-story brick block. The carved stone lintels above the windows, their elaborate cornices, and the rusticated stone pilasters on the corners illustrated a more ostentatious style than had previously been seen on Main Street. Binder was born in Germany and came to Ann Arbor at the age of 21. He started out by running a profitable hotel located near the Michigan Central Depot and later ran a saloon on the ground floor of this Main Street building. As he prospered, he "made judicious investment in city property and erected many of the store buildings now on Main street. These brought him a good rental, adding materially to his income." Curiously, despite his wealth, his biography noted that when he died in 1894, his wife and 11 children "were residing over one of his store buildings on Main Street."

Around 1877 S. and J. Baumgardner's Bakery, Grocery, Flower and Feed Store replaced Dinger's Saloon. Baumgardner's was so successful that they built a brick bakery in the back in 1880. An 1881 biography of the company states that the brothers came to Ann Arbor from Germany in 1877 "scarcely knowing any of the English language. The success which has crowned them in this line of business is ample proof of their honesty and integrity." Despite their reputation as being one of the best bakeries in Washtenaw County, their business closed and by 1892 the storefront was rented as showroom space to the Ann Arbor Organ Company, another German enterprise (see 49) which was then the second largest employer in town.

In 1908, the building was remodelled into the basic form it has today, shedding its frilly Victorian look for the staid appearance of a Roman-style facade. The German -American Savings Bank opened in the ground-floor space. In 1916 the bank moved out and was replaced by Hutzel's Ladies Apparel and occupied the corner for the next 70 years.

The Selo-Shevel Gallery purchased the building in the late 1980s and successfully obtained a variance from the sign ordinance to keep the 30-year landmark sign, simply changing the name.

MSHD

122

319-325 South Main Street

Marchese Brothers Building

1925

Ann Arbor architect Hermann Pipp designed and built this pleasing brick and terra cotta commercial building for the Marchese Brothers. Related to the Art Deco style in its developmental period, the sculptural details of the facade give the building a Gothic character, adding texture and charm to South Main Street.

Demetrio and Anthony G. Marchese had their tailoring shop on the first floor with residences above, but the Depression years proved too difficult and ownership passed to Henry A. Whitker. Rentals during the 1930s were sporadic until Grinnell Brothers opened a combined musical instrument and appliance store in 1936 in the center section. In the course of time Grinnell's restricted sales to musical instruments and sheet music. The store expanded to occupy the entire ground level, until the firm moved to Briarwood in 1975. The ground floor now contains various retail shops with the upper floors converted to office use.

MSHD

Kip Miller

120 Packard Road

William W. Wines House (Dean House)

127

Circa **1848**

William Wallace Wines and his brother Daniel E. Wines, natives of Connecticut, married two sisters and took them West, to the new frontier of the Michigan Territory. Daniel arrived in Washtenaw County in 1837 followed by William in 1841 and together they operated a lumber mill in Ypsilanti. William moved to Ann Arbor in 1848 and built this charming vernacular cottage, reminiscent of houses common "back East." Daniel came to Ann Arbor two years later and built himself a house next door at 126 Packard. He then entered the sash, door and blind business, and became a contractor and builder while his brother William co-founded a clothing business known as Wines and Worden.

Biographies of Daniel stress his importance as an early local builder, ranging from comments that he "has erected many of the best business houses and private residences in Ann Arbor" to Fiske Kimball's comment that "two fine old residences out Washtenaw Avenue, built by Daniel Wines" were "much appreciated by their owners of the faculty" and were "masonry covered with warm stucco."

This house, which may have been built by Daniel for his brother William, is a simple clapboard structure with a center entry and its long side facing the street — features common in New England. It is probably an I-house, a folk form two stories high and one room deep, though it has quite a large addition on the rear which may be original to the house. The scallop edging is an unusual touch — perhaps new designs made possible by machinery just beginning to make its appearance, perhaps a later embellishment. Old-fashioned construction details include brick nogging found in the walls, a primitive form of insulation (see 116), and wooden pegs for the framing.

The house was purchased by another pioneer, Nelson Strong, in the early 1870s after William built himself a grand brick Italianate house on the corner of Packard and Main Streets. (It was demolished in the 1960s and is now the site of Baker Commons). Shortly thereafter, Strong sold it to his son-in-law Sedgewick Dean. Dean ran a grocery store on Main Street, but the family's name has been perpetuated by his daughter Elizabeth, who willed the City of Ann Arbor over a million dollars in 1964 for the special care of the city's trees. The Elizabeth Dean Fund perpetuates the memory of this fine lady who astonished the town with her generous bequest.

Elizabeth Dean had left this house long before she died, but her earliest years were spent here. A scene from her daily life is revealed in the diary of visiting nurse Emily Hollister, who wrote in July of 1890: "I come to Mr. Sedwick (sic)

CONTINUED on next page

Dean's place to nurse Mrs. Stebbins' (Elizabeth's aunt) daughter Emily who is sick with typhoid fever. She is a lovely girl — The family is very pleasant. Clara Dean is 14 years old — very interesting. Miss Elizabeth is 5 years old. Her mother has been dead for 5 years and Mrs. Stebbins has been with the family. Mrs. Stebbins is a daughter of Dr. Strong."

Elizabeth eventually sold the house after World War I to Reverend E. C. Stellhorn, a Lutheran minister. Stellhorn altered the interior considerably and probably changed the window to the right of the doorway so he and his wife could enjoy a more modern lifestyle. They occupied this house for almost half a century. After their deaths, the house was purchased by Donald Van Curler, a local architect and developer. He had originally intended to demolish the house and build an apartment building, but was so enchanted when he toured the interior and noted the high ceilings, chandeliers, and marble washstands, that he changed his mind and moved in instead!

Kip Miller

100 North State Street

1882

First Unitarian Church
(Hobbs & Black Assoc. Inc.)

Dr. Jabez T. Sunderland came to the ministry of the First Unitarian Church in 1878. During his twenty-year tenure he and his wife Eliza (who taught history and political science at Ann Arbor High School) were leaders in the religious and intellectual life of the town. They soon initiated the project of a new church building and were successful in raising the $19,000 required. The building was dedicated in 1882, the *Ann Arbor Register* of September 13 noting that "The structure is thoroughly churchly in look, picturesque in outline, and certain to be one of the most admired, architecturally, of our public buildings." Donaldson and Meier of Detroit were the architects and the fine stone work was done by the Walker Brothers of Ann Arbor, stone masons also for the Michigan Central station.

The Romanesque design is strongly reminiscent of the work of the influential Boston architect, Henry Hobson Richardson. The tower is much like that on Boston's Trinity Church, the building which launched Richardson's career in 1872. The new house of worship contained an audience room or chapel, Sunday-school rooms, a parlor, and a spacious and well-furnished reading room. A legacy left by Judge Ezra C. Seaman of Ann Arbor provided for the establishment of a Liberal Religious Library "to be accessible to all persons who desire to read the best liberal-religious thought of the age."

In the early 1930s, during the ministry of the Reverend Harold P. Marley, the original draft of the Humanist Manifesto was authored by congregant Roy Wood Sellars and read in the church. The church took an assertive lead in the civil liberties movement and in the Ann Arbor Community Forum, which debated and lobbied for means to end the Depression, for public school improvements and for upgrading city services.

During the decade before World War II the city and university doors were by and large closed to the emerging anti-war and peace movement groups as well as to the labor groups which were organizing. The Unitarians, always staunch supporters of free speech and civil liberties, voted to provide space for these groups to meet. In 1937, the Fellowship Room of the church was designated "Unity Hall" and the church was opened seven days a week to accommodate educational programs in labor problems and leadership skills for labor union activists. *The Washtenaw Progressive*, a "people's front" newspaper, with a governing body drawn from the workers' unions, was published in the church offices.

CONTINUED on next page

During World War II the Unitarians collaborated with the Unitarian churches in Detroit to serve the large number of workers coming in to Ypsilanti to work in the bomber plant. These services not only included a "Wayside Pulpit" but provided a nursery, playground and recreational facilities, giving social work experience to numbers of young people eager to serve in non-military programs.

In 1946, when the Unitarians moved to Washtenaw Avenue, the congregation of the Grace Bible Church purchased the building and used it until 1975, when they built a new sanctuary on South Maple Road. In 1985 the building, badly deteriorated inside and out, was purchased by D. B. Associates Ltd. The exterior stone work was restored to its original appearance and the entire structure reroofed. The interior was totally rebuilt to house the architectural firm of Hobbs and Black, Associates, Inc. In the rebuilding process, a Tiffany window was uncovered, much to the surprise of the new owners. Installed to commemorate the loss of a child in the 1890s, the window had been boarded over in the 1930's and forgotten when the building was sold. Hobbs and Black had the window restored by Tiffany experts and it graces the east wall of their reception room.

NR, OFW

Hobbs & Black Assoc. Inc.

110 North State Street

First Unitarian Church Parsonage

138

1883

Only one year after the Unitarians completed their church at Huron and State Streets (see 137) in 1882, they began work on a parsonage for their dynamic leader Jabez Sunderland. The Detroit firm of Donaldson and Meier, who also designed the church, chose a modest Queen Anne style for the house. Characteristic is the use of different materials on the exterior, including brick veneer on the first story and cut shingles on the second, intersecting gables, and an asymmetrical floor plan. Unusual details include the stone quoins around the first floor windows (giving the building a Gothic effect) and two large chimneys, one of which had to be removed during renovation.

Sunderland was not without input, however. Diaries of local mason Warren Walker, now housed at the Bentley Library, give us day-to-day descriptions of the work: "Sunderland asking for brick veneer and boulder stone trimmings around the doors and windows and also to build corner of stone for first story only. I told him we could" (entry for March 5, 1883). In a September entry, Walker also noted that Sunderland had changed his mind about the color of the mortar: it was to be red, not black.

The history of the parsonage basically follows that of the church. When membership in the congregation declined in the mid-20th century, both the buildings fell into disrepair. In 1946 the Unitarians sold them to the Grace Bible Church and moved to their present home on Washtenaw Avenue (see 171). After Grace Bible built its new church out on Maple Road, they continued to use the buildings for meetings, youth recreational programs and, briefly, a bookstore until the late 1970s when the deteriorating conditions forced them to close first the church and then the parsonage,

Long an eyesore, the parsonage, the church and several houses on Huron Street were meticulously restored in 1986 by the architectural firm of Hobbs and Black, Associates, Inc. to serve as their corporate headquarters. This restoration was given an award in 1987 by the Ann Arbor Historic District Commission. Today all the buildings in this complex have given this highly visible corner a new lease on life and have added immeasurably to the revitalization of the Old Fourth Ward Historic District (see previous photograph).

NR, OFW

139

200 and 322 North State Street

Wil-Dean and Duncan Manor Apartments

1928

Apartment buildings were never common in Ann Arbor before World War II and the few that were constructed were built in the 1920s. Demand for housing for the burgeoning population of students and medical personnel at the newly built hospitals prompted owners to tear down or move older houses and erect what was for Ann Arbor very high-density housing. These two buildings are almost identical twins and were built by Harold Zahn and Dugald Duncanson, two real estate salesmen. Duncanson hired architect Gardiner Vose, a 1927 graduate of the University of Michigan School of Architecture, and had him prepare the designs. They differ only in color: sandy-beige for the Wil-Dean at 200 North State Street, which Zahn owned, and red for Duncan Manor at 322 North State Street, which Duncanson owned.

Kip Miller

The buildings are in the Tudor Revival style, popular in the 1920s. They have steeply sloping roof lines, half-timbered gables, round arched entries, tapestry brick and the general asymmetry common to the style. Multi-paned steel casement windows were another popular feature of this period. Now drafty and rusted out with age, they are being replaced with carefully researched copies in aluminum.

Both buildings were begun in 1928 at the height of the Roaring Twenties. Zahn and Duncanson never stinted on materials or details: the roofs are slate, the expensive accents are pierced brick work, color tiles and sandstone details, and some windows even had canvas awnings.

Unfortunately, the stock market crash of 1929 sent their dreams to the dustbin. Duncanson lost title to Duncan Manor but Zahn managed to hang on to the Wil-Dean until 1946 when he sold it to Elizabeth Lueck, who eventually acquired Duncan Manor as well. The Lueck family have remained the owners ever since and have maintained the buildings in excellent condition, providing low-cost, high quality housing to many. Long thought of as two of Ann Arbor's most intriguing and romantic buildings, these apartments maintain their attractiveness to renters despite their lack of parking.

OFW

307 North State Street

Hanorah and Ellen Morse House

140

1882

A dynamic woman named Ellen Morse was responsible for the building of many rooming houses along this stretch of North State Street in the 1860s to 80s. Local Ann Arbor historian Louis W. Doll quotes an 1879 newspaper article about her: "This [house being constructed] makes the seventh large and commodious house erected by Miss Morse... [She] is entitled to thanks... She is a business woman and orders all her own lumber... and personally supervises the erection of her houses ... in the words of one of our hardware merchants 'She is as sharp and close a purchaser as I have to deal with."

Kip Miller

In 1881 Morse and her mother Hanorah purchased a large property on North State Street where she subsequently built both 301 and 307 in 1882. As with her other houses, the builder was probably William Lawrence, and the tenants were students.

After the Civil War the University of Michigan grew tremendously and, according to Doll, returning veterans boosted enrollment to over 1,200 making it then the largest university in the country. Morse's houses were designed to fill the tremendous need for housing and the fact that both she and her mother lived in them, moving often from one to the other, meant that they were constantly looked after.

Miss Morse charged $1.75 per week with the students furnishing their own wood for heat. According to Doll, she often did her own housecleaning and was a daily sight on State Street with her mop, pail, and brushes. Morse could have been a rich woman had it not been for a disastrous investment which left her almost penniless. Despite her near poverty, she managed to hang on to a few properties and live to the age of 87. She donated her last, and most permanent home at 419 North State Street, to the Sisters of Mercy who started St. Joseph Mercy Hospital there.

Miss Morse sold the house at 307 North State to Alexander and Lena Wallace in 1915. Their daughter, Minnie Wallace, continued the boarding house tradition established by Miss Morse. In 1970 the house was purchased from her estate by the Intercooperative Council for co-op housing. The esteem in which she was held by generations of students led to the naming of this house after her. Known for years as Minnie's, the house is a local landmark partly because the co-op's constitution requires the house to be painted purple.
OFW

141

406 North State Streeet

Enoch and Keziah Terhune House

1858

This house shows the transition in architectural styles between the Greek Revival and the Italianate. In plan, massing, and square shape, the house resembles an "Italianate cube." Its central entry/center hall construction, engaged corner columns, wide architrave, and rectangular six-over-six windows (some still with original glass) all point, however, to a Greek Revival sensibility.

Kip Miller

It was built by Enoch Terhune, whose wife Keziah purchased the property in 1858. Terhune was the son of pioneers from Seneca County, New York who had settled in Pittsfield Township in 1831 when Enoch was 14. He was educated in Washtenaw County and became a builder and contractor in Ann Arbor in 1842. In 1846 he branched out into agricultural implements and owned a "sash and blinds" factory on Detroit Street. The 1881 *History of Washtenaw County* states that Terhune was the first to bring planing machinery to Ann Arbor, "thereby calling down on his head the wrath of numerous workmen who thought this would spoil their business." After his first wife died in 1857, he married Keziah with whom he had one child. Terhune's grandfather, an ensign in the Revolutionary War, is buried in the tiny Terhune Cemetery in Terhune Park owned by the City of Ann Arbor and maintained by the Pittsfield Chapter of the Daughters of the American Revolution.

After the turn of the century the Terhune property passed into the hands of grocer Jay Herrick of Herrick and Bohnet. Mrs. Herrick was an active suffragist, as indicated by a program of the Ann Arbor Equal Suffrage Club from 1911 which lists a meeting at this house.

The house was converted into apartments in the 1950s.

OFW

410 North State Street

Society of Friends Meeting House

142

1851-2

An 1851 deed confirms that Richard Glazier and Robert B. Glazier, trustees of the Society of Friends (Quakers), purchased this property on behalf of the Society for a meeting house. The 1853 map of Ann Arbor indicates the building, the only house on this stretch of State Street, and labels it "Quakers Meeting."

Robert B. Glazier (sometimes spelled Glasier) was originally from New York State. He was an active Quaker and one of the best conductors on the Underground Railroad helping slaves escape to Canada. His home was a station on this system and part of the 300 acres he once owned east of town remains some of the most unspoiled land in the area. Robert also gained notoriety for being the first man imprisoned for war resistance in the United States. The name of the road fronting his former land was recently renamed Glazier Way to honor and perpetuate the name of his family.

Kip Miller

Judge Noah Cheever, in his *Stories and Amusing Incidents in the Early History of the University of Michigan*, noted that in the winter of 1860-61, Parker Pillsbury came to Ann Arbor to speak on the abolition of slavery. "He appointed a meeting in the old Free Church on the east side of North State Street, near the brow of the hill, now a dwelling house." This house thus had a strong association with abolition in its earliest years.

The Quakers sold the house in 1866 to tobacconists Charles and Frederick Horn. When the Horns sold it ten years later for $2000, they doubled their investment. The house changed hands frequently after that and by 1931 it had been divided into 10 apartments.

Passersby often notice the brackets on the first floor bay windows and under the eaves of the roof, and the elegant door. These features were probably added in the 1870s, while the Colonial Revival porch dates to the early 20th century. The door frame, however, with its plain pilasters, wide entablature and sidelights, is probably original.

OFW

143

418 North State Street

Newton A. Prudden House

1854

The Newton A. Prudden house is one of a small group of stuccoed Greek Revival houses built in this neighborhood in the 1840s and 1850s. Built in a simple style with a side entry, the house dates to the mid-1850s and was constructed of adobe brick like its neighbor at 602 Lawrence Street (see 95). As such it is one of only two known examples of adobe houses in Ann Arbor proper. It originally had a gable roof that was altered into the present hipped shape after the Civil War. No elaborate details exist on the house save for the transom and sidelights around the entry.

Prudden was a local fruit dealer, bee keeper, and manufacturer of water filters. After his death, his nephew Newton F. Prudden took over the business and lived in the house with his aunt until 1893 when he traded the house for a farm in Chelsea. The diary of visiting nurse Emily Hollister from 1889 gives us an unusual perspective on this family. She noted that she had come to nurse Mrs. Prudens [sic] and that she made a will in which "she gave away some relics [being] a card and a comb to her nephew [and] her flax wheel to the M. E. Church art loan program, her feather bed with blue patch to Mr. Pruden [sic] and...a dollar to a cousin that she owed it to for...years." Mrs. Hollister went on to comment about the house: "[It] is old and has been neglected. It reminds one of old mansions with many rooms, that one reads of in books and it gives one a creepy feeling. Well, death comes today, January 6."

Kip Miller

Like most of the other houses on this block, this house was converted to a boarding house in the 20th century. Celebrated local author Louis W. Doll purchased the house in 1938 from the Home Owners Loan Corporation, an agency handling the property of banks that failed during the Depression. Doll remarks that during his renovation of the house he was surprised to find that the hipped roof had been built over the original gable roof. He tore out the older roof and re-used the oak beams to level the ceiling. An addition on the side was so deteriorated that it had to be demolished. Doll also replaced the old entry with a "colonial" door that was featured on the cover of House Beautiful in September 1937.

OFW

231 South State Street

State Theater

1940

This former movie theater, with its jazzy Art Deco exterior stretching 132 feet along State Street, has been an Ann Arbor landmark since it opened in 1942. An impressive sketch by the architect C. Howard Crane was front page news in November 1940 when construction began.

Crane began designing theaters in a highly ornamental style in the 1920s. The Fox Theater in Detroit, recently restored, illustrates art of the Far East, India and the Mediterranean. The State Theater, however, is in the later stream-lined Art Deco style popular in the 1930s and 40s. Except for the missing red vitrolite glass panels that once sheathed the first floor, the unique facade is relatively intact. The Ann Arbor Bicentennial commission recognized it with an award in 1976.

The theater was constructed for the Butterfield Company, a chain which owned many theaters in Ann Arbor and throughout Michigan. In the late 1970s when multi-unit theater complexes opened on the outskirts of Ann Arbor, Butterfield divided the interior of the State into four smaller units and ended operations in 1989. The building was sold a week later to Hogarth Management who gutted the first floor interior for retail space, retaining the proscenium arch and the original ceiling lights and mosaic floor tiles in the lobby. The second floor theaters are scheduled to reopen soon with minimal remodeling. In 1990 the Ann Arbor Historic District Commission presented Hogarth Management with a Special Merit Award for restoring the marquee with its original brilliant yellow and red colors and re-activated neon. The sign is an icon, visible for blocks along both State and Liberty Streets, a potent symbol of the vibrancy of this commercial area.

SSHD

Sturgis Collection

326-328 South State Street

145

Nickels Arcade

1916

This small but charming example of the glass-roofed shopping arcade popular in Europe, but rare in the United States, was designed by Ann Arbor architect Hermann Pipp. Other existing Pipp designs include the Barton Hills Country Club and the Marchese Building.

The Arcade's State Street facade, faced with terra cotta, is essentially Beaux Arts Classic in design and proportion with details anticipating the Art Deco designs of a few years later. The Maynard Street facade is similar in design but it is of yellow brick with terra cotta trim. A glass skylight illuminates the passageway of the steel and brick structure. Of the eighteen shops which open into the 265 foot tiled arcade, three - Van Boven's, the Caravan, and the post office - have been there from its earliest days. Shops and offices occupy the second and third floors.

Frances Wright

The land extending from State Street to Maynard was owned by John H. Nickels, proprietor of a meat market on State Street. When his son, Tom E. Nickels, inherited the market, he razed the building and bought out other portions of the property left to his brothers and sister. A man with strong feelings about Ann Arbor's need to grow, Nickels began the Arcade in 1915. He moved to a residence at 513 East William to be near the construction, which took three years to complete.

The Farmers and Mechanics Bank, which originally occupied the south corner on State Street, owned its portion of the Arcade. Only after its successor institution, the Ann Arbor Bank, moved its branch to Liberty Street in 1960 did the Nickels family finally complete its ownership of the entire structure.

Today, some seventy years after its construction, the Arcade remains essentially unchanged. In 1987, when the building was listed in the National Register of Historic Places, a thorough refurbishing was done. The terra cotta interior and exterior were repointed, the mosiac tiles reset in the floor, and new lamps were hung. It is today, as when it was built, one of Ann Arbor's unique and most attractive structures.

NR, IHP

434 South State Street

Newberry Hall

146

1888

This picturesque building was designed by architects Spier and Rohns for the Students' Christian Association as the headquarters for its work on campus. The building's name, Newberry Hall, appears on the east gable end, in memory of railroad magnate John S. Newberry (class of 1847), whose widow, Helen, contributed a substantial part of the building fund in his name.

Kip Miller

The building material is fieldstone, trimmed with Ohio blue stone and Forest City brown stone. A staircase of oak leads to the second story, originally a hall seating 550 persons, which was embellished with a beautiful Tiffany window. The grand hall is now divided into smaller rooms. The Romanesque design with its heavy stone work, round arches, and decorative detail demonstrates the influence on architects of the work of H. H. Richardson. They also followed Richardson's pioneering use of cast-iron columns and Carnegie steel beams supporting wood joists and floors.

The Student Christian Association was reorganized in 1904 as the YMCA and the YWCA and affiliated with the national organizations. On campus the title Student Christian Association was maintained, with the same Board of Trustees governing both organizations. Newberry Hall became the home of the YWCA. By 1919 the building was again available to all religious groups within the university community. In 1920 the SCA could no longer afford to maintain Newberry Hall, and the University was allowed to hold classes in the building in exchange for maintenance. The archaeological collections gradually became housed in the building and in 1937 Newberry Hall was sold to the University. Latin Professor Francis W. Kelsey, in his constant search for papyri, had noted the promising ruins at Karanis, Egypt. In 1923, he led an expedition to excavate the site. The Francis W. Kelsey Museum of Archeology was established to hold the many treasures recovered by that expedition. It now houses over 100,000 of the finest of art and archaeological artifacts.

NR

206 North Thayer Street

148

Thomas Ready House

1858

When Thomas Ready constructed this Greek Revival cottage in the late 1850s, its only neighbor was the former Ellsworth Boarding house up the street at the southeast corner of Catherine and Thayer Streets. Both were built after the University of Michigan decreed that students could no longer live on campus. President Tappan's edict in 1852 prompted a mad scramble by local citizens to accommodate the new demand for housing (see 78). This overlapped with the expansion of the Irish community into this neighborhood.

The chain of title for this property reveals an almost unbroken string of Irish names, from Ready to Timothy Keating, James Evans, and Patrick O'Hearn. O'Hearn purchased the property in 1885 and his family owned it for the next 70 years. In 1888 O'Hearn built another house on the north half of this property (see 149) which he used as a rental and never lived in himself.

Simple in shape and style, the main attraction of this clapboard house is its beautiful, intact Italianate porch with the filigree scroll work and thin chamfered columns typical of the style. Also characteristic is the absence of any porch railing. The house is an excellent example of vernacular architecture in Ann Arbor.

The current owners have taken meticulous care of their home and were given a preservation award in 1989 by the Ann Arbor Historic District Commission. They too are of Irish descent, though not related to the earlier owners.

OFW

Kip Miller

210 North Thayer Street

Patrick O'Hearn House

149

1888

Kip Miller

Patrick O'Hearn built this elegant Queen Anne house in 1888 in the side yard of his home at 206 North Thayer (see 148). With intersecting gables, different materials (clapboard and shingles), windows of various shapes and sizes, and an elaborate porch with turned columns and carved trim, the house is a fine example of the Queen Anne style from the late 1880s.

O'Hearn must have believed there was a rental market among the faculty for such housing, for his first tenant was Dr. Jacob Reighard, a Professor of Zoology at the University of Michigan. Around 1905 Dr. Reighard became the Director of the Zoological Laboratory and Museum and built himself a much grander house in Burns Park. After a decade with Reighard as its tenant, the house was rented for many years to a series of occupants until it was sold to two widows in the 1940s. In 1969 the owners of 206 purchased it, thus re-uniting the two houses under single ownership.

OFW

151

331-339 Thompson Street

St. Mary's Student Chapel

1924-25

The building was designed in 1924 by Albert J. Rousseau, professor of architecture at the University of Michigan from 1917 to 1931. Rousseau was trained in his native city of Quebec and at the Ecole Nationale et Speciale des Beaux Arts in Paris. Basically an innovator, Rousseau made no attempt to camouflage with fake buttresses and arches the modern construction methods used in the chapel. The half-story basement contains rooms for social and recreational use, while the main floor houses a plain auditorium. The present fittings of the chapel are not original. The exterior has a strong Art Deco flavor, note particularly the large stone crosses and windows. Rousseau was also the architect of the facade of the Land Title Building at 106 North Fourth Avenue (see 52), as well as one of the architects of Ann Arbor's Art Deco Masonic Temple, demolished in 1975, which had similar brick work and decoration.

The Student Chapel was established for students and faculty in 1919 under the direction of the Reverend Michael Bourke, who was also chaplain of St. Joseph's Mercy Hospital. The first chapel, which was independent of the St. Thomas parish, was in a home on South State Street where the University of Michigan Administration Building now stands. When Father Bourke sold the old chapel to the University and bought the property at 331 Thompson, he had the building designed and the contract let. The day before construction was to begin, Father Bourke learned of a diocesan plan to block the plans. He hurriedly got out contractor Pipp at 11 o'clock at night, had him move a big shovel to the lot and dig out a shovel full of dirt. The next day, Father Bourke attended the diocesan meeting and informed the members that construction had begun. In 1928 St. Thomas and the Student Chapel were consolidated under Father Carey. In 1940 St. Mary's again became a separate parish for Catholic students attending the University.

Sturgis collection

201 East Washington Street

Hoelzle Meat Market

156

1893

Kip Miller

The octagonal corner turret, crowned by a tent-shaped metal roof, has served as the signboard for most of the occupants since the building was built in 1893. The original Hoelzle Meat Market proudly proclaimed its occupation with a cow weather vane crowning the turret. Sun Cleaners and Laundry boarded up the original windows and used the side of the turret for signage. By the 1970s a short-lived business called the Dragon Inn added stripes, described by the *Ann Arbor Observer* as being "a psychedelic fantasy in wavy red, blue and yellow."

The building is a brick structure in the Queen Anne commercial style, with a large arched window taking up the second floor width on the Washington Street side. An 1893 photograph shows the newly finished structure in its original form before the bricks were painted. By 1913 it was Geisendorfer's Meat Market and in the 1930s it was the Washington Meat Market. A large portrait of George Washington was painted at this time on the Fourth Avenue side of the building, and this is probably when the building as a whole was first painted. The small brick addition at the rear along the alley was added by the mid-1930s.

By the early 1960s the building housed the Sun Cleaners and Laundry, in the 1970s a gem and mineral store followed briefly by the Dragon Inn. Harry's Army Surplus proved more successful, staying until 1990. Bob Andrus, Jim Davis and Tom White, who purchased the building in 1982, cleaned up the exterior and unblocked the turret windows.

Metzger's Restaurant, a next door neighbor since 1936, purchased the building in 1984 and expanded into it in 1991. "Metzger" means butcher in German and thus seems appropriate for this building with its butcher shop heritage. John Metzger, the grandson of William Metzger who opened the restaurant in 1928, attributes the success of the project to architect Paul Green, straw boss Russell Kaercher, and woodworker Wilhelm Roth of Saline (originally from Bavaria).

In May of 1991 the Ann Arbor Historic District Commission presented an award to John Metzger for excellent rehabilitation.
MSHD

157

216-218 East Washington Street

Frederick Sorg Block

1871

When Frederick Sorg completed the brick block at 216 for his paint and glass depot in 1871, he realized such instant success that he built a second store next door in 1872 at 218 East Washington. One of the local newspapers, the *Peninsular Courier*, remarked in July of that year that a "new brick block is going up rapidly." It joined the ranks of Ann Arbor's other brick commercial blocks that were sprouting up in downtown during the boom years of the early 1870s.

Sorg was so proud of this building that he featured it in many of his advertisements. In the 1874 *Atlas of Washtenaw County* an engraving shows in delicate shadings the second-floor arched windows separated by thin brick pilasters. It also shows the floor-to-ceiling plate glass storefront windows that were the newest rage among businesses.

Sorg advertised himself as a "house, sign, and ornamental painter, dealing in paints, oils, varnishes, glass etc." Paper hanging, printing and glazing also were his specialties and by the late 1870s he had added graining and gilding. His work was carried on by his son Albert until 1886. In the 1890s Edgar Munyon and his wife Addie ran a millinery shop here and lived upstairs, just as the Sorgs had. Throughout the 20th century the building housed a succession of businesses including a barber shop, a tape recorder store, a donut company, a shoe store and a coal store.

Milton Kemnitz

In 1985 Robert Tisch, owner of Tisch Incorporated, an insurance and investment services firm, purchased the building and hired architect Daniel H. Jacobs to remove the porcelain enamel panels that had covered the front since the 1950s. The original facade was then restored using the drawing in the county atlas as a guide.

Recognizing the great improvement both to the building and to the street as a whole, the Ann Arbor Historic District Commission awarded Tisch a Rehabilitation Award in 1986 for his sensitive restoration of the building's interior as well as its exterior.

MSHD

219-221 East Washington Street

Weinmann Block

Circa 1867, 1892

Kip Miller

Just after the Civil War Michael Weinmann and John Gall were able to build the elaborate brick building at 221 East Washington to house their lucrative meat market and their families. Only two stories high, it nevertheless made a strong architectural statement with its fancy bracketed cornice, oculus window under the pediment, and shuttered windows. Originally numbered as 31 East Washington, this building continued to serve as the Weinmann Meat Market until 1892, when the owners were prosperous enough to build an even fancier building just to the west (219 East Washington). Decorative pressed sheet metal storefronts were an innovation of the late nineteenth century - an inexpensive and practical way to simulate cast iron or stone pillars and carved decoration. Only a few survive in the entire state of Michigan. When building their new addition, the owners were careful to carry the cornice line over from their older building.

The Weinmann Meat Market occupied the new building after 1892 and the older building was leased to other businesses. The butcher shop, known in its later years as the Weinmann-Geisendorfer Meat Market, survived until 1937. Known for the best frankfurters in town, it was a popular stop for high school students on their way to school.

In 1937 another venerable Ann Arbor institution took over the space. This was the Jno C. Fischer Company, a hardware store whose antecedents could also be traced back to the 1860s. "Fischer Hardware" remained until 1982, when the buildings were purchased by real estate developer Peter T. Allen. Allen immediately began to restore the buildings to their 1890s appearance. The cornice was rebuilt, windows were unblocked, shutters replaced and the storefronts redone to emphasize the differences between the two structures (changes made in the 1960s had attempted to obliterate this distinction).

NR, IHP

315-323 East Washington Street

159

Michigan Bell Telephone Company

1925

The design of this building is attributed to William Kapp of Smith, Hinchman and Grylls, a Detroit firm of architects which has designed several buildings for Michigan Bell. A graduate of the University of Pennsylvania, trained in the Beaux Arts tradition, Kapp incorporated in his design many of the characteristics of that style. Notable is the use of terra cotta tiles instead of carved stone (a relatively new technique at the time), outstanding capitals and arches, and bricks curved at the windows. The molds for the terra cotta tiles were designed by Mr. Kapp.

William Kapp's other buildings include the University Club and Players Club in Detroit, the Country Club in Grosse Pointe, Meadowbrook Hall, and the Rackham School on the University of Michigan campus.

Kip Miller

322 East Washington Street

1887

Jacob Hoffstetter House

160

Frances Wright

The Jacob Hoffstetter house is one of the most handsomely detailed of Ann Arbor's 1880s houses. A rare survivor of the nineteenth century neighborhood that once surrounded it, it is one of the best preserved of any age remaining in the downtown. Built of red brick and set high on a coursed ashlar foundation, its windows are capped by segmental arches and carved stone keystones. Oculus windows and kingpost gable ornaments with pierced trefoil designs decorate the front and side gables, while bracketed cornices crown the bay windows, all features of the Queen Anne style popular in this period.

The structure was built for Jacob Hoffstetter, who settled in Ann Arbor in 1854 with his parents, Christian and Mary. The family was among a large number of German immigrants whose settlement had a great impact on the early development of Ann Arbor. They were also part of a small group of Germans who converted to Presbyterianism shortly after their arrival.

Jacob Hoffstetter established a grocery store and saloon on Main Street in 1872, worked hard, and eventually became prosperous. Until the mid-1880s, he and his wife and two sons lived above the store. In 1887, he sold the family business and moved into this new house. One year later he rented part of it to the newly organized fraternity of Alpha Tau Omega, which made its home here from 1888-1894.

When the house was divided into apartments in 1937, a new entrance was constructed at the southeast corner. Though interior remodelling was extensive, much of the original wood trim remained intact. In 1980 the house was purchased and restored by Peter Heydon who also restored the former parsonage next door (see 161). Mr. Heydon was honored the next year by the Historical Society of Michigan for his work "in preserving and developing... historic properties on Washington Street and for finding an adaptive reuse for them."

NR, IHP

161

332 East Washington Street

Methodist Episcopal Parsonage

1858

This former Methodist Episcopal parsonage is architecturally significant as one of a small number of well preserved Greek Revival homes remaining in downtown Ann Arbor. Its unusual exterior detailing is indicative of its late date and suggestive of the general transformation in architectural taste from classical to picturesque that was taking place in the 1850s.

A two-story, front-gable clapboard structure with a one-and-a half story rear wing, distinctive details include the entry with sidelights and transom, the triangular window in the gable, and the full entablature decorated with dentils. The building's late date within the Greek Revival idiom is most evident in the scalloped trim on the front eaves.

The house also possesses local historical importance in having been constructed to house the Reverend Seth Reed, one of the leading lights of Methodism in Michigan in the 19th century. Reverend Reed was admitted to the Michigan Conference of the Methodist Episcopal Church in 1844 and served as pastor of various churches in southeast Michigan. In 1857 he was appointed to serve the Ann Arbor congregation, established in 1827. During his short but successful pastorate (1857-59), the church, a large frame building on the southeast corner of Ann Street and Fifth Avenue, was enlarged and modernized and the Washington Street parsonage constructed. The house seems to have served its original purpose until about 1881.

Frances Wright

The next owner was English immigrant William Allaby, a shoe merchant, who purchased the property in 1882 and lived there until his death in 1910. Albert M. Graves acquired the property in 1924 and the following year established Grave's Garage at the rear of the site. Graves died in 1927 but Mrs. Graves continued to live there until her death in 1962, dividing the house into apartments in 1957.

Mr. Peter Heydon restored the building in 1980, and rehabilitated its interior for office and residential use. A year later, the Historical Society of Michigan honored Mr. Heydon for his efforts (see 160).

NR, IHP

411-413 East Washington Street

1848

Albert Polhemus House

162

This well-built Greek Revival house has a characteristic classic entry with side-lights. The elegantly restrained porches are later additions. The house was built in 1848 for Albert and Leah Polhemus and their family of six, who had come to Ann Arbor from thc statc of New York.

Kip Miller

The Reverend Maltby Gelston, Jr. family moved into the house in 1861. Mr. Gelston and his brother, Mills B. Gelston, were "supply" ministers for small churches in lower Michigan. Maltby's son, Joseph Mills Gelston, was pastor of the First Presbyterian Church of Ann Arbor from 1888 to 1909. After Maltby Gelston's death in 1893, his daughter Sarah converted the house into apartments, which at the time were reserved for single or widowed ladies. It has now been converted into offices.

Germania Hotel — *text on next page*

Kip Miller

163

119-123 West Washington Street

Germania Hotel

1885

Farmer Michael Staebler of Scio Township had timber on his land, so he started a sawmill. He needed coal, so he set up a rural coal yard. He dealt in farm implements, too, and operated a threshing machine, cider press, and a flax seed press. Then he moved to town in 1885, investing his profits in a new building quite impressive by Ann Arbor standards: a hotel that would also house his business offices, while it provided a livelihood for six sons and a son-in-law. George B. Schwab was the architect.

Staebler's Germania Hotel contained the largest "sample rooms" in the state, where traveling salesmen could exhibit sample goods. On the first floor, #119 contained the Staebler coal and farm implement businesses, a saloon and the hotel kitchen were in #121, with the hotel lobby and dining room in #123. Outside on the sidewalk, a ten-ton chunk of coal served as notice of the enterprise within. The high third-story windows belonged to the club rooms of the Germania Verein, where Ann Arbor audiences were often entertained by visiting concert artists.

By 1895 the German society had moved, possibly as a result of financial difficulties. Remodeling replaced the hotel's mansard roof with a fourth story and the clubrooms were divided into guests rooms. The cornice appears to have been moved to the top of the new parapet. The name was changed to the American House. The Staeblers added a bicycle shop and then an automobile dealership. In 1901 they were the only auto agent in Ann Arbor, selling the Toledo car. The Staebler and Son garage building was attached to the rear of the building in 1918 to serve the dealership. Showroom windows were put in the Ashley Street facade in 1927. In 1954 the hotel was renamed the "Earle" after Earl Milner, Ann Arbor native and head of the Milner hotel chain, which leased the place in its declining years. In 1971 code violations forced the hotel's closing.

Harding and Burgess purchased the building in 1973 and began renovations and restoration. Paint was stripped from the north and west walls to reveal the natural brick. The three first floor store fronts have been somewhat altered but retain their original proportions and some of their iron trim. Original windows have been replaced. Major alterations were made in 1975 to the basement and first floor to accommodate the Earle Restaurant in the basement level. In 1989 an entrance canopy was added to the center structure. The entire interior has now been handsomely renovated to provide shop space and offices on the first floor, with the Ann Arbor Area Community Foundation and other offices on the upper floors.

NR, IHP

122 West Washington Street

John Wagner Jr. Blacksmith Shop

1869

Blacksmithing and related crafts were already concentrated along Ashley Street (called Second Street until 1889) when John Wagner Jr. undertook the construction of his carriage and blacksmith shop in 1869. He was not only expanding the craft into more elegant quarters but was also carrying on a family tradition. His father, John Wagner Sr., trained as a blacksmith in his native Wurttemberg and was one of Ann Arbor's earliest blacksmiths, arriving from Germany in 1837. He lived kitty corner from this shop, at the southwest corner of Ashley and Washington. John Jr. must have succeeded at his trade, for the 1872 City Directory contained the follwing advertisement: "John Wagner, Jr. CARRIAGE AND BLACKSMITH SHOP, keeps on hand and manufactures to order all kinds of CARRIAGES, WAGONS AND SLEIGHS. Customer work and horse shoeing done promptly and in a satisfactory manner...Corner Washington and Second Streets."

Kip Miller

By 1874, probably due to the Depression of 1873, the shop became the property of John Schneider Jr., another early German pioneer and blacksmith. In 1878 Schneider was in business with his brother Louis, but by 1883 he was by himself. Three years later Schneider's horse shoeing business moved around the corner onto Ashley Street (where Wagner's business had moved earlier), and the building was named the Union Hotel. In 1888 a bottling works shared this building with the hotel and by 1899 only the bottling works remained.

CONTINUED on next page

After 1895, the storefront portion was operated by Oswald Dietz as Deitz's Saloon. Throughout the 20th century, saloons and restaurants operated here under a half dozen different names: Barrell House, Dietz's Soft Drinks (during Prohibition), Flautz's Restaurant, Metzger's German-American Restaurant, Flautz's Cafe, LaCasa Restaurant, and Del Rio Restaurant and Bar, the present tenant. Charles Miller, in his 1982 biography of W. H. Auden, recounts going with Auden in 1941 to "the then popular Flautz Tavern" and having him comment, "This is all right, but isn't there a common place where, uh, the workers go? A kind of beer hall?" (They ended up going to another bar on Ashley Street.)

This commercial Italianate building is typical of many built just after the Civil War in Ann Arbor. It is of local red brick, three stories high, with a fancy bracketed cornice surmounting brick pilasters which divide the facade into three bays. True to the Italianate style, the upper story windows are tall and narrow and capped with curved window heads and keystones.

The ground floor facade was sympathetically remodeled in the mid-1970s. Using an old photograph, the new owners eliminated earlier changes inappropriate to the building's style.

IHP

First Congregational Church — *text on next page*

Kip Miller

608 East William Street

176

First Congregational Church

1872-1876

The First Congregational Church of Ann Arbor was organized on March 23, 1847. According to the 1947 history of the church written by Calvin O. Davis, "...its founding was the result of a schism within the membership of the local Presbyterian Church, the separation taking place primarily in protest against the stand maintained by that church on the question of Negro slavery." The secession was led by a small group of liberals who also differed with the Presbyterians on questions of faith and dogma. In 1849 they built a church on Washington Street at Fifth Avenue, but by March of 1870, having outgrown their church building, they voted to build a new one. They chose the corner of State and William Streets, and in June of 1872 the cornerstone was laid. The dedication of the finished church was held on May 10, 1876.

Detroit architect Gordon W. Lloyd, also the designer of St. Andrew's Episcopal Church (see 33), chose the Gothic style in multi-colored cut fieldstone and Indiana limestone. The elaborate slate roof with lozenge motifs in contrasting colors is a hallmark of the Gothic style, as are the wooden hammer or collar beams on the inside. In 1942 the interior of the building was refurbished, and in 1946 stone entrance steps and 21 stained glass windows were added. Dr. Leonard Parr began the effort to add a parish house to the original building. Its cornerstone was laid on May 10, 1951.

The Douglas Memorial Chapel, named after Dr. Lloyd C. Douglas, minister of the church from 1916 to 1921, and the parish house were designed by University of Michigan Professor of Architecture Ralph Hammett and completed in 1953. Famous for his preaching abilities, Douglas was also the author of two popular novels, *The Robe* and *Magnificent Obsession*, which were later made into movies.

In 1986 the church completed a three-year renovation, which included the restoration of the collar beams in the main sanctuary, the installation of the Wilhelm Tracker Pipe Organ, and a ramp and elevator for handicap access.

The church complex is of remarkable beauty and interest. It graces a major traffic corner and provides a balance to the University campus just across the street, as well as a fitting transition to the State Street commercial district to the north.

IHP

177

611 East William Street

DKE Shant

1878

Constructed in 1878 by the Delta Kappa Epsilon fraternity as a meeting place for its members who lived in rooms scattered around the campus, this was the first fraternity building at the University of Michigan.

The "Shant" was designed by William LeBaron Jenney during his tenure as professor of architecture at the University of Michigan (1876-79). Later Jenney returned to Chicago, where he achieved fame for the pioneering use of a steel skeleton frame in the Home Insurance Building, generally considered to be the world's first skyscraper. The DKE Shant, built in what was described by Jenney as a thirteenth century French style, resembles the Grace Episcopal Church in Chicago, designed by Jenney a few years earlier. It is thought to be Jenney's only remaining work in Michigan.

After the Dekes' chapter house on Geddes burned in 1968, the chapter ceased to hold regular meetings and the empty Shant was repeatedly vandalized. In 1971 the late Detroit industrialist Wilfred V. Casgrain and other Omicron chapter alumni renovated the structure to function again as an on-campus club for DKE student members.

Ivory Collection

The original stone foundation, woodwork, and Jenney's characteristic brick work have not been altered. The building is a gem of nineteenth century Victorian eclecticism, having a basic Gothic character with Italianate trim. The interior is now contemporary. The high brick wall that was added in 1901 shelters a tiny marble tombstone in memory of the dog "Abe," the Dekes' long-time mascot.

DSHD

NORTH

Ann Arbor

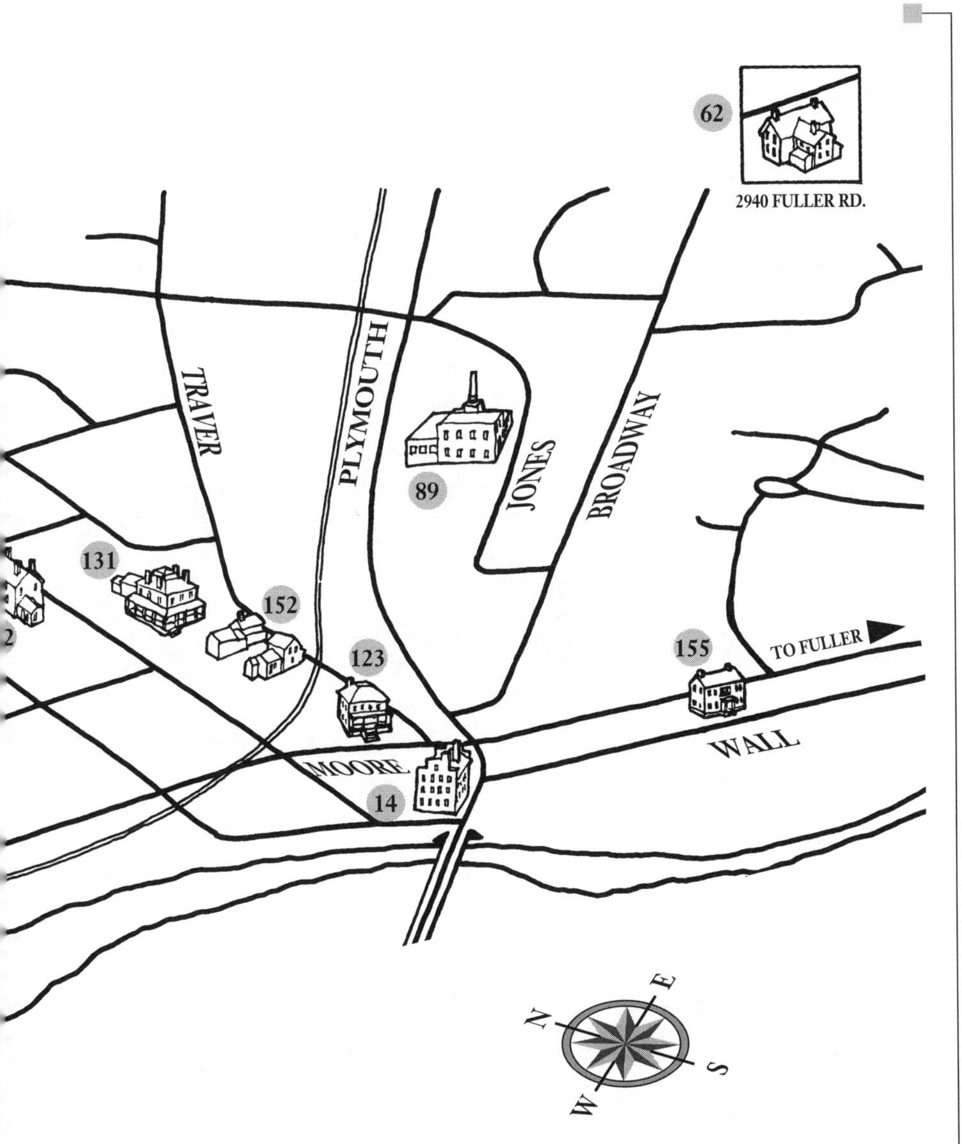

62
2940 FULLER RD.
TRAVER
PLYMOUTH
JONES
BROADWAY
89
131
152
123
155
TO FULLER
WALL
MOORE
14
N
E
S
W

1001-1007 Broadway

Anson Brown Building

1832

This building, the oldest surviving commercial structure in Ann Arbor, has a symmetrical front facade, and parapet end walls characteristic of eighteenth century Dutch-influenced buildings on the east coast. Hand-hewn timber framing of oak is visible in the attic.

Anson Brown had worked for seven years on the Erie Canal before he arrived with his fortune in Ann Arbor, where he became the principal landowner of Lower Town, north of the river. He wanted his business district to be the commercial center of a fine metropolis, and he named his streets Broadway, Wall, Maiden Lane after the major avenues of the Empire City of his native state. He erected as a merchandising center this building and two similar blocks (The Exchange Building and, across the street, the Ingalls Block, replaced in 1959 by a motel and restaurant). The Washtenaw Hotel nearby was one of the largest hotels on the route from Detroit to Chicago, a comfortable stop before crossing the Huron River. The new buildings were an attraction to trade, and Brown was successful in securing an appointment from the Territorial Governor to be postmaster of the town. His brief but intense rivalry with the "hilltoppers" for control of Ann Arbor's development ceased abruptly when Brown died in the cholera epidemic of 1834.

Frances Wright

The upper town regained political dominance, the new University of Michigan drew development in that direction and the railroad came through on the south side of the river. Brown's building outlasted all the other commercial structures of his time and is the only survivor of the town he envisioned and partially built.

The well-maintained building, somewhat European in flavor, was owned by the Colvin family for more than sixty years until it changed hands in 1989.

IHP

2940 Fuller Road

Orrin White House

62

1836

In 1823, merchant Orrin White of Palmyra, New York, came to the newly opened Territory of Michigan to locate a farm. Choosing 176 acres on the north bank of the Huron River, he registered his claim in July. After winding up affairs in Palmyra, White returned in 1824 with his wife Ann, father-in-law Nathan Thayer, and three children. They erected a slab shanty on the site now covered by Huron High School, and moved in on July 4. The Whites were the first settlers in Ann Arbor Township outside the village of Ann Arbor, founded only five months before.

During the 1820s the family nervously shared the farm's flatlands with several hundred Indians who camped there annually while enroute to Windsor to receive treaty gifts from the British, their allies in the War of 1812. White was appointed the second commissioner of Washtenaw County in 1827, sheriff in 1832, and associate Circuit Court judge from 1833-37, often holding court in his log cabin. In 1835, as the Territory moved toward statehood, White was a delegate to the first constitutional convention. In 1842 he was elected to the state legislature. A lieutenant-colonel in the militia, White defended the Territory during the Black Hawk scare and the abortive "Toledo War," a boundary dispute between Michigan and Ohio.

In 1836 the Whites built this L-shaped cobblestone house on Fuller Road, using stones gathered nearby. Stones on the north facade are set in a herringbone pattern while horizontal courses provide contrast on sides and rear. The deep-set center front doorway is enhanced by delicately incised columns, handmade glass sidelights and a massive lintel of oak. Wooden eaves with hex-like symbols decorate the gables.

Louisa Pieper

Robert and Nan Hodges did a magnificent restoration of the house during their ownership in the 1970s and 1980s. Nan Hodges lovingly researched the history of the house and of its original owner.

NR

1327 Jones Drive

Northern Brewery

1886

A brewery had existed on this site on Traver Creek at least since 1872, when George Krause opened his brewery for business. When Herman Hardinghaus took over the running of the brewery in 1884, he had already operated breweries in Cincinnati, St. Louis, and Ypsilanti. The son of a brewer, he had attended upper-level schools in Germany before deciding to emigrate and make his fortune in America. By 1886 Hardinghaus was able to construct a new brewery building and a separate bottling works as well. An 1891 biography states he "manufactures a superior quality of ale which he ships to different cities and towns." He made his home next door on Jones Drive (then known as Mill Street) at what is today 1317 Jones Drive and commonly referred to as the "brewmaster's house."

Prohibition doomed the brewery business so other uses were found for the building. Ernest Rehberg was the last to brew beer here and after 1908 he ran an ice business from this location. The building was used as a creamery for a while and from 1922 to 1972 was the location of the Ann Arbor Foundry.

The foundry was a unique enterprise in many ways, most notably in that it was operated by Charles Baker and Tom Cook, an African-American and a Jewish immigrant from Russia. Their 50-year partnership provided work opportunities for minorities and preserved an unusual industrial forging operation. In 1954, it was doing a flourishing business according to a local newspaper feature, despite the fact that, in the rest of the country, iron foundries that filled individual orders were fast disappearing. Both men worked in the forges until well into their eighties.

After Cook's death in 1971 and a state citation for air pollution, the foundry was closed. The building remained empty until 1978 when the architectural firm of Fry/Peters purchased it and restored the building for their offices.

NR, NBHD

Kip Miller

723 Moore Street

Waite-Kellogg House

1838/1865

Atlas of Washtenaw County, 1874, page 54

Behind its unappealing asbestos siding and fire escapes, this house is a gem waiting to be uncovered and restored. Built in approximately 1838 by Joseph Waite, it was originally one room deep — an example of the type of folk house known as an I-house. Although built as a private house, and adorned by a very handsome Greek Revival doorway, it soon became a rooming house for workers at the nearby Jones and Foley paper mill. Times were tough in the country after the Panic of 1837 and large houses like these quickly became a heavy burden for individuals.

A very individualistic citizen, however, saw fit to purchase the house in 1865 and enlarge it into its present Italianate configuration. This was Daniel B. Kellogg, clairvoyant physician. Dr. Kellogg was famous enough — and his home was grand enough — to be featured in an engraving in the 1874 *Atlas of Washtenaw County*. From this engraving one gets a true image of the treasure which lies beneath the surface.

CONTINUED on next page

Kellogg was born in Pittsfield Township to pioneers from Oneida County, New York. His first encounter with his "gifts" for clairvoyance (or "clear vision") came when he was 17 and encountered a traveling hypnotist. Kellogg was a quick study and soon his neighbors in Pittsfield visited him to "join hands, hear rappings, witness automatic writing and watch the parlor furniture dance as if bewitched." Word of his supernatural perceptions spread quickly and his diagnoses were often linked with remedies. He moved to Ann Arbor in 1865, set up his office on nearby Broadway, and did a brisk business in mail-order diagnosis, answering letters from all over the country and even from Europe. To keep up with demand for his services, he enlisted the aid of his brother Leverett and sold a line of "family medicines" as well, including Kellogg's Liver Invigorator, Kellogg's Magic Red Drops, Kellogg's Family Cathartic Pills, and Kellogg's Lung Remedy.

Unfortunately Kellogg's success was short lived. He died in 1876, at the young age of 42. Undaunted, Leverett continued to sell the patent medicines while Daniel's son Albert C. Kellogg continued to practice his father's unusual profession. An 1891 biography of Albert stated that he continued to manufacture Dr. Kellogg's Family Remedies, which were handled by druggists throughout the State of Michigan, and that his pleasant home in the old part of the town was where he and his wife "keep up the old homestead."

By the 1890s the house had once again reverted to a rooming house, and tenants came and went in rapid succession. As in the rest of the area known as "Lower Town," the decline persisted as businesses and residents moved closer to campus and to the thriving shops on Main Street. But the house did not go unnoticed. In 1936, Emil Lorch of the University of Michigan School of Architecture, noted the unusual entrance and added: "plus or minus good stairs, interior doors and trim." At that time the house was owned by Louis Goffe, a tenant for over 25 years. It remains a rooming house today.

1324 Pontiac Trail

Jonathan Lund House

1847

Ten years after Jonathan Lund and his wife arrived in Ann Arbor in 1837 they built this large and gracious Greek Revival house with its sweeping view of the Huron River valley. A matter of interest at the time and to historians since is the fact that the stucco was mixed with barrels and barrels of skim milk to give it a particularly adhesive quality. The builders, Robert and John Davidson, finished in time for the Lunds to celebrate Thanksgiving in their new home.

The fine details and fixtures of the house aroused envy and exaggeration in the village. Known as "The Place" during the years when the Lunds were famed for hospitality, the house was surrounded by gardens and groves. White pillars at the street marked the entrance to the drive. Peacocks strutted on the lawn; turkeys and Spanish chickens scratched among the bushes. Family letters tell of an excess of cream, eggs, and strawberries which were sent into the village for sale.

Frances Wright

Lund was a man of many enterprises. He built the first paper mill on the river in Lower Town, manufacturing papers for books and tobacco, as well as colored and wrapping papers, which were sold in Chicago and beyond. In the 1850s Volney and Charles Chapin, father and son, bought into the firm and another mill was constructed at Geddesburg, a small town on the Huron River east of Ann Arbor. The partnership was a happy and prosperous one until ill health forced Lund to sell in 1858. Lund's office was an attractive little building with classic columns which stood for many years at the northwest approach to the old Broadway bridge.

After Lund's death the house passed through a number of hands and in the 1890s the Weeks family purchased it. Weeks wrote that he so much appreciated the plantings and flowers that one fine Decoration Day he filled his carriage with flowers and placed them upon the Lund graves.

In 1908 young Fremont Ward came to Ann Arbor to supervise the construction of the Main Street Post Office. He and his wife Flora spied the house on an evening's walk, admired it, bought it, and settled in Ann Arbor, remaining in the house for nearly half a century. Early in the 1930s they divided the home into apartments without affecting the outside appearance. In 1936, in one of the apartments, University student Arthur Miller regaled an election night faculty party with humorous readings from some of his recent "finger exercises."

IHP

132

1425 Pontiac Trail

Guy Beckley House

1842

The Reverend Guy Beckley, a devout abolitionist, came to Ann Arbor in 1839 with his wife Phyla and their eight children. In 1840 he purchased 28 acres of land adjoining the farm owned by his brother Josiah, to whom he sold all but the plot on which this house stands.

The New England Georgian style of this house is unique in Ann Arbor. The walls are sixteen inches thick and made of field stone in the first story, bonded and veneered with hand-made brick. (Beckley's brother, Josiah, had a brick yard, see 133). The heavy oak timbers which make up the interior framing are carefully doweled together. The trim is done in oak and glossy black walnut. Instead of the customary fireplaces, the house was entirely heated by Franklin stoves, an innovation of its day.

Beckley was a man of firm and ardent beliefs. He was well established in Ann Arbor as a minister and lecturer, active in the antislavery movement. He published an influential abolitionist paper, *The Signal of Liberty,* edited by Theodore Foster. Beckley's house was an important "underground" station on one of the routes from the south.

Lester Fader

The Reverend Beckley's time was short, however, as he died in 1847, followed by his wife in 1850. The house thereafter changed hands many times, although the Pascal Mason family remained there from 1862 to 1915.

Ralph W. Hammett and his wife purchased the house in 1933, by then sadly misused and run-down. Hammett, a professor of architecture and an authority on architectural history, took great pleasure in restoring the beautiful home we see today. The many windows with their small panes are original as are the front door and its sidelights. The front porch is a restoration true to the shape and size tracings on the brick work. The modernization of the interior was done with a minimum of change to the structure. The Bertoni family who followed the Hammetts valued the history and the architecture of this home as do the present owners.

IHP

1709 Pontiac Trail

Josiah Beckley House

133

Circa 1834

Kip Miller

Josiah Beckley and his family were members of that intrepid group of early settlers who left New England for the Michigan Territory just after the opening of the Erie Canal in 1825. Beckley arrived in Ann Arbor in 1827 with his wife Minerva, a son Luke and an infant Charles. In October of that year, he purchased 73 acres from Isaac Hull in what was then Ann Arbor Township. According to the family's history, the house was built either in 1834 or 1836, though it could be even older.

Josiah's large brick house has two stories and a classical center entry, and in form resembles a New England house. It has brick end chimneys and an elaborate doorway (not original) with no portico, which is probably how it originally looked. The current windows in the house were added in the 1980s. The black metal stars on the exterior signal the presence of tie rods — iron rods that span the width of the building and help hold it together.

It is not surprising that Beckley built his house of brick, for an 1835 newspaper advertisement indicates he was in the brick business: "Brick! Brick!! Brick!!! Brown and Co. having made an arrangement with Josiah Beckley for brick we are prepared to supply their customers and all others who may wish, with any quantity of the article on reasonable terms. (Signed) Ann Arbor, (on the Huron), April 20, 1835."

Josiah Beckley died in September of 1843 at the age of 53. His wife Minerva and their children continued to live in the house for a few more years but it appears that the house had to be sold to pay Josiah's debts. In 1847 Warren Millard purchased the house and his descendants lived there for almost 100 years.

Today the house remians on its large lot, surrounded by mature trees and looking almost as it did when Ann Arbor was just emerging from the wilderness of the early Michigan Territory.

1219 and 1223 Traver Street

152

Solomon and Jacob
Armstrong Houses

1843 and 1851

Frances Wright

Solomon Armstrong was born in 1821 in Ballston Spa, New York. He arrived in Ann Arbor in 1843 to work as a carpenter and millwright together with his father Jacob and his sons John and Frank A. Armstrong. Solomon's papers are now housed in the Bentley Library in Ann Arbor and include notebooks of his work on houses such as the Jonathan Lund house at 1324 Pontiac (see 131) and the Kellogg Mill. Even his recipe for paint is included.

The house at 1219, probably built in 1851 when the Armstrongs purchased the two lots, represents the more common style of Greek Revival house with its simple rectangular massing and side gables with returns. The house at 1223 is an example of an unusual Greek Revival house form known as "hen and chicks." Said to be unique to southern Michigan, this house type has a tall central portion with a roof gable facing the street, flanked on either side by shorter wings giving the overall appearance of a mother hen sheltering her baby chicks. "Hen and chicks" houses were popular during the 1830s and 1840s, so this is probably the older of the two houses and may have been moved from Armstrong's original property down the road.

Armstrong sold 1219 in 1861 to Amos Corey, another carpenter. In the 1920s, 1219 passed into the hands of the Schlemmer family, who occupied it until the mid-1970s. The house at 1223 was occupied by the Hatch family for almost the identical period and then by Mrs. Adaline Barbiaux for several decades.

Frances Wright

The houses have been featured in books on Ann Arbor's historic buildings, most recently in *Ann Arbor Architecture*, A Sesquicentennial Selection, published by the University of Michigan Museum of Art in 1974. Unaltered until recently, the two buildings form a unique grouping and present an idealized version of our rural and unhurried past.

IHP

947 Wall Street

Nathan Burnham House

1837

In 1834, Anson Brown, his wife Desire, and her brother Edward Fuller began selling land just north of the Huron River. Brown planned to have a new commercial center develop in this area known as "Ann Arbor on the Huron". He would have made a "killing" selling real estate lots to settlers pouring into the area had he not died in the cholera epidemic of 1834. Brown's widow soon married Caleb Ormsby and by 1836 the firm, now Ormsby and Fuller, continued selling house lots to settlers at a brisk pace. Nathan Burnham purchased lots 10 and 11 from Fuller and Ormsby in June of 1837 for $600. When he sold the property back to them two years later, he received $1000, indicating that the house had probably been built in the interval. Burnham built the house in an old "New England" style with a high brick foundation, two fireplaces at each end, four rooms on each floor, a central hallway, and an unusual three-part window on the second floor.

The entry is a beautiful example of the carpenter's craft with its finely carved pilasters and intricately mullioned side lights.

Kip Miller

When Dr. Mark Hildebrandt purchased the house in 1969, he removed a more modern door and late 19th century porch and installed this entry which he had salvaged from a house of the same period being demolished. He hired an architect to design the new portico, put in fire stairs and a new entrance off the parking lot in the rear, changing the official address to 940 Maiden Lane. Patients who visited his office enjoyed the unique cobblestone smokehouse with brick quoins that Hildebrandt preserved in its original location in the rear of the house. While renovating the house, he noted that it was constructed with oak beams and pegs, and that the trim was tulip poplar, a wood commonly used in the early settlement period. The house still serves as a doctor's office, now for Dr. Edward Pierce, a former Mayor of Ann Arbor and well-known political and health activist.

EAST

Ann Arbor

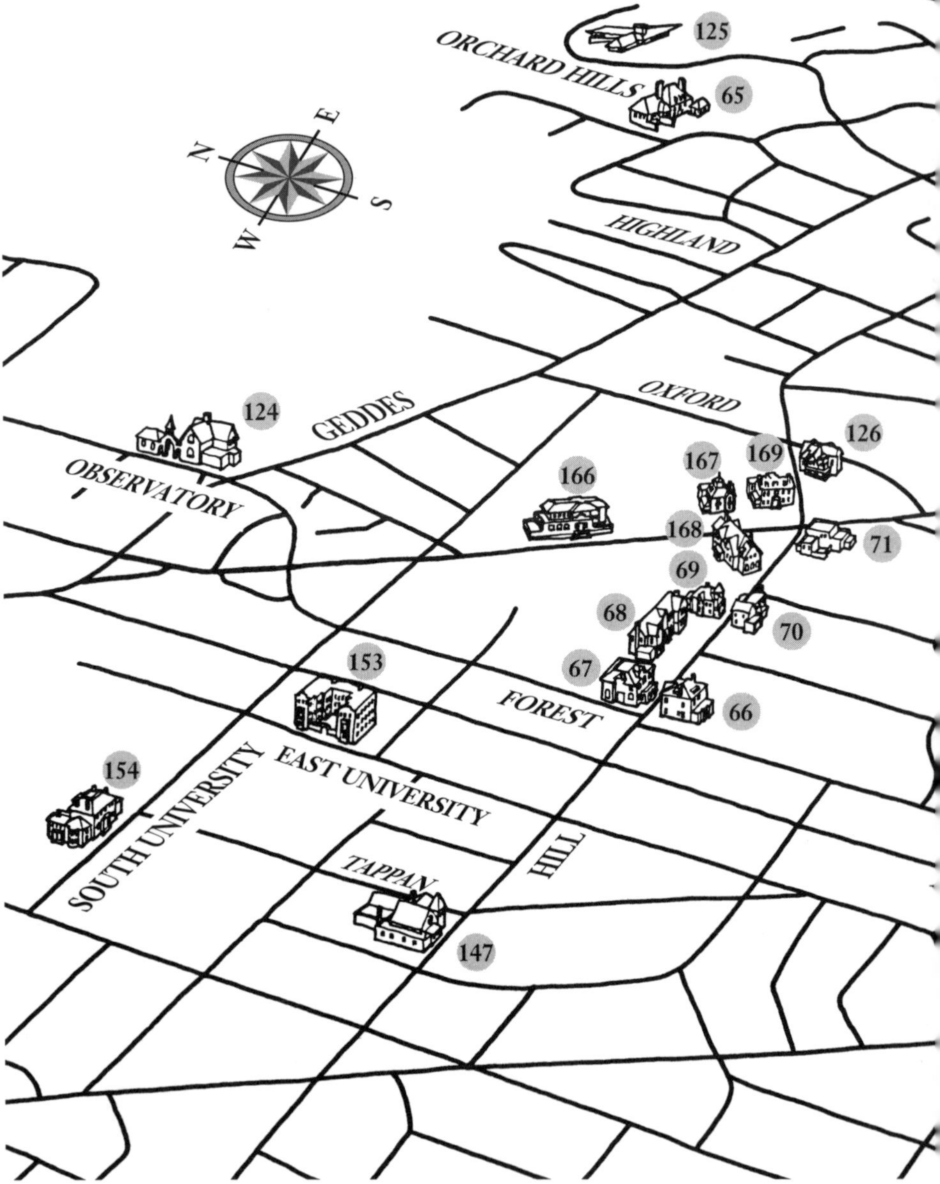

125
ORCHARD HILLS
65
N
E
S
W
HIGHLAND
OXFORD
GEDDES
124
126
169
167
166
OBSERVATORY
168
71
69
68
70
153
67
FOREST
66
154
EAST UNIVERSITY
SOUTH UNIVERSITY
HILL
TAPPAN
147

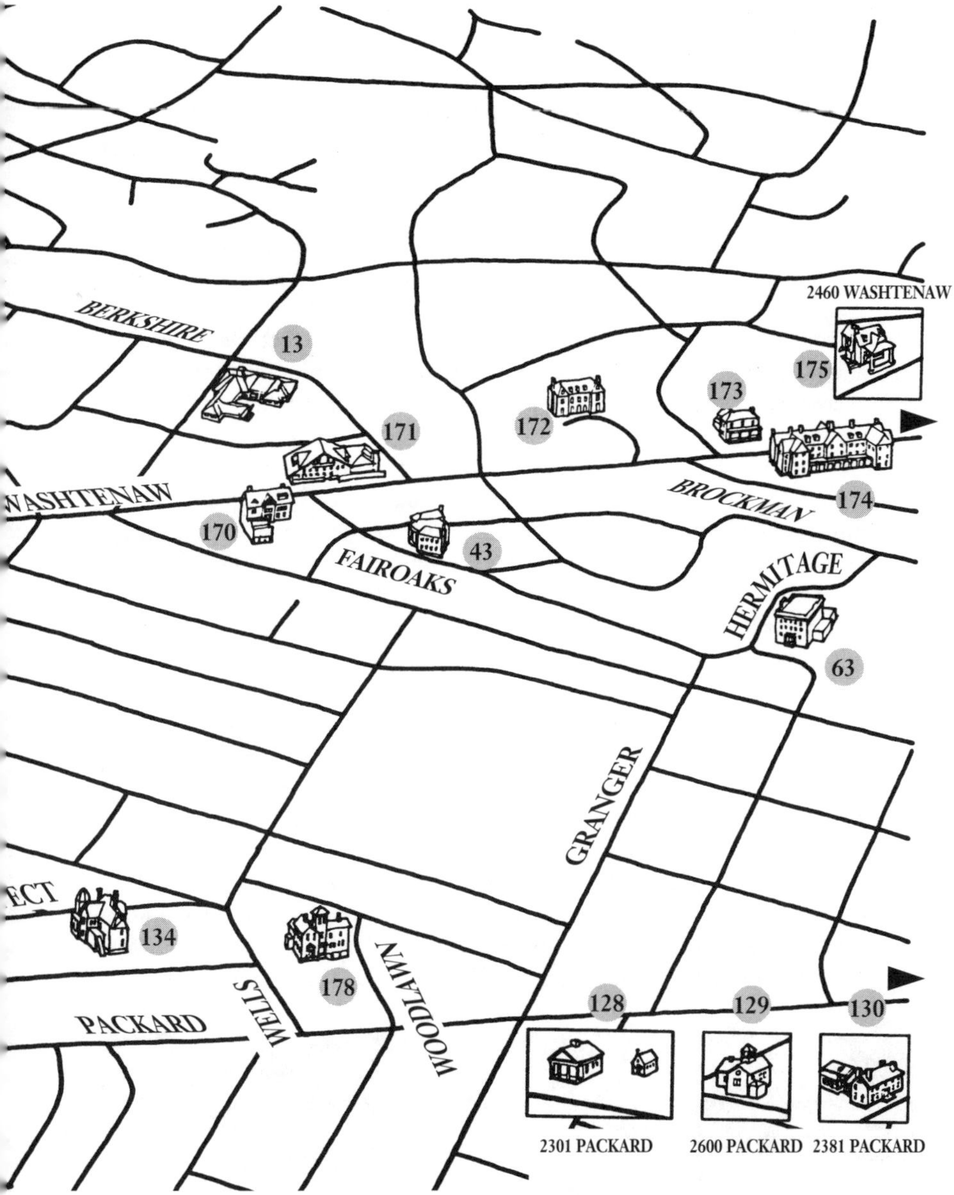

2460 WASHTENAW
BERKSHIRE
13
175
173
172
171
WASHTENAW
BROCKMAN
174
170
43
FAIROAKS
HERMITAGE
63
GRANGER
ECT
134
178
WOODLAWN
WELLS
PACKARD
128
129
130
2301 PACKARD
2600 PACKARD
2381 PACKARD

13

1000 Berkshire Road

Harry and Margaret Towsley House

1932

Well-known Michigan architect Alden B. Dow designed this house in 1932 for his sister, Margaret, after her marriage to Dr. Harry Towsley. According to Katharine Mattingly Meyer's 1971 AIA *Architecture Guide to Detroit*, it is the first residence in the country designed with an attached garage facing the street. It is a long, low brick structure topped by a standing seam roof of greenish copper. It marks the beginning of the "modern" movement in architecture in Ann Arbor and retains a remarkably fresh and exciting look today.

Alden B. Dow was a student of Frank Lloyd Wright and incorporated many of Wright's ideas into his designs. This included an emphasis on honesty, love of nature and a passion for individuality. He produced some 300 buildings in his 47 years of architectural practice. Shortly before he died in 1983, he was named Michigan's architect laureate. His home and studio in Midland, Michigan were designated a National Historic Landmark in 1989.

The Towsley home is one of several buildings in Ann Arbor designed by Dow. These include the Ann Arbor City Hall, the Ann Arbor Public Library, the building and greenhouse complex of the Matthaei Botanical Gardens, the University of Michigan Administration Building, and Greenhills School. The Towsley home was highlighted in a 1952 Ann Arbor Women's City Club Tour and has been photographed for the Detroit Free Press Magazine.

The Towsley family have made their mark on Ann Arbor in many ways. Dr. Towsley worked as a pediatrician and professor at the University of Michigan Medical School. Mrs. Towsley has been an activist in many causes including early childhood education, Planned Parenthood, the Ann Arbor Community Center, and the Republican Party. Well-known philanthropists, they have endowed numerous scholarships, professorships, and buildings dedicated to art, medicine, and science. Like her father, Herbert H. Dow, founder of the Dow Chemical Company of Midland, Michigan, Margaret Towsley built a comfortable home for her family and never moved. More than 50 years after its construction, the Towsleys still reside in their "modern" house.

Kip Miller

1111 Fair Oaks Parkway

James Petrie House

Early 1914

In early 1914 developer Charles Spooner planned a subdivision named Scottwood that promised to be: "a group of handsome residences... amid a landscape setting not hitherto attempted...Unlike most additions to the modern city, platted with straight streets and small lots giving scarcely breathing room between the houses, it has winding roads (and) a large garden space... indeed, each house stands on a little knoll, commanding a pleasing view." Such was the setting for the James Petrie home.

Kip Miller

All the houses in Scottwood were designed by Dr. Fiske Kimball, at that time an Assistant Professor of Architecture at the University of Michigan and later nationally famous as the head of the Museum of Art in Philadelphia. Since this lot was at the intersection of Norway and Fair Oaks, Kimball chose to place the house facing the corner, rather than either of the streets. The unique floor plan combines circular rooms in the center of each floor flanked by rectangular wings set at an acute angle to the main axis. The round portico in front with its elegant two-story columns exhibits Kimball's fondness for classical detailing. As stated in the brochure for the development, Kimball's designs were to have the "quiet unobtrusiveness of good taste. Each completely individual, they nevertheless harmonize in charm of design and refinement of detail."

The house was built for James N. Petrie, Esq. and his son Warren, and was described in detail by Fiske Kimball in a 1918 issue of *Architecture*. By 1920, Mrs. Dorothy Sellards and her husband Thomas, both osteopaths, lived here with their two sons. Widowed in 1923, Mrs. Sellards continued to live here, on and off with her sons, until 1940. After World War II, Dr. Norman Maier, Professor of Psychology at the University of Michigan since 1931, moved in with his wife. He lived in the house well into his retirement in the late 1970s.

1808 Hermitage Road

Marvin A. Ives House (The Hermitage)

1914

"I built this house about 1914" wrote Levi D. Wines on an old photograph now housed in the Bentley Library. This 28-room structure, set on a hilltop in 10 acres of large trees, exemplified the estate of a country gentleman. The Georgian style house, with its rigid symmetry, its imposing mass, and its arched windows, corner quoins, stucco walls, and pedimented entry, was built for Marvin Ives, a soap manufacturer from Detroit. Ives was born in Detroit in 1859 but his family had long associations with Ann Arbor. His grandfather, Marvin Allen, had been one of the first members of the University of Michigan Board of Regents. His sister Jennie married Edward Campbell (see 66 and 169). Ives moved into 1808 Hermitage in 1915 with his wife, son and daughter, commuting to Detroit to tend his soap business which he eventually sold to Proctor and Gamble. While the family lived here, from 1917 to 1924, the address was on Ferdon.

The 1923 subdivision of Ives Woods, which created 20 lots, paved the way for houses that now surround the Ives mansion. When Ives sold the house to the Hermitage Fraternity after the death of his wife in 1923, the new street took their name. The Hermitage fraternity remained in the house until 1934. The house was home to several fraternities including Phi Sigma Delta from 1949 until it was sold to University of Michigan Professor Jesse Gordon and his wife Anitra in 1970.

Kip Miller

The Gordons attempted to restore the house to some semblance of its former grandeur after its rough years as a fraternity house but the task was unending. In 1981 they put the house up for sale. In 1982, a Designer Showcase, similar to that held for the Hoover Mansion (see 172), was held here to raise money for scholarships for theUniversity of Michigan School of Art. The Gordons rented out the apartment on the third floor to Joseph Brodskey, a celebrated Russian dissident poet who later became poet laureate of the United States.

2301 Highland Road

James Inglis House

65

1927

This imposing residence, near the University of Michigan Arboretum, was built in 1927 for James Inglis as part of an exclusive subdivision on the eastern edge of town. It was situated on the rear acreage of a farmstead that had been in the Inglis family since 1901. It reputedly cost $250,000 to build and was designed to resemble a French Chateau. Nestled away from the bustle of town, the Inglis House today is owned by the University and is used as a guest house and reception center for visiting dignitaries.

Kip Miller

The four story residence is Ann Arbor's only true "country estate," an architectural as well as a social landmark. It has 12 rooms plus servants' quarters, a caretaker's cottage, a three-car garage, a greenhouse, a workshop, and a pumphouse. It was designed by Lilburn "Woody" Woodworth, at the time a young architect and friend of the family whose only other building had been the Arch Diack residence at the bottom of Geddes Heights. Unusual features when it was built included electrically operated garage doors, separate wash bowls for the parents in their bedroom, tennis courts, a golf course, and a panelled library, filled to the ceiling with fine volumes.

Today the French Chateau style building, with its steeply pitched slate roof, irregular brick and stone, and elegant accoutrements, sits amidst the lush foliage of the original gardens. It elicits praise from many of the world famous scientists, musicians, government leaders and kings who have wined, dined and lodged there. In 1986 it was featured on the Ann Arbor's Women's City Club House Tour and in 1988 was designated as a significant historic building by the City of Ann Arbor.

James Inglis, a successful Detroit industrialist, owned the American Blower Company. In 1901 his sister Kate and her husband Frank Smith, had purchased a farm in the "country" near Ann Arbor in order to live a simpler life. Kate's niece, Carol Inglis Spicer, remembered her aunt's grapevines strung along Geddes Street as well as the farm's apples and pears and chickens. The farm house still stands at 2105 Geddes.

CONTINUED on next page

In the 1920s the farmlands were subdivided for development and the "back seven acres" with the best view was chosen by James Inglis as the site of his grand country home. With his wife Elizabeth, who designed the elaborate formal gardens, they created a country estate almost fit for royalty. As Mrs. Spicer described it "... it was truly a 'creation'... building that house... and most particularly that garden, where there had been before only long grass and wild blackberries... In my aunt's later years... in California... it has been the garden ... that looms in her memories of those halcyon days."

James Inglis died in 1950, leaving the house to his wife for her lifetime and then to the University of Michigan. In 1951 Mrs. Inglis moved to Kalamazoo and donated the house to the University. Mrs. Inglis' gardener, Walter Stampflei, remained to tend the gardens, living in the caretaker's cottage until his death. After some years of inattention, University horticulturalist Charles Jenkins put the gardens back into shape, restoring them to their former glory. This only adds to the splendor of the estate and makes it a real hidden treasure in Ann Arbor.

IHP

Kip Miller

1310 Hill Street

Edward Campbell House

66

1890

This spacious and attractive house is of Queen Anne vintage, but its symmetry and classical detailing are in sharp contrast to Queen Anne buildings. Inspired by the centennial celebrations of 1876, a renewed interest in earlier design led to adaptations called Colonial Revival. The house was first occupied by Edward D. Campbell, junior professor of metallurgy, when he was called to his position at the University of Michigan.

In 1901, when the Campbell family moved to 1555 Hill Street, Margaret Lydecker, a widow recently arrived in Ann Arbor, purchased the home and opened a boarding house which was famed for its style and elegance and for providing the "best food in Ann Arbor." Her daughter, Margaret, married Professor Earl S. "Doc" Wolaver, and they raised their family in this house. It remains a single family dwelling.

WHHD

AAHDC

67

1315 Hill Street

Amariah Freeman House

1908

This is a textbook example of the Italian Renaissance style as described by the McAlesters in their *Field Guide to American Houses*. It was built by local attorney Amariah Freeman in 1908 and features a triple-arcaded entry with free-standing columns. It has large arched windows on the main floor with smaller ones on the second floor, red brick quoins at the corners contrasting with pebbly light stucco walls, red clay tiles on the hipped roof and dormers, and bracketed eaves.

Louisa Pieper

Freeman and his wife built a second house six years later at the corner of Hill and East University and sold this house to Alpha Sigma Phi fraternity. Photographs taken in 1915 by University of Michigan photographer George Swain, show a stone balustrade on the roof of the porch entry (now gone) and a wonderfully wooded setting, still somewhat in evidence today. Although large houses like these were requisitioned for use as barracks during World War I, it remained the fraternity's home until 1941. It was then sold as a "League" house, or boarding house for women students under the direction of Mrs. Marie Maddy.

From 1949 to 1962 Alpha Kappa Kappa fraternity owned the house, renting it out during the early 1960s for a series of University-related institutes. By the mid-1970s, Paul and Edith Nickel occupied the first floor and rented out about 15 rooms to graduate students. It is now the home of Delta Sigma Phi fraternity.

The house has an unusual floor plan which is hardly suggested by the exterior. The interior is designed like an Italian palazzo with a completely open courtyard in the center. One wall on each floor has windows facing on this open court, which gave the whole an extraordinary feeling of light and air.

WHHD

1331 Hill Street

Delta Upsilon Fraternity

68

1903

Albert Kahn designed this building in 1903 for the men of Delta Upsilon fraternity, and it is significant for two reasons. It is the oldest fraternity house in Ann Arbor still being used by the organization that built it and it is one of the earlier surviving examples of non-industrial, non-commercial designs by Kahn.

It is built in a Tudor Revival style, in an "E" shape, with half timbering and stucco on the projecting gable portion in the center exemplifying the most distinctive elements of the style. Adding to the "English" effect are the slate roof, shingled accents, carved verge boards, and casement windows grouped in units of two, three and four. The interior also has features derived from late 16th and early 17th century English architecture including ornamental woodwork and plasterwork, a fine panelled recess framed by Tuscan columns with built in seats, a Pewabic tile fireplace with an elaborately carved mantel, and overmantel with an inset of the fraternity logo.

Delta Upsilon was founded as a non-secret fraternity at Williams College in 1834 and its University of Michigan chapter was chartered in 1876. In the October 1, 1902, issue of their magazine, it was reported that "the crisis in the struggle for a new chapter house is past, and thanks to the generous aid of loyal alumni, the finest fraternity building in Ann Arbor is in the process of construction." Albert Kahn's specifications were executed by the local construction firm of Koch Brothers, well known for their many campus projects and other major public buildings.

Louisa Pieper

A 1909 postcard as well as photographs taken in 1916 by University of Michigan photographer George Swain show that the house has changed little through the years. On September 29, 1991, the fraternity celebrated the listing of the building on the State Register of Historic Sites and the public was able to see firsthand why this building warrants its many distinctive honors.

SR, WHHD

69

1335 Hill Street

Farwell Wilson House

1894

Louisa Pieper

Though the Farwell Wilson house was built in 1894 for a lumber dealer and his wife, Mrs. Wilson unfortunately was widowed shortly afterward. By 1914 the house had been sold to Professor Clarence Johnson and his wife Bessie. Johnson, who was Director of the Davis Engineering Company, lived here for well over fifty years.

We can get a feeling for the type of social activity participated in by upper class women from a 1911-1912 program of the Ann Arbor Equal Suffrage Club. The program lists the meeting of February 1 to be held at Mrs. Wilson's residence. It featured "Women, their Organizations and Why?" by Mrs. Field and "Great Leaders, Past and Present," by the President, Mrs. Plummer, with helpers. The club met, usually twice a month, both at members' homes scattered throughout the neighborhood (see 141) and most often at the high school.

The house is a typical high style Queen Anne with a round corner tower topped by a conical roof and finial. Turned posts with brackets and unusual railings and foundation screening enhance both the two story front porch and the long porch on the east side. Alternating bands of fish-scale shingles and clapboard carry out the typical Queen Anne exterior decoration.

In 1970 neighboring Delta Upsilon fraternity purchased the house and currently uses it as an annex (see 68). The Ann Arbor Historic District Commission honored the fraternity in 1992 for the sensitive way in which it repaired and replaced the porches and exterior trim.

WHHD

1410 Hill Street

Paul C. Freer House (Shearer House)

1898

Ralph Latimer, when writing about Ann Arbor architecture in *The Inlander* of 1901, drew particular attention to several of the houses recently constructed on Hill Street, remarking that "the residences of Mr. Rolfe and Dr. Freer are also good examples of houses in quite a different style (than the colonial) and are particularly pleasing in their air of solidity and competence to meet the climatic conditions of the place; though largely built of wood they look strong, warm and comfortable and have not that air of summer cottages unoccupied during the winter which is so depressing."

This house, with its intentional asymmetry, its half gable interrupted by a turret with no tower, and its use of many different size windows in odd relationships, was designed by the well-known Chicago architecture firm of Pond and Pond for the equally renowned Professor Paul C. Freer, Director of the Laboratory of General Chemistry. Pond and Pond was an architecture firm consisting of two brothers, Irving Kane and Allen Pond, sons of local newspaper editor Elihu Pond. Other buildings in Ann Arbor designed by them include the University of Michigan Union, the Women's League, the Student Publications Building, the first YMCA Building at 110 North Fourth Avenue, and several private residences.

AAHDC

Professor Freer only remained here four years. In 1901 he was soliciting renters for his house: "We built it four years ago. It contains ten rooms, hardwood floors, laundry in the basement, a 30x15 living room, large fireplace, and a 20x20 veranda opening off the living room with an awning protected by vines... The dining room is alt Deutsch... The rent will be fifty dollars a month, and if necessary, I am willing to lease it for two years."

Freer sold the house in 1902 to Professor Albert Stanley, head of the School of Music, and his wife Emma. After five years, the Stanleys sold it to insurance agent Chauncey Shearer, and his wife Louise, who made it their home and their daughter's until the early 1970s. Since 1972 it has been the home of Professor Frank Casa and his wife Julie who have received awards for their preservation efforts and maintain a beautiful garden in front.

WHHD

71

1530 Hill Street

J. D. Baldwin House

1848

J. D. Baldwin came to Ann Arbor in 1847 from Detroit, where he had been engaged in the hardware and leather trade. He purchased 154 acres outside the city and built this unique brick villa, a Greek Revival house with a nearly flat roof rather than the more familiar slope-roofed temple form. It was covered with salmon colored stucco and was known as "the pink house with the blue-green blinds," a landmark on the old middle Ypsilanti Road which later became Washtenaw Avenue.

Baldwin made his land into a profitable fruit and berry farm. An active member of the Washtenaw Agriculture Society and a leader in the Washtenaw Pomological Society, he was often called upon to speak as an authority on the culture of peaches, strawberries, and the apples for which he was best known.

In the 1876 he sold the home and 78 acres to Olivia and Israel Hall, who later subdivided their acreage, and with great foresight, placed the restrictions on the property, including the 60 foot setback, which give Washtenaw Avenue some of its grace and character. The Halls' son Louis and his bride Elizabeth moved into the house in 1885. Mrs. Hall lost no time in changing the color of the stucco. Fireplaces replaced the original stoves and the sloped-roof porches were added for family comfort.

AAHDC

Louis Hall studied dentistry at the University of Michigan and was soon a prominent member of the Dental School faculty. Their daughter, Mrs. J. R. Hayden, resided in the family home until her death in the 1980s.

In the late 1980s, a new owner thoroughly remodeled the interior and restored the exterior of this fascinating home.

WHHD

415 Observatory

Forest Hill Cemetery

1858 and 1867

In 1856, a Cemetery Company was formed to choose a site for a new cemetery in Ann Arbor. The cemetery then in use (now Felch Park) was too small and was hemmed in by the expanding town and university. After offering $50 for the best plan, the Company chose a hilly part of town south of the Observatory, known as the Taylor farm, to construct a new type of cemetery. No longer to consist of rows of tombstones next to the church, the new approach called for a scenic setting, reflecting the peacefulness and repose of death. In the 1850s, this new view of cemeteries saw them as places for contemplation. In fact, the movement towards the creation of the public parks system in the United States began in the picturesque or "romantic" cemetery movement.

Forest Hill was inspired by the first and most well-known of the Romantic cemeteries in America, Mt. Auburn Cemetery in Boston, Massachusetts, which had introduced the naturalistic English landscape style to American cemeteries. Like Mt. Auburn, Forest Hill has a varied topography. While it is flat along Geddes and Observatory, it has several hills and vales in the interior. And also like Mt. Auburn, it features curved paths that follow the slopes, many of which bear the same floral names: verbena, myrtle, snowdrop, eglantine, and moss.

Although the $50 does not appear to have been awarded to anyone, we do know that the original map of the cemetery was drawn by Colonel J. L. Glen of Niles who is also believed to have been the designer. Colonel Glen was a civil engineer who had surveyed and laid out the city of Lansing and had been in charge of the construction of the State Capitol.

The new cemetery was dedicated on May 19, 1859 and what a dedication it was. It is described by O. W. Stephenson in his 1927 *Ann Arbor The First Hundred Years*: "...Under the direction of George D. Hill... a great procession marched to the grounds. First came a band, then several military companies, officiating clergy, the orator for the day, the President of the Cemetery Board, William S. Maynard, and other members. In order after these came the Common Council, the faculty of the University, the members of the Board of Education, teachers of different schools, editors and printers, the student body of the University, members of the fire companies, another band, the Masons, Oddfellows, private citizens and children of the public schools."

After the dedication, the graves of many early settlers buried in the old cemetery were moved to Forest Hill. In its 103-year history over 17,000 people have been buried there, from Elisha Rumsey, co-founder of Ann Arbor, to

CONTINUED on next page

University presidents, prominent citizens, and foreign students. The first person permanently interred was Benajah Ticknor, the Navy surgeon who built Cobblestone Farm (see 130).

In 1866, the Cemetery Board instructed the Building Committee to solicit designs for an office, gatehouse, and caretaker's house at the entrance to the cemetery. The plans selected were those of James Morwick, a local architect who had recently built the chapel addition to St. Andrew's Episcopal Church (see 33) and the home of Dr. Alonzo Palmer at the corner of Division and Ann Streets (see 29). Designed in the Gothic Revival style, these buildings exhibit typical features including lancet windows, slate roofs with colorful lozenge and diamond patterns, a quatrefoil window in the gable of the caretaker's house, and wavy bargeboards curving under the roof eaves of each gable. The original metal roof cresting is some of the last remaining in Ann Arbor.

The walls are cut fieldstone of various soft colors and the entire effect is one of picturesque beauty, further enhanced by the charming cemetery gate: a pointed stone arch capped by a copper topped belfry. Two stone pillars flank the entrance on which are inscribed: "J. Morwick, Builder" and " Walker Bros, Masons."

Sturgis Collection

Forest Hill today retains much of its original design. Flat gravestones along Observatory preserve the open view to the large monuments. As trees and shrubs have matured, however, the contrast between the wooded areas and the grassy meadows has been obscured. Just beyond the gateway and dominating the entry stands the Washtenaw County Civil War Memorial, moved here from the courthouse lawn at Main and Huron Streets when the new courthouse was built in 1954.

IHP

227 Orchard Hills Drive

William and Mary Palmer House

1952

125

Balthazar Korab

It is said that Frank Lloyd Wright was a romantic. He must have felt he had met with two kindred spirits when he was approached by Mary and William Palmer and asked to design a house to fit their newly acquired hilltop site above the river. Now, forty years later, the home, surrounded by its spacious "stroll garden," would surely have pleased his romantic soul. Bill Palmer, retired Professor of Economics, says that Wright was not only a great architect, he was a wonderful human being, and joy to have as a guest.

This is one of Wright's Usonian houses, designed in 1950 to be built in a pattern of equilateral triangles. It was ready for the Palmers and their two children, Adrian and Mary Louise, in 1952. The living area is open, with repeated panels of glass, including mitred-glass corner windows, leading the eye to the garden beyond. Perforated ceramic blocks run the length of the long, low house, adding detail and a sense of mystery to the exterior. At eye level in the kitchen, they provide a view of the living area on one side and the entry way and carport on the other. Cantilevered roofs of cedar shingles shelter the house with deep overhangs.

The house was built by local contractor Erwin Niethammer. The "claycraft" brick as well as the perforated ceramic blocks were made in Upper Sandusky, Ohio. Wide board-and-batten walls and ceilings are of red tidewater cypress, beautifully constructed by Niethammer's son-in-law Paul McDowell. In the living area the ceiling rises to a point from three directions. The cypress throughout was finished by Oswald Herz, a prominent decorator of that time. The soft reds of the brick and the cypress are picked up in the triangles scored into the concrete floor, under which radiant heating was installed. The unusual finish of the floor was produced by broadcasting red granules over wet concrete and troweling them in to give the floor the appearance of polished leather. The focal wall of the living area contains a huge, open fireplace that gives dramatic effect to even a small fire.

126

700 Oxford Road

Albert Lockwood House (Sigma Nu)

1910

Albert Lockwood came to the University of Michigan School of Music in 1901 as the Head of the Pianoforte Department. When his parents, Charles and Albertine Lockwood, joined him in Ann Arbor he built this remarkable Tudor Revival house to be the center for their musical interests. Although the building is composed of multiple units, the facade presents the appearance of symmetry with front-projecting gables at each end of the main roof. Adding to the apparent symmetry is the central entry located under an open-gabled portico. All roof gables, including the main and secondary porticos, are flared and covered by terra cotta tile. In keeping with the Tudor style, the exterior of the building is faced with light stucco and dark half-timber beams forming cross and loop patterns. The second story jetty further evokes medieval England.

Kip Miller

Every Tuesday at four o'clock, Albert, a gifted pianist, held recitals at one of the two grand pianos in the spectacular three-story dining room while students and neighbors listened from the surrounding carved wooden balconies and staircases. During colder weather a cheery fire burned in the impressive fireplace, offsetting the chill of the tall windows. Albert's own master bedroom, and a nursery opposite it, opened onto the dining room by way of the balconies. These are the finest rooms in the house, one with a bay window overlooking the back garden, the other with a handsome fireplace.The interior is rich with floors, balconies, banisters and ceiling beams of black walnut. Shaped plaster, painted black, and carved walnut decorate the rooms and a large iron chandelier hangs from the ceiling.

Charles Lockwood died not long after the house was completed. When his mother Albertine died in 1919, Albert Lockwood sold the house to the Sigma Nu fraternity. Sigma Nu is proud of their house, and recently replaced on the balconies thirteen plaster gargoyles, stolen in a fraternity prank over 30 years ago. As former president Jim Doyle wrote: "700 Oxford was already magnificent when it was built —Today, that magnificence is increased by the knowledge it could never be recreated."

IHP

2301 Packard Road

128

Circa 1846, 1940

William Anderson House and Wisdom Chapel

Pioneer John Anderson purchased Pittsfield Township farmland in 1831, but it was his son William who erected this small Greek Revival home. A modernist who wanted the best for his family, Anderson used stoves instead of fireplaces and installed a closet, an innovation in those days.

As county sheriff, William Anderson had carried on a public feud with Probate Judge Robert S. Wilson, who built a larger Greek Revival house on Division Street. "A dastardly coward," Wilson had called Anderson. Wilson soon left Ann Arbor, but the Anderson family lived in this house through three generations until in 1937 it was sold to Dr. Inez Wisdom.

Frances Wright

Dr. Wisdom was a prominent local physician who served as President of Washtenaw County Medical Society and the St. Joseph Mercy Hospital Medical Society. She was especially active in Episcopal Church affairs. In 1941 she erected a small chapel for private prayer next to the house on the south side which was patterned after those she had seen in Europe. In 1953 she and her joint tenant and companion, Miss Gertrude Griffith, gave the chapel and grounds to the Episcopal Diocese of Michigan, establishing the St. Clare of Assisi parish. The parish later erected its meeting house next door. In 1968 Miss Griffith obtained full title to the house and later gave it to the church.

Frances Wright

As on the Kempf House, four square columns support the pediment above which is a frieze containing three window openings with wooden ornamental grilles. A notably pure temple style, the house was drawn and photographed for the Historic American Buildings Survey.

NR, HABS, SR, IHP

129

2600 Packard Road

Stone School

1911

Constructed in 1911, this is one of the most picturesque rural schoolhouses left in Michigan. One-story with a high attic, the building is of uncoursed field-stone with a terra cotta tile roof, topped at the intersection of its four gables by an open belfry complete with school bell. White boxed cornices vividly contrast with the multi-colored stone and red tile. Oculus air vents are located in each gable. This building replaced an earlier fieldstone school dating back to 1853.

The Stone School District dates from 1826 when a small band of pioneers who had settled around the present intersection of Packard and Platt Roads decided their children needed schooling. They selected a site in an oak grove on the Nordman farm and hired Miss Elzada Fairbrother as teacher. By 1827 a building had been constructed that was called the Mallett's Settlement School.

Kip Miller

In 1853 the district was divided because of an increasing number of children. The new district was called Pittsfield District No. 7 fractional, and the first stone building was erected on this site by volunteer labor using materials from nearby farms. This building served until 1911, when a larger school was needed. With great enthusiasm the people of the district tore down the old structure and helped build the new school. Stones were salvaged from the old building, and additional stones donated by the Ticknor and Hutzel farms.

Over time additional wooden buildings were erected to accommodate the growing school population. From 1918 to 1927 these buildings were used as a training school for student teachers from Michigan State Normal College (now Eastern Michigan University) in Ypsilanti. By 1947 the school population had greatly increased and a bond issue was approved to build a new school across the road. The old stone school was boarded up after the new school was completed in 1949.

Countless people, seeing the charming school unused, sought to acquire it but it remained empty until 1958 when Miss Jean Dickinson opened a nursery school in the building. To this day it remains a nursery school—and a building which is regarded with affection by local residents.

IHP

2781 Packard Road

1844

Benajah Ticknor Farm (Cobblestone Farm)

130

This farmhouse is an example of an unusual building style that began in the 1830s in western New York and moved westward with the frontier. Erected in 1844 for Dr. Benajah Ticknor by Stephen Mills, a mason trained in New York, the house combines the restrained elegance of the Federal style with an extravagant facade of cobblestones, laid in herringbone rows.

The front door, flanked by columns and glass sidelights, opens into a wide central hall with a staircase and "grained" woodwork. A parlor and library, sitting room, and bedrooms complete the stone portion of the house, which contrasts sharply with the simple wooden New England kitchen wing. The section of that wing containing the dining room and maid's chamber is probably the original tiny house which Heman Ticknor bought from farmer Charles Maynard in 1835. Heman purchased the farm for his brother, Dr. Benajah Ticknor, a U. S. Navy surgeon. After years at sea off South America and in the Far East, Dr. Ticknor wanted land in Michigan as an investment and for a retirement home.

In 1840 Benajah and his wife Gessie paid their first brief visit to Ann Arbor. The sight of Heman, his wife Eliza, and seven children crowded into so small a

Kip Miller

CONTINUED on next page

house may have prompted Benajah to build the larger stone house for both families. In 1845 a kitchen, pantry, milk room, hired men's dormitory, toilets and a woodshed were added to the frame house, which was joined to the stone house at the same time. Several outbuildings (destroyed by fire in 1924) completed the farm.

From 1844 until his death in 1858, while accepting several assignments at sea and in naval hospitals, Benajah Ticknor called Ann Arbor his home. A self-taught classical scholar, mathematician, philosopher, and diarist, Dr. Ticknor participated in the social and intellectual life of the University community and was sought after for medical opinions. Ticknor's classical and medical library was left to the University of Michigan. Yale's Sterling Library preserves the handwritten journals of his voyages and other experiences between 1818 and 1854.

In 1860 Ticknor's widow sold the farm to Horace Booth, who passed it to his son. Nelson Booth enlarged the 183 acres, added barns for thoroughbred race horses, installed a front-yard fountain, and added an Italianate front porch.

In 1881 the farm was purchased by Scottish immigrant William Campbell, an Ypsilanti merchant, who soon achieved renown for his pure-bred cattle. Campbell, his son Clair, and grandchildren William, George, and Mary kept the house essentially unchanged for 91 years. After World War II most of the farm's acres were absorbed by housing developments and park land. In 1972 George and Mary Campbell sold the house and the last 4.5 acres to the city to complete Buhr Park.

Since 1974 a volunteer citizens group, the Cobblestone Farm Association, has provided research, planning, and fund-raising for restoration of the house and grounds as a working farm museum.

NR, HABS, SR, CFHD

1136 Prospect Street

Samuel Miller House

134

1893

This house, which current residents refer to as "the castle" was built by Samuel and Harriet Miller. It appears to be modeled loosely after Design No. 27 in Goerge F. Barber's *The Cottage Souvenir, Revised and Enlarged* (1892). It is a particularly fine example of the Queen Anne style, with a very tall curved chimney enveloping an oriel window on the first floor. Adding to the effect of grandness is the conical topped tower to the right of the entry. The use of different materials and shapes of windows and roofs in odd relationships with one another adds to the effect of extravagance.

Frances Wright

The Miller house site was created from the acreage of Christian Eberbach's vast estate on Packard named "Woodlawn" since Harriet was Christian's sister. The 1874 map of Ann Arbor shows a tree-bordered drive running east from Packard to Eberbach's estate of orchards and gardens. The Millers' romantic Victorian house was placed on a hilltop at the edge of the orchard. Prospect Avenue was opened as an access road and the drive from Packard became a part of the Miller Addition to the City of Ann Arbor.

Although Samuel and Harriet Miller died early in this century, their daughter Aura lived in the house until 1936. Older residents of the area remember her, the orchard (of which a few trees remain) and a bog at the bottom of the hill which closed off Church Street in wet weather. Despite some unsympathetic alterations to the front as a result of the conversion to nine apartments, the house is still considered a major neighborhood landmark in the Burns Park area.

IHP

147

730-734 Tappan Street

Memorial Christian Church

1891

When Mrs. Sarah Hawley Scott of Detroit left a large sum of money to the Church of Christ and the Christian Women's Missionary Society, the entire amount was put at the disposal of the Christian Women's Board of Missions. Under great pressure to locate a mission church in Ann Arbor, they used the money to erect a building on South University near State Street. At the dedication services on October 11, 1891, Ann Arbor church leaders made an eloquent plea for Christian unity.

The church was built in the Shingle style of the late nineteenth century, a simpler, quieter and purely American derivative of Queen Anne design. Ground story walls are typically of stone with wood shingled walls on the upper level. In this handsome church built for the Disciples of Christ congregation, red slate was used instead of wood shingle siding. The arrangement of the pews reflects the Disciples' emphasis on lay participation in the service. The pews surround the projecting front chancel area in a wide sweep to achieve a sense of intimacy and group unity. The cost of the original building, with furnishings and the spectacular rose windows, was $17,000.

In 1923 the University of Michigan, in its need to expand, purchased the land on which the church was standing in order to construct the University Law Quadrangle, with the provision that they would reproduce the church building at a new location chosen by the congregation. In 1925, after the church set a new foundation at the Hill - Tappan Street site, with a basement "high enough to ensure its being well-lighted," the University reconstructed their church, using the original materials, stone by stone, as much as possible, including the organ. In 1924 the Christian Women's Board of Missions deeded the building to the Church of Christ in Ann Arbor.

Lester Fader

In 1950 the organ pipes were concealed and the beams and pews were painted. A wing was added in 1969. In 1991, the church celebrated its centennial year.

IHP

619 East University Avenue

Anberay Apartments

153

1923

Kip Miller

When the student population dramatically increased after World War I, there was a boom in the construction of apartment buildings. In 1923 the Anberay was the first to be completed.

Built in a style referred to as "Chicago," perhaps because its U-shape is similar to many apartment buildings built in Chicago during this period, it is a simple, straightforward building of yellow brick with stone trim decoration. Its U-shape plan forms a central courtyard, with two gateways that flank a wall with the name "Anberay" carved in stone. Each of the 21 units has its own balcony with stone and brick balustrades, each with a slightly different design. The number of vertical units in the balustrude decrease in number as one moves from the top floor down to the ground. This rhythmical design is further accented by the stepped-in pattern of each of the two sides of the "U" giving the whole a feeling of movement and energy.

The earliest tenants of the Anberay were definitely from the better set in Ann Arbor. They included the Athletic Director of the University of Michigan, Fielding Yost, Elizabeth Dean (see 127), and Dr. A. C. Furstenberg, as well as University of Michigan Professors Palmer Christian, DeWitt Parker, Ermine Case, and Francis Kelsey. Many tenants spent their entire lives here, even after retirement. Often they came as new faculty and never left the comfortable, spacious, modern units.

After the collapse of the stock market in 1929, many builders could not meet their mortgage payments. For the price of back taxes, buildings were bought very cheaply, often by well-known landlords Rosa and Harold Lueck. Rosa started their apartment building empire in the early 1930s with the purchase of this building. She had come from Germany almost penniless and worked as a washerwoman, scrimping and saving until she had enough to buy buildings such as this. Harold did the plumbing and general handiwork, even years later when they were millionaires. The building is still owned by their son who lives in Seattle and maintains an interest in the properties.

154

815 South University Avenue

University of Michigan President's House

1840

This is one of the four houses constructed in 1839-40 on the new University of Michigan campus square as dwellings for its professors. Constructed by a local contractor, Haspier Lum, it was, like the other three, a two and one half story structure with a low pitched roof, a cupola, and a long, inviting porch facing the square. The interior, built in reserved classical style, had a central hall on each floor with two rooms opening off each side. The seven fireplaces which heated the rooms are still in place. At the back of the house were gardens, a small orchard and a stable.

Lester Fader

The modest brick home, covered with stucco to resemble mortar courses, acquired its present appearance in the early 1860s when the upper half story became a full third story. The house took on an Italianate style, much in vogue at the time, with the addition of the truncated hipped roof, double brackets, and a balustrade replacing the original cupola. The artificial mortar courses were filled in. The four chimneys were unchanged from the original structure, and the front entrance of two Doric columns and entablature is believed to be the same. Indoor plumbing and a kitchen wing were a part of the renovation.

In 1891 a two-story west wing with a circular library and upstairs bedrooms was built, and the house was wired for electricity. In 1920 President Marion Leroy Burton replaced a small east porch with a sunroom and upstairs sleeping porch. During Alexander Ruthven's administration (1929-1951) a second story and rear study were added to the east wing. A glassed-in plant room dates from that time as well.

The President's House is the only building remaining of the original four houses and two dormitory-classroom structures and is the oldest building on the University campus.

NR

1443 Washtenaw Avenue

Phi Kappa Sigma Fraternity (Trotter House)

1924

Kip Miller

"The Phi Kappa Sigma house was lavishly built at a cost of $125,000 in 1924," wrote noted writer and University of Michigan alumnus Edmund G. Love in a 1988 article in the *Ann Arbor Observer* on what he called his "depression education." Love also wrote: "By 1932, its members were so financially pressured that I was given a job in the house only after I recruited half a dozen new members." Love was the son of a Flint lumberman whose finances during the Depression forced his son to drop out of college and work at menial jobs. Love was determined to finish college, however, and in 1932 he returned to Ann Arbor and to his former fraternity. "No matter how broke I was, however, I spent the fall in a very posh atmosphere. The Phi Kappa Sigma house... sat on a huge plot of land... on Michigan's fraternity row, and had sweeping lawns, front and rear, with a stand of great trees surrounding it."

This fraternity house, purportedly designed by noted local architect Albert J. Rousseau, is in a style reminiscent of Frank Lloyd Wright and the Chicago School with its wide sweeping porch and low sloping roof. Rousseau also designed a number of other buildings in Ann Arbor including St. Mary's Student Chapel (see 151), the facade for Lawyers Title (see 52), his own home at 2001 Vinewood. The fraternity was and is extremely elegant in its simplicity of design and materials. The site today could still be described in Love's words of 1932.

In the 1970s following the Black Action Movement on campus, the University of Michigan purchased the house for a center where African-American student groups could hold meetings and cultural events. The house was renamed Trotter House after journalist and African-American activist William Monroe Trotter. Born in 1872, Trotter graduated *magna cum laude* from Harvard University after growing up in the white suburbs of Boston, and was the first African-American to receive a Phi Beta Kappa key at Harvard. After earning a master's degree at Harvard, Trotter dedicated his life to battling oppression and to educating other African-Americans on important issues of the day.

1547 Washtenaw Avenue

167

Henry Simmons Frieze House

1860

When Professor and Mrs. Henry Frieze located their country estate east of town on the main Ypsilanti Road, across from the J. D. Baldwin farm, they acquired seven acres with a fine stand of trees. Skilled stone masons from Guelph, Ontario, worked on the house, which features the soft colors and solid textures of locally cut stone. It is unique in the Ann Arbor area since few houses designed in the Italianate mode are articulated in such fine masonry work. The cornices, balconies and porch add elegance, charm, and a dramatic play of shadows to the stately residence. The generously sized rooms with eleven foot ceilings are finished with walnut and butternut woodwork. The landscaping is characteristic of the man for whom the house was built, for Frieze was devoted to nature and art and gave the turf, trees and rose hedges his personal attention.

When Frieze, a Professor of Latin at the University of Michigan, became acting president of the University in 1869, he sold the estate to "Deacon" Augustus Scott, a wealthy and retired gentleman from Toledo, who for almost thirty years made it the center of Ann Arbor social life. Scott added the cupola.

Kip Miller

In 1898 the Frieze house was purchased by Horace L. Wilgus, professor of law. The Wilgus daughter married geography professor Stanley D. Dodge and they lived in the house, keeping it in the family until the William G. Shepherd family acquired the home in 1969. The Shepherds restored the slate roof and were active in a local group organized to protect and preserve the character of the Hill-Washtenaw area until they left Ann Arbor in the 1980s.

NR, WHHD

1550 Washtenaw Avenue

1921

Phi Kappa Psi Fraternity (Zeta Tau Alpha Sorority)

Louisa Pieper

This multi-gabled house, nestled among trees with a deep setback from Washtenaw Avenue, was built in 1921 in the popular Tudor Revival style. Since 1892 Phi Kappa Psi had occupied an older home on the site, the estate of local clothing merchant Chauncey Millen, a spectacular example of an 1860s high style house, combining features of the Italianate and Gothic styles. According to a local architectural historian, it was built from a design from Samuel Sloan's *The Model Architect* (1861) and was the only one of its kind built in the U.S.

Replete with half timbering on the upper floors (exposed beams separated by stucco), steeply pointed gables, tall narrow casement windows with many panes of leaded glass, and a low arch framing a recessed entry, the new house was a textbook example of the Tudor Revival style.

In 1971 the house was sold to the Zeta Tau Alpha sorority, which occupies it today. The three pairs of brick pillars lining the driveways have an interesting history (despite the fact that they are a target of graffiti artists). Five of the pillars have the Greek letters for Phi Kappa Psi, the sixth has the initials JCK. These refer to Jerome C. Knowlton, a well-known law professor, who lived next door to Millen. He and Millen shared a driveway, and when the old house was pulled down, Knowlton's initials were inscribed on one pillar to honor his memory.

WHHD

169

1555 Washtenaw Avenue

Edward Campbell House (Campbell-Hays)

1899

This Georgian Revival style house was built in 1899 for Edward DeMille Campbell, a distinguished professor of chemistry at the University of Michigan and Director of the Chemical Laboratories. Campbell's father, Judge James Valentine Campbell, was the first Dean of the University of Michigan Law School and later became one of the first Supreme Court Justices in Michigan. Edward and his wife Jennie, sister of industrialist Marvin Ives (see 63), had originally lived at 1310 Hill Street, just a few blocks away (see 66). After a chemical explosion blinded Campbell in 1892, his architect, Albert Kahn of the firm of Nettleton, Kahn and Trowbridge, altered the Hill Street house to help him get around more easily. Many of these ideas were later used in the Washtenaw house. According to Emil Lorch, Director of the University of Michigan School of Architecture, this home was the first designed by Kahn after his firm was organized.

AAHDC

The house, with its red brick and white trim, its strict symmetry, its central entry, end chimneys, and dormers, has fine interior woodwork, wide stairways and a panelled study. Nearly all the original details remain including porcelain keyholes and door handles and marble bathroom fixtures. It is one of the few houses Kahn designed in Ann Arbor and the only one with both the exterior and interior intact.

When Campbell and his wife died their six children inherited the house in equal shares: In 1929, daughter Mary and her husband James Griffith Hays moved in. Significant renovations were made including replacing the wiring and plumbing though great care was taken to preserve the original interiors and the design created for her blind father. The Hays lived here until their deaths when again several family members inherited the property jointly. Unable to buy each other out, yet concerned that new owners not destroy the house or convert it to another use, the heirs worked to establish the Washtenaw Hill Historic District. In 1980 Robert and Holde Borcherts purchased it and thoroughly renovated it.

SR, WHHD

1850 Washtenaw Avenue

Edward L. Adams House

170

1917

This noble Georgian Revival house was built in 1917 for Edward Larrabee Adams, Professor of French in the Romance Languages Department at the University of Michigan. Adams, whose specialty was Old Provencal, joined the faculty in 1904 as an instructor and retired as Professor in 1949. In 1917 Adams hired local architect Samuel McCoskry Stanton to design his house. Stanton created this side-gabled, center-entry brick structure to resemble early 18th century American houses. The balanced design, end chimneys, central roof dormer flanked by eyebrow dormers, and the porticoed entry with Chinese Chippendale railing are all features of this style.

Stanton, the grandson of the first Episcopal bishop of Michigan, was born in Detroit and educated as an architect in Paris and Stuttgart. He came to Ann Arbor around 1900 and had a fairly well-established practice by the time he designed this home. His other well-known local buildings include the University of Michigan Homeopathic Hospital (now known as North Hall), the Hobbs house at the corner of Hill and Oxford Road, and his own family home at 501 Onondaga. He also supervised the construction of the Equitable Building in New York City. He practiced in Ann Arbor for over 40 years and died in 1946.

Professor Adams lived on in the house after his retirement until his death in 1958. A few years later it became the home of his son, Edward L. Adams, Jr., a consulting psychologist, who lived here with his wife until 1986. He and his brother Dwight perpetuate their father's name through an endowment to the Romance Languages and Literatures Department which is used to support the department's alumni newsletter. Due to this long continuity of ownership, the house has remained in almost pristine condition.

Kip Miller

1917 Washtenaw Avenue

171

Dean Myers House
(First Unitarian Universalist Church)

1917/1956

Probably the only Swiss Chalet-style house in Ann Arbor, this cut fieldstone house was built by local contractors Weinberg and Kurtz for Dr. Dean Myers, a prominent eye, ear, nose and throat specialist. The builders were so proud of it that they featured it on their checks for years.

Myers was a 43-year old widower when he moved in and shared the house with his daughter Dorothy and his mother-in-law. In addition to his private practice, he was active in community affairs and served on the Ann Arbor City Council, the school board, and as chair of the Democratic party. After six years in the house, he married Eleanor Sheldon, who had been the first house director at Betsy Barbour dormitory. In 1946 Dr. and Mrs. Myers sold the house and moved out to Hildene Manor (see 174). He died in 1955, and she followed a few years later.

The purchaser of their house was not another couple, but a church. The Unitarian Church had occupied a large building at State and Huron since 1883 (see 137) but seriously declining membership and maintenance problems led them to sell the church and purchase this home in 1946. Ironically, a new pastor spurred church growth to a point where not only did they need to build a parsonage on the rear of the Myers' house in 1948 (expanded in 1955), but a wing for holding services as well.

George Brigham, a well-known local architect of modernist sensibilities, member of the architecture faculty at the University of Michigan, as well as of the church congregation, designed the new sanctuary in 1956. Brigham's design was successful, as each building complements the other and yet stands as a product of its own time. Apparently, even Frank Lloyd Wright was pleased with the results for he declared, "That's good!" in one of his rare expressions of approval.

Milton Kemnitz

2015 Washtenaw Avenue

Leander J. Hoover Mansion

172

1918

This beautiful mansion, designed by Ann Arbor architect Rupert Koch, has survived a difficult history. The original owner, Leander J. Hoover, founded the Hoover Steel Ball Company in Ann Arbor in 1913. Very much a self-made man, Hoover learned about the manufacture of ball bearings as he worked his way up the ladder from the age of 16. He established his first plant, the Grant Hoover Company, at Merchantville, New Jersey in 1906. The fine quality of Hoover bearings, and the advent of World War I led to the brilliant success of Hoover's company. He became very rich very quickly.

Kip Miller

Hoover began his $350,000 "French Chateau" in 1917. Set in extensive beautiful gardens, his new home had a small theater and a ballroom on the third floor. The 24 acre site also included a greenhouse and gazebo. Sadly, after a long illness complicated by influenza, Hoover died in September of 1918. His family remained in the house a very short time thereafter.

In 1922 the house was purchased by the Kappa Sigma fraternity. It was vacant during the 1930's and in 1945 it was almost razed by the city. Instead Mr and Mrs. Carroll Benz purchased it at auction in 1946. They renovated it and later sold it to Tau Delta Phi fraternity in 1950.

In 1968 the house became the headquarters for Youth for Understanding, a cultural exchange program for students worldwide. When Y.F.U. moved to Washington, D.C. in 1978, the house again stood empty. Later that year, just prior to its purchase by Group 243 Inc., an advertising firm, the house received a cosmetic makeover as a "designer showcase" to raise funds for Mott Hospital.

In 1983 the Patton Corporation bought the mansion and leased it to General Automotive Corporation. The house and its sweeping front lawns, as impressive as the house itself, have been renovated and the original carriage house reunited with the property.

IHP

2117 Washtenaw Avenue

173

Bell-Spaulding House (Tuomy House)

1854

This is a well-preserved early farmhouse that reflects the change in local architectural tastes in the decade between 1854, when the rear ell was constructed for George W. and Jane E. Bell, and 1864, when the present front section was built for Frederick A. and Almina S. Spaulding. Its transitional Greek Revival style with Italianate finish typifies the better class of frame farmhouse of that period.

Some of the original finishes of the original Greek Revival home still exist: the wide floorboards of pine, simple baseboards, squared door and window enframements, and stair balustrade. The additions, most likely built in 1864, overshadow the original portion of the residence in size and design. The formal entryway was reoriented toward Washtenaw Avenue with the construction of a two-story, Italianate styled block. Other additions made that year include shed-roofed extensions on the south side and another on the east extension, which was fitted out as the new kitchen. The back door was moved to an off-center location and fitted with a small porch. Several other modernizing changes have been made since that time.

Very little is known of the Bells except that they consolidated pieces of land in Ann Arbor township to create a farm, and they were the first to have an interest in developing the property rather than buying it for speculation. The Spauldings were descendants of early east coast settlers, coming to Ann Arbor from New York state in 1863. Since Frederick Spaulding was already in his mid-60's, they led a quiet farm life until his death in 1874. Two of the Spaulding sons became well-known in Ann Arbor, Frederick Austin Spaulding, Jr., as a Doctor of Medicine, and Volney Morgan Spaulding as a Professor of Botany at the University of Michigan and founder of the University Botanical Gardens.

In April of 1874, Patrick and Cornelius L. Tuomy purchased the 214 acre Spaulding farm. Cornelius L. Tuomy, one of nine children of Timothy and Joanna Roach Tuomy, was raised on a Scio Township farm where his father had cleared 367 acres in the 1830s. Cornelius lived as a bachelor on the former Spaulding farm for eleven years before he married Julia Ann Kearney, described by a biographer (Beakes, 1906) as a "woman of rare intelligence, social power and popularity." Cornelius was a good agriculturist with varied interests. He was a successful dairy farmer and, with Patrick, was well-known for his ownership and breeding of several prize race horses. His sheep were sometimes reported in the local press as wandering down Washtenaw Avenue. Two of their children, Kathryn and Cornelius W. (Bill) Tuomy, formed a part-

CONTINUED on next page

nership and as the city grew, they developed the property and sold insurance from an office in the house. In 1930 they built the unusual and picturesque fieldstone Tuomy Hills Service Station (see 175) down the road at the junction of Washtenaw and the "cutoff" (Stadium Boulevard).

When Bill Tuomy died in 1966, his will provided that the house be given to the City for some historic purpose. On March 16, 1968, by agreement with the City, the executors deeded the house and two acres of land to the University of Michigan. The University furnished some of the rooms in elegant Victorian style and arrangements were made for the house to be headquarters for the Historical Society of Michigan and the Academy of Arts, Science and Letters. In 1982 the house was transferred with its contents to the Society. The Society has worked since on the total restoration and maintenance of the house.

NR, IHP

Frances Wright

174

2220 Washtenaw Avenue

Hildene Manor

1926

Kip Miller

This Tudor Revival style building is actually eight six-room apartments, cooperatively owned. When it was built it was the only cooperatively owned apartment house in Ann Arbor. The large roomy apartments reflect the 1920s when apartment living was chic and largely confined to the wealthy. The builders of this venture, the Group Homes Apartments, chose the Tudor Revival or "Olde English" style as a way of expressing their taste, their refinement, and perhaps their lineage. Half-timbered with stucco on the exterior, it has symmetrical stone arched entries, a steeply pitched roof punctuated by chimneys, and groups of double hung windows with small panes of glass.

The owners of each unit are free to decorate them individually while the group as a whole maintains the grounds and the exterior. Though many such cooperative ventures fail, this one succeeded, "because of the spirit of the people living there."

The apartments adopted the name Hildene Manor in 1927, a year after the building was completed. A newspaper article from that year stated that it acquired a name because it was located outside the city limits, and no number could be given to it for mail delivery, "so the residents decided to name it to avoid confusion." Perhap they also liked the idea of referring to themselves as living in a "manor."

Recognizing that Hildene Manor has never fallen into disrepair and has always been maintained in the high standards with which it was built, the Ann Arbor Historic District Commission gave it a Preservation Award in 1990. Though it has long been part of the city of Ann Arbor, its setting on Washtenaw beneath massive trees still gives the sense of a country estate today.

2460 Washtenaw Avenue

Tuomy Hills Gas Station

175

1927

Frank Carson, the architect of many fine Ann Arbor homes and winner of the Prix de Rome in 1925, designed this gas station in 1927. Local businessman Cornelius "Bill" Tuomy had it built in a residential style to show that a business could blend gracefully into a residential area. Long a beloved landmark, it not only blends in, but enhances the point where two prominent Ann Arbor roads converge. Some architectural scholars see it now as a unique remnant of the American roadside.

The structure most resembles an English gatekeeper's cottage, with its heavy masonry walls sixteen inches thick—eight inches of brick faced with eight inches of stone. With an eighteen inch thick concrete floor, a heavy slate roof, and sturdy hand-hewn oak pillars supporting the roofs of its two porte-cocheres, it was built to last for centuries.

Tuomy and his sister Kathryn had inherited the large Tuomy farm on Washtenaw, famous for its horses and dairy cattle (See 173). They went into business together as Tuomy and Tuomy, selling real estate and insurance. Their offices were in a little building behind their "Tuomy Hills" gas station, a name which refers to the subdivision they developed from their farm's vast acreage.

In 1927, with a new bypass (Stadium Boulevard) in the offing, they decided the area needed a gas station and built one to be a credit to the city. The Standard Oil Company, which leased the station, was so proud of it they displayed a model of it at the Century of Progress Exposition in Chicago in 1933. When Mr. Tuomy died in 1966, Standard Oil (now Amoco) acquired ownership of the building. In 1988 Amoco closed the station and boarded up the building. The continuing deep concern of local residents made it clear that demolition was not an option. Now for sale, the future of Ann Arbor's famous "gateway" finally looks much brighter.

Frances Wright

IHP

1115 Woodlawn Street

178

Christian Eberbach House

1863-69

Constructed in the 1860s, this former farmhouse was beyond the southern limits of the city. The site was chosen so Christian Eberbach's children could benefit from an education in Ann Arbor and still enjoy the healthful air and active life of the countryside. Eberbach was already a trained pharmacist when he came to this country in 1838 at the age of 21. At first he worked in the W. S. Maynard store, but in 1842 he founded Eberbach and Company to manufacture articles sold by pharmacists and opened the Eberbach Drug Store on Main Street.

Sturgis Collection

A pioneer of great industry, he not only presided over his successful pharmaceutical enterprises and a productive farm, but was also a founder of the Hutzel Plumbing Company and the Ann Arbor Savings Bank. An early organizer of the Republican Party, he was a member of the Electoral College which confirmed Abraham Lincoln's election. Christian and his wife, Margaretha (Laubengayer), had eight children, of whom five lived to maturity.

The house is Ann Arbor's best example of the Italianate Villa style, a T-shape with a three-story tower rising directly over the front entry. From the second floor a narrow winding staircase led to the children's playroom at the top. The windows exhibit formal treatment with characteristic Italianate corbeled brick crowns, but both the segmental shape of the crowns and the inset wooden enframements reflect Eberbach's German origins in use of the Rundbogenstil motif.

In one of the upstairs bedrooms there is a marble fireplace featuring a scroll keystone and panels with bas relief floral patterns. Under the parlor end of the house a large vaulted brick storeroom kept the grains and fruits of the harvest. Built in at one end is a brick chimney originally used for smoking hams.

IHP

WEST

Ann Arbor

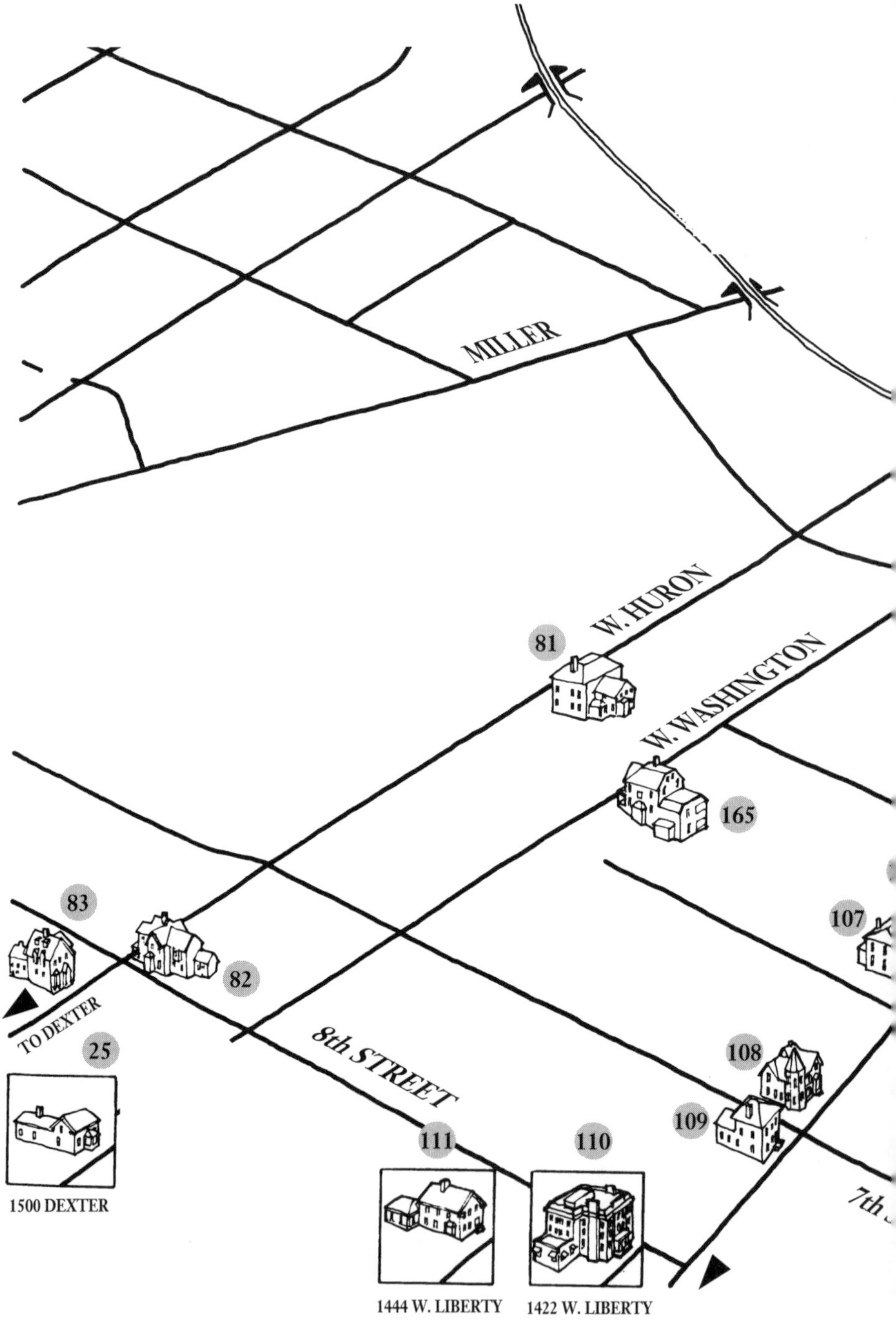

MILLER
W. HURON
W. WASHINGTON
81
165
83
82
107
TO DEXTER
25
8th STREET
108
109
111
110
1500 DEXTER
1444 W. LIBERTY
1422 W. LIBERTY

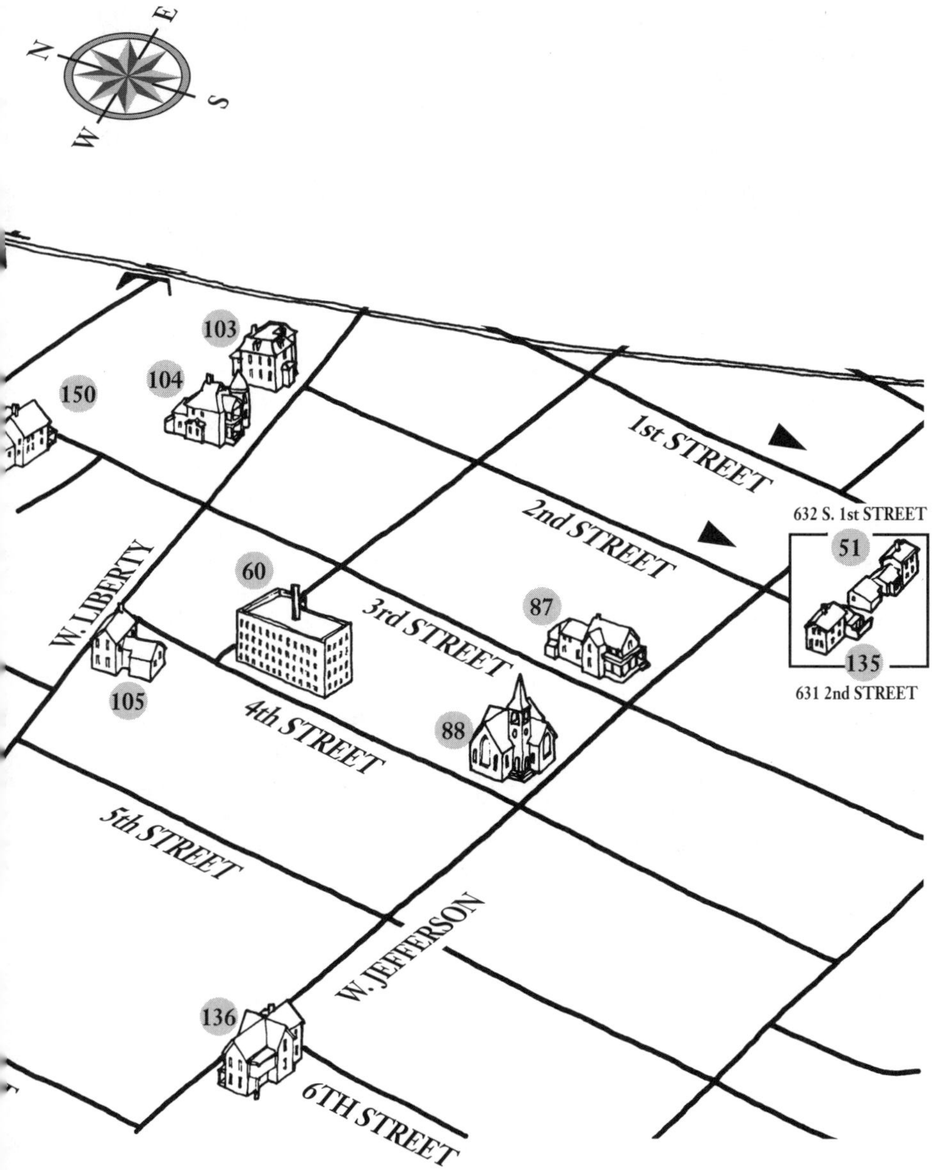
N
E
S
W
103
104
150
1st STREET
2nd STREET
632 S. 1st STREET
51
135
631 2nd STREET
W. LIBERTY
60
3rd STREET
87
105
4th STREET
88
5th STREET
W. JEFFERSON
136
6TH STREET

1500 Dexter Avenue

Eunice Baldwin House

1850

Kip Miller

This small Greek Revival house shows its original 12 by 12 timbers and stone walls in the basement. Some fifty years ago, when it still had its original narrow clapboards, its pleasing appearance won the attention of the Historic American Building Survey. Drawings and photographs in the Library of Congress show the Baldwin House as it looked then. Its position at the "Forks" and its eye-catching proportions make it an Ann Arbor landmark.

The house was probably built by carpenter and builder Norman B. Covert for Eunice Baldwin, the mother of his new bride, on an eighty-acre piece of farmland. Their two properties were separated by a road which has now become Revena Boulevard.

When Mrs. Baldwin died in 1868, she left her house and land to her two daughters, Nancy Baldwin and Lucy A. Covert. In 1887, Andrew Heimerdinger acquired the property. The original eighty acres has long since been divided into residential lots, but this small farm house is now owned by a fourth generation Heimerdinger.

HABS, IHP

632 South First Street

Raab-Harlacher House

51

1885

Among the many historic homes designated by plaques during the Ann Arbor Sesquicentennial celebration in 1974, this is the only one which was still occupied by its original family. The Charles Raab family moved into their new home in 1886. In 1915 their youngest daughter, Matilda, married William Harlacher, and they continued to live in the family home until recent years.

Architecturally, the house is an excellent example of vernacular or "folk" building. While architects were designing large asymmetrical Queen Anne houses using a multitude of different ornamental materials, houses like this one were being erected by their owners without formal plans. Based on ethnic traditions, in this case German, the houses found throughout the Old West Side Historic District were intended to be solid and functional. The front porch is an addition to the original facade, and recent changes include a contemporary wing and window replacement. It is interesting to compare this house to the Wiegant-Hochrein house at 631 Second Street, which has been entirely renovated. The two houses were once identical.

NRHD, OWS

Kip Miller

60

405 Fourth Street

John Keck and Company (Argus Building)

1866-1884

Situated in the heart of the Old West Side Historic District, this red-brick building began as a furniture factory. It was constructed in three phases, beginning with a wood-frame building facing William Street built in 1866 by John Keck and Company and now covered with brick veneer. In 1879 additional stock in the company was sold in order to finance a four-story brick building along Fourth Street. More construction followed in 1884 when the company was reorganized as the Michigan Furniture Company and a four-story building was built at the corner of Fourth and William, thus connecting the two older structures.

Keck came to America from Wurttemberg in 1854 at the age of 15 and apprenticed to cabinetmaker and coffin builder Florian Muehlig. By 1866 he was able to establish his own furniture factory with his brothers Frederick, George and Martin. The 1860s and 70s had been decades of rapid mechanization in the furniture industry. The steam engine had replaced water as a power source and specialization accompanied expansion as machines became more and more specialized. Despite the Depression of 1873, Keck employed 40 to 50 men and became one of the town's major businesses.

By 1879, when Keck formed a stock company, the decision had been made to specialize in bedroom suites (pronounced "suits"). They concentrated on making bedsteads, commodes and dressers and would continue this emphasis until they ceased operations in 1929. Unfortunately for antique collectors, Keck never marked his furniture and thus his products today are, in the words of journalist Mary Hunt, "distressingly anonymous."

Keck's designs were in the then-popular Renaissance Revival style, massive pieces with layers of elaborately carved woodwork, topped by carved pediments. A collection of Keck's drawings, recently discovered in the Grand Rapids Public Museum, gives a sense of the range of designs he produced. In 1884 the prominence of the buildings of the Michigan Furniture Company was noted in a local paper, which asserted that every visitor to Ann Arbor always inquired "What is that large four-story building?" Keck, who was no longer with the company, had opened another factory on Detroit Street in the mid-1880s. His success there was short lived, however, and he spent the rest of his life working in Detroit and Grand Rapids.

After furniture making ceased in 1929, Charles Verschoor acquired the building and began manufacturing his popular Kadette tabletop radios. Never one

CONTINUED on next page

Kip Miller

to sit on his hands, Verschoor traveled to Germany in 1936 to study camera manufacturing. When he returned, he began to mass produce a small 35mm camera — the famous Argus Model A. The camera was an instant success, selling 30,000 units in its first week on the market. In 1939 the name of the company was changed to Argus and the Argus C-3 camera was introduced. It remained the staple of the company until 1957.

During World War II, Argus received many contracts from the government for telescopes, binoculars, periscopes, and gunsights. However, after the war Argus was unable to compete with Japanese cameras and the company was sold to Sylvania. In 1963 the building was sold to the University of Michigan which used it for various research institutes including an amphibian lab.

The recession of the 1980s prompted the University to sell the building in 1983 to C-3 Partners who undertook the enormous task of restoring and renovating this historic structure in 1986. Quinn/Evans Architects provided the expertise and the newly renovated space preserves the best of the old and the new. O'Neal Construction, one of the C-3 partners along with First Martin Corp., is now headquartered here and their offices feature the original heavy timbers and red brick walls that characterized these simple factory buildings.

NRHD, OWS

709 West Huron Street

John N. Gott House

1861

Begun in the 1850s by William C. Voorheis, this Italianate brick mansion was completed in 1861 by a creditor, attorney John N. Gott, who lived here for three decades. In 1890 it was sold to Dr. William James Herdman, a prominent member of the University of Michigan's medical faculty, who converted it to a private hospital while maintaining his residence there. Fond of experimenting with medical uses of electricity in his laboratory, at home Herdman was a Victorian autocrat. "I'll do the thinking around here!" he admonished his daughter when she hesitatingly prefaced a statement with the words, "I think —" His son, school and city physician E. K. Herdman, inherited the property in 1906. After 1925, Dr. William Koch, who claimed to have a cure for cancer, treated patients in his clinic on the premises.

When the Eugene Hannahs bought the place from Koch in 1941, they named it the "Martha Washington House" as it provided lodgings for women only. Acquisition of a second rooming house for men, to be named for George Washington, was contemplated but never accomplished.

When Donald and Lorraine Haugen purchased the house in 1971, they hoped to reopen some of the seven original fireplaces, one of which has a lovely marble mantel, but were disappointed to find that the chimneys had been removed when the roof was resurfaced. Later in the 1970s, the firm of Bishop and Shelton purchased the house and, with practically no change to the interior or the exterior, converted it to law offices.

The cast iron window grilles in this stately landmark are identical to those in the Kempf House. Apparently a stock item available to local builders, the same grilles have been found on several farmhouses in rural Washtenaw County.

NRHD, OWS

Lester Fader

921 West Huron Street

Martin and Helena Noll House

82

1888

Kip Miller

A winning lottery ticket from Germany provided the source of funds for this magnificent Queen Anne house. Martin Noll, a shoe repairman who had emigrated from Germany, used his winnings to buy a lot on the west side of town and build this house in the current high fashion of the late 1880s. Unfortunately Noll died the next year, but his wife and children occupied the house until 1913. The Canadian family of Wilson Sherk purchased it and sold it in 1975 to the present owners, who effected a true restoration of its Victorian character.

Barbara White and Richard Green undertook what proved to be a monumental task. Not only have they restored the exterior trim and clapboard siding in an authentic three-color paint scheme, but many interior elements as well. Fish-scale shingles, diagonals, and Chinese Chippendale porch railings enliven the exterior while glowing woodwork with bullseye corner blocks fill the interior. The owners set high standards, having broken or missing elements remilled, and restoring even small details such as shutter hinges. In 1985 the Ann Arbor Historic District Commission presented them with a restoration award, to acknowledge and applaud their fine work. The house was also featured in a 1986 calendar of historic houses published by the Washtenaw County Historical Society.

NRHD, OWS

1020 West Huron Street

83

John M. Wheeler House

1859

Kip Miller

When local historian and school teacher Lela Duff first encountered this house, it piqued her curiosity because it was so different from the others in the area. She noted that it seemed "closed and aloof" with its gray paint, sharply pointed gables, and fancy mill work around the eaves, reminding her of Nathaniel Hawthorne's House of Seven Gables. People remembered its grounds surrounded by a low picket fence with a deep wooded ravine at the back and a mysterious Dutch windmill. (In the late 1930s the West Side Women's Club voted to restore this windmill but, for reasons unknown, never did so.) By the time Duff wrote an article about the house for *The Ann Arbor News* in 1960, the house was "teeming with apartments" and had lost its fence and windmill. A bulldozer was working nearby, busy subdividing the grounds.

The house was probably built in 1859 for attorney John M. Wheeler. He was admitted to the bar in Indiana in 1843 and practiced there for 15 years before settling in Ann Arbor. After retiring from his legal practice, he became Treasurer of the University of Michigan in 1872.

The house was once a fine example of Gothic Revival, a style rare in Ann Arbor. It is often compared with the Douglass House (see 75), as both houses are stucco over brick and may even be the work of the same architect. Early photographs show the elaborate porch entry with its Gothic clustered columns and quatrefoil balustrade, features which appeared on the former porte cochere. These distinctive Gothic style details were unfortunately destroyed in the 20th century. Hints of the former grandeur still remain, however, in the ornamental "gingerbread" or barge boards under the eaves.

NRHD, OWS

420 West Jefferson Street

J. Frederick Schaeberle House

Circa 1880

Particularly notable for its ornamental porch, gabled roof and fishscale siding, this inviting wood frame Queen Anne house was built about 1880 for the J. Frederick Schaeberle family.

Frederick came to Ann Arbor in 1853 at the age of nine. While a youth he worked in Christian Mack's department store, then made harnesses with his father. His leisure time was devoted to music, and he was sent eventually to study with a master in Chicago. He finished his education in Germany where he also found his bride, the former Katherine Kemmler. Returning to Ann Arbor, Schaeberle began a long and distinguished career as a music teacher. His music store at 114 West Liberty, which opened in 1896 carried musical instruments "from the best houses." Townspeople relied upon his piano tuning and his performing, which a biographer noted was "far beyond mediocrity in the interpretation of the masters."

After Mr. Schaeberle's death in the late 1920s, his widow Katherine continued to live in the house for a few years. Their son, Ernst, kept a music store in Ann Arbor well into this century.

In 1944 Jacob F. Fahrner converted the house to four apartments. Ownership has changed frequently and it is still a multifamily home. In recent times the house has been faced with aluminum siding. Its porch has been rebuilt with care to maintain the decorative details. It is a part of the Old West Side Historic District.

NRHD, OWS

Kip Miller

520 West Jefferson Street

First German Methodist Church
(Reorganized Church of Jesus Christ of Latter Day Saints) 1896

Kip Miller

German settlers in Ann Arbor maintained cultural unity through close religious ties formed in their homeland. Their faith was a rock, an unwavering refuge of strength for immigrants in this strange new land. Key to their faith and traditions was the mother tongue, the language of their Bible, catechism, and beloved hymns. So even though Ann Arbor already had a Methodist Church, Germans of that denomination petitioned for one of their own, and a congregation *the Erste Deutsche Methodisten Kirche* was organized by the Ohio Conference in 1847, with their church building at the southwest corner of Liberty and Division.

Erected in 1896, this was the second building for the congregation. It later changed its name to the West Side Methodist Church with services conducted in English, after early generations of German-speaking members had passed away. Today's West Side Methodists worship in larger quarters on South Seventh Street.

Since 1951 this cheerful little building, an example of simplified Gothic Revival style, has been the home of the Reorganized Church of Jesus Christ of Latter Day Saints. The Gothic windows and the tower with matching single doors at the base distinguish the building. Careful maintenance seems to assure its continued presence as a neighborhood landmark.

NRHD, OWS

326 West Liberty Street

Peter Brehm House

1870

Peter Brehm, proprietor of The Western Brewery located on Fourth Street near William Street, built his mansard-roofed brick home in the Second Empire style around 1870. In choosing this particular style, Brehm was participating in a short-lived trend in Ann Arbor architecture. The 1860s and 70s witnessed a flurry of building activity, especially in the central city. A few of the more affluent chose the Second Empire style, the most elaborate examples of which were Hill's Opera House at Main and Ann Streets (now demolished as were most residential examples of this style), and the Raja Rani restaurant at Division and William Streets, built as the residence of architect Peleg Marshall in 1860. This boom turned to bust in the Panic of 1873 and newspapers began to fill up with mortgage sales and business failures. Building activity virtually ground to a halt. Brehm's residence remains a rare survivor of this style.

The mansard roof that is the hallmark of this fashionable style was popularized by French Renaissance architect Francois Mansart, revived by Napoleon III in the 1850s and copied throughout Europe and the Americas. Brehm's residential version is a simple domestic expression of the wealth, and monumentality reflected in more elaborate examples. The roof, it should be noted, tops a building more Italianate in character with typical round-headed windows, hood-moldings, overhanging eaves and decorative brackets. Such combinations of styles were common for Midwest American architecture.

Brehm founded the Western Brewery in 1861 after arriving in Ann Arbor the same year. By the 1880s, under different ownership, it was the largest brewery in Ann Arbor. Brehm became wealthy as a brewer and in 1868 was able to purchase the property at 326 West Liberty, demolish an old house on the site, and construct his Second Empire building. Another brewer who also became wealthy in this period was John Adam Volz, who built an elaborate Italianate house at 716 North Fifth Avenue (see 46).

Sturgis Collection

Brehm's quick rise to wealth is almost as puzzling as his decline, for by 1872 he no longer owned

CONTINUED on next page

the Western Brewery. Equally mysterious is his suicide in 1873, though the Panic of that year may have been the root cause. (Volz also lost his brewery in the same depression.) No hint of scandal, however, was mentioned by either newspaper when they noted his death: "Peter Brehm, former proprietor of the Western Brewery committed suicide on Friday last, by shooting himself in the forehead with a pistol. He had been for some time laboring under a sort of mania induced by hard drinking... The particulars of the melancholy death of Peter Brehm... are these: suffering from temporary insanity, he thought he should be sued by someone... Last Friday he came home and informed his wife that he had been sued and must go to court. Changing his clothes, he started towards the Court House, but soon returned going directly to his room, shooting himself through the head, dying instantly. Mr. Brehm was a kind-hearted and very generous man, respected by all who knew him"

After Brehm died his wife, daughter, and son Gustav, who served two terms as City Clerk and County Treasurer, continued to live here. In 1894, Gustav joined forces with a former competitor of his father and started the Ann Arbor Brewing Company, of which he was secretary.

Two years later he sold his Liberty Street property to William Arnold, a local jeweler and a descendant of early immigrants from Germany. Arnold and his wife Siona raised five sons and continued to live in the house until their deaths in 1930 and 1932. William Sr., a well-known and prosperous merchant, owned the German-American savings Bank, the State Savings Bank, and the Artificial Ice Company, one of the major industries in Ann Arbor in the early 20th century. Other businesses associated with the Arnold family included Ann Arbor Asphalt, Ann Arbor Construction, and Abbott Gasoline.

In the 1930s and 40s the house was used by family relations attending the University of Michigan and as a summer home for Arnold family members. In 1952 the International Order of Odd Fellows purchased it and converted it to a meeting hall. When the Moveable Feast restaurant bought it in 1978, Emil Arnold reminisced about growing up in the house, remembering that at the turn of the century electricians and plumbers had trouble wiring and plumbing the house due to its thick brick walls.

Today Peter Brehm's, without its original porch, front door, or roof brackets has been partially restored both inside and out. The interior has its original shutters and bannister which add to the ambience and form an elegant backdrop for dining.
NRHD, OWS

408 West Liberty Street

Albert Mann House

104

1891

Kip Miller

Built of brick instead of the more customary wood siding, this house has the usual Queen Anne characteristics: a very irregular and steep pitched roof, projecting bays on both sides of the house, and a fine turret with crenelated brickwork decorating the upper portion. The two-story porch to the left side appears to be original but has been renovated. Of interest, too, are the large oak double entrance doors and the "sunburst" design with which the carpenter decorated each of the two front gables. Note that they "burst" in opposite directions.

The area described as "east by Allen Creek, south by Eber White Road (West Liberty Street), west by Lord's Estate, north by Territorial Road (West Huron Street)," was subdivided into residential lots in the late 1880s. John Koch, a builder, bought this lot and probably constructed the house which was purchased by Albert and Henry Mann in 1891. Albert's family occupied their castle-like house for more than forty years.

The Mann family has been a part of Ann Arbor from its early days. Albert's father, Emanuel, came to Michigan in 1830 at the age of 16. In 1842 he joined Christian Eberbach as a partner in a pharmacy and drug manufacturing company and later opened a drug store on Main Street. Albert and his brother Eugene eventually took over the store.

In 1958 the house was converted to a four-family dwelling. The present owner has added two dormer windows.
NRHD, OWS

105

603 West Liberty Street

John and Andrew Jackson House

1847/1863

John and Andrew Jackson wasted no time in purchasing this lot from William S. Maynard after he platted the land and added it to the City of Ann Arbor in 1846. It is likely they built the Liberty Street portion of this house sometime in the fall of 1847, for, when they sold the property eight years later in 1855, they tripled their money.

The south wing, which appears on the 1866 "birds-eye" view was probably added by laborer John M. Weitbrecht, who purchased the property in 1862. The Weitbrecht family occupied this corner until the turn of the century. The estate sold the property to John and Lydia Kuehnle (she may have been Weitbrecht's daughter) for $1400 in 1898 and it remained a single family house throughout the 20th century. By the 1930s it also had a commercial use. The rear portion facing Fourth Street housed the Lunsford Bakery, famous for its cinnamon rolls, from 1935 to 1970.

Louisa Pieper

The main part of the house, which is clapboard, is the New England folk form known as an "I" house: two stories high, two rooms wide, one room deep, with a central hallway. The fieldstone foundation of this portion is much lower than the brick foundation of the south wing, where the land slopes away from the house. This rear section also has a central entry, but is only one story high. The four-over-four windows in the wing appear to be original as does the glass.

William and Susan Johnson, the present owners, restored the exterior by removing the asphalt siding and corrugated canopy that had hidden the classical front doorway and original clapboards. Today the Johnsons are extending the south wing and the house remains a fine example of the vernacular type of house built in the Old West Side up to the Civil War.

NRHD, OWS

626 West Liberty Street

William and Katherine Kuhn House

106

Circa 1850

This tiny "cabin" appears to have been built around 1850 by William and Katherine Kuhn. It is an example of the very simple, small dwellings constructed by Ann Arbor's working class in the mid-19th century. Its only hints at style are the Greek Revival returns on the side gables. The original clapboard and multi-paned windows also hint at an early date of construction.

Kip Miller

The house is first mentioned specifically in William Kuhn's will: when he died in 1879, he bequeathed a "dwelling house" and the land to his wife and their eight children. The fact that a family of ten might have lived in what was essentially a one-room house with a sleeping loft, makes one ponder the privations suffered by the average family in this era.

The house had long been recognized as charming— both by academics who included it in a 1974 Sesquicentennial publication entitled *Ann Arbor Architecture*, and by neighbors who remembered Mrs. Hattie Holter, occupant from around 1950 to 1980, who kept the place in immaculate condition. This is why, when demolition was proposed in 1985, citizens in the neighborhood were so concerned. During public hearings, many spoke in favor of saving the house, despite its small size. The Ann Arbor Historic District Commission tabled action on the demolition request, and at last a rescuer came forward. Douglas Trubey, a lifelong resident of Ann Arbor who had already renovated an abandoned house in Scio Township, purchased the house.

Describing it as a "house that fell out of time," Trubey built a two story carriage house in the rear for storage and immediately began renovating the house. In 1989, the Ann Arbor Historic District Commission gave him a restoration award by for his efforts. Trubey proved the impossible — that someone could and would live in this "cabin" and make it look like a home again.

NRHD, OWS

107

706 West Liberty Street

John Christian Burkhart House

1867

Kip Miller

Charly Rieckhoff purchased the John Christian Burkhart home in the late 1980s and discovered the outline of an earlier porch when he removed the wide aluminum siding. With the aid of a neighbor's old snapshot and the scars left on the clapboard, Rieckhoff began his transformation of this center-entry Italianate structure. Using skills he acquired while working with his father on old houses, he added insulation and replaced the clapboard with new redwood the same width. He even crafted the trim by hand to match the outlines of the original woodwork uncovered when the siding was removed.

This was in keeping with the tradition established by Burkhart, a German carpenter and skilled cabinetmaker who reportedly moved to Ann Arbor from his farm in 1848 to help construct the first Bethlehem Church. Margaret Murawski, in a 1968 article in the *Huron Valley Ad-visor*, claimed that Burkhart built this house and the church in the same year. Since this house dates to 1867, this oral tradition probably refers to another house Burkhart owned across the street at 707 West Liberty.

After her father's death in the 1880s, John's youngest daughter Mary remained to take care of her mother and then lived there with her husband Christian Overbeck after their marriage. They raised their two children here and one son, Erwin, owned and operated Overbeck's Books on South University for half a century. Casper Enkemann, Chief of Police in Ann Arbor from 1948-1960, later purchased the house and lived here with his wife Gladys until his death in 1982.

When Rieckhoff completed the exterior restoration he began to work on the interior and then on the grounds. With the help of landscape historian Scott Kunst he has added an authentic 1870s garden to the front yard, and built a wooden picket fence to enclose it. In 1990 Rieckhoff was given a Rehabilitation Award by the Ann Arbor Historic District Commission.

NRHD, OWS

818 West Liberty Street

John Hagen House

1888

Born in Prussia in 1819, John Hagen came to the Ann Arbor area in 1844. He married in 1848 and soon had increased his farm on Traver Road from 200 to 725 acres. A fever took his first wife, Catherine, leaving him with four children. It was with his second wife, Johanna, that he moved into this fanciful Romanesque "castle" which had been built a year earlier by John Koch. Here he raised a second family, commuting regularly to his farm on Traver Road where most of the older children remained to work the land. (A part of Hagen's farm is now the Leslie golf course.)

Described in an 1891 biographical album as "a fine specimen of the German people," Hagen was also a staunch and active Democrat, "taking delight in the fact that the local offices have been taken from the Republicans who formerly controlled the official patronage of Ann Arbor."

A son of his second marriage, Herman Hagen, occupied the house with his family for some years. Divided into four apartments, the house was owned by John Hagen's granddaughter, Cora Haas, until her death in 1977.

NRHD, OWS

Lester Fader

109

902 West Liberty Street

Christian Walker House

Late 1850s

Kip Miller

Old Ann Arbor directories indicate that Christian and Katherine Walker lived here beginning in 1870. Christian Walker and his brother were partners in a prosperous wagon manufacturing business on West Liberty near Main Street.

Time and various owners were not kind to the house. At some time along the way the brick was painted and two covered porches removed. The two-story square Italianate structure retains its basic character and still has its bracketed`eaves and dentil trim. Observers should note the difference in design of the first and second story windows, twenty-three of which have antique glass. Dr. John Hatch bought the house in 1979 and with painstaking care has removed and restored all of the interior trim, with the woodwork copied exactly and the original nail holes used for the baseboards. He has also stabilized and restored the exterior.

NRHD, OWS

1422 West Liberty Street

110

1916/1927

Robert MacKenzie House
(Anna Botsford Bach Home)

Dr. Robert MacKenzie, a prominent physician and head of the University of Michigan's Obstetrics Department built this neo-classical Italian villa in 1916. Unlike most of his colleagues, MacKenzie and his wife preferred to be in the "country" and have more acreage. Thus they built their new home on the far west side of town where many of Dr. MacKenzie's patients lived. Dr. MacKenzie was fluent in German, which made him popular among the many Germans living on the West Side.

When construction began in 1916, the architect suggested a third floor with a ballroom, but Mrs. MacKenzie vehemently objected to such ostentation. Even without a ballroom it was a grand house, with spacious rooms, verandas, a central hall big enough to play football, and two large fieldstone fireplaces. Ten years later Dr. MacKenzie's health began to fail and in 1926 he and his wife moved to their summer house in Frankfort, Michigan. He died there in 1930.

The spacious house soon proved it could handle a larger family. MacKenzie had been instrumental in expanding St. Joseph Mercy Hospital from its beginnings in a house on North State Street. That house later became the first Old Ladies Home. After the addition of a third floor, the Old Ladies Home moved into the MacKenzie house in 1927 and has been here ever since. The name soon changed to the Anna Botsford Bach Home, in honor of the energetic woman who had worked tirelessly to create a home for elderly women.

Today, more than 75 years later, the goal of the Anna Botsford Bach Home remains the same: to provide a homelike atmosphere for its sixteen elderly residents. The women are friends and companions, and there is a sense of affection and respect for the special care provided there. Through careful maintenance by the Board of Trustees, this structure and its beautifully landscaped site provide grace and charm to Liberty Street, one of the city's main thoroughfares. In 1990 much of the original interior woodwork in the dining room was restored by Jim Stacey. The Ann Arbor Historic District Commission presented the Home with a Preservation Award in 1989.

IHP

Louisa Pieper

1444 West Liberty Street

111

Jacob Beck House

1864

Lester Fader

Jacob Beck built this Greek Revival house in 1864 on twenty acres he had purchased from Eber White, a pioneer farmer in Ann Arbor Township. Beck had been a farmer himself for many years in Scio Township, where his family had settled in 1832. This was his retirement home, and he and his wife spent their last years here. "While residing in Ann Arbor he had no business cares, but enjoyed the rest which he had truly earned and richly deserved," a biographer wrote in 1906.

Interior living space was gained when the roof of the house was raised to permit the addition of the upper story. The bay window on the west is a recent embellishment. Well preserved after more than a century on its hill, the Beck house remains a private residence.

631 Second Street

Wiegant-Hochrein House

Circa 1885

The vernacular character of this house establishes it in no specific style group but it is an attractive house, representative of its type in the area. When built, it was identical with the home at 632 South First Street, (see 51).

Cabinetmaker Christian Wiegant and his family were the first occupants. Cousins of the Wiegants, Michael and Mary (Graf) Hochrein, came with their children in 1884 from Germany where Michael had been a baker and an overseer on a nobleman's demesne. Their third son, Ferdinand, was apprenticed to cabinetmaker Wiegant and together with his wife, Caroline (Radtke), became members of the household. In the 1890s the Wiegants moved around the corner to Mosley, leaving Ferdinand and Caroline to raise their seven children in this house. Ferdinand worked in the Allmendinger organ factory and later became an assistant to Silas Douglass at the Ann Arbor Gas Company.

The brickwork had already been painted when Mathematics Professor Fred Gehring and his wife Lois purchased the house in 1956. They replaced the dirt floors of the fieldstone basement with concrete and contemporized the house. Later Clarence and Ruth Roy renovated and landscaped the house in a charming and harmonious fashion. Clarence, a landscape architect, selected a ground cover of pachysandra for the front yard. Ruth, an interior decorator, chose shutters rather than curtains to show off the unusual framing of the living-room windows. Bricks for the back yard wall were salvaged in 1965 from the wreckage of Ann Arbor's old City Hall.

Kip Miller

NRHD, OWS

502 Sixth Street

136

John Lucas House

1882

John Lucas was born in 1841 in Hesse-Darmstadt near the Rhine river, where his father was a skilled stone and brick mason. The family emigrated to Canada in 1852. After learning the mason's trade at his father's side, John was apprenticed in all the building skills. Around 1870, after the death of his Canadian-born wife, he moved to Ann Arbor with his four small children. Married again to Elizabeth Wagner in 1872, a union which produced six additional children, he used his expertise to build this fine brick residence in 1882. Newspapers of the day took note of the "modern" Queen Anne style and the beautiful surroundings of the home.

A prominent Ann Arbor builder, Lucas erected several commercial structures and homes, as well as two large buildings (now gone) for the Medical Department of the University of Michigan. His widow lived in this home until it was sold in 1908 to the Koch family.

Karl H. Koch was also well known in Ann Arbor as a building contractor. Descendants of the Koch family are still in the house.

NRHD, OWS

Kip Miller

212 Third Street

Katherine Staeb House

150

1895

This is one of the homes which makes the Old West Side an area of special architectural interest. Built in the Queen Anne style popular in the late Victorian period, this charming house is particularly notable for the contrasting geometric patterns in the wood siding of the upper story and for the ornamentation of the porch. Katherine Staeb, widow of J. George Staeb, was the first resident and continued to live in the house until the 1930s.

Present owner, Susan Fisher, is taking great care to restore and maintain the exterior wood trim. She is adding a kitchen wing on the rear with care not to impair on the two principal facades.

NRHD, OWS

Kip Miller

165

719 West Washington Street

David F. Allmendinger House

1890

"A 1-1/2 acre Paradise on Washington Street," is how local journalist, Mary Hunt, summarized the David F. Allmendinger estate after reading in a 1905 newspaper article: "There is no prettier sight in Ann Arbor at this time of year than the magnificent grounds of David Allmendinger on West Washington — Mr. Allmendinger has a little Belle Isle park of his own."

David Friedrich Allmendinger was a true American success story. Born in Waiblingen, Wurttemberg, Germany in 1848, he came to America with his parents in 1851. They joined a large extended family which had been immigrating to Washtenaw County from Swabia since 1829. In 1867, Almendinger was apprenticed to organ builder Gottlieb Gaertner, who taught him the art of organ making and wood carving. He founded the Allmendinger Organ Company in 1872, and his earliest commissions were for organs for the two German churches in town. His real success, however, lay in selling organs to German farm families throughout the county.

He began modestly in the back rooms of his house at the corner of Washington and First Streets. He later built his brick factory here (see 49) and became Ann Arbor's second largest employer. In 1890 he was successful enough to build this house a few blocks to the west, in a still undeveloped part of town with creeks running through it. The house was a large, white rambling affair with a wrap-around porch and decorative wood trim in the front gable. Allmendinger needed a large house for his family of 13 children but did not believe in ostentation, so his house is simple by comparison with others from this era. He put most of his time and energy into creating his little "Belle Isle," his Garden of Eden.

Sturgis Collection

Early 20th century photographs capture the idyllic lifestyle. The family posed together under a massive oak tree for a portrait in 1905. Allmendinger's interests in landscape gardening were second only to organ making and he created from that acre and a half a dining terrace, a grape arbor, a goldfish pond with water lilies, a larger pond for carp, a croquet lawn, a log cabin, and the rustic gazebo and bridge, not to mention vegetable gardens and fruit trees of many varieties including plum, cherry, pear and apple, and a chicken coop and barn. Most of this he did by damming the creeks that ran through the property, creeks that are now part of the Allen Creek storm drain system.

David Allmendinger died in 1916. His daughter Julia, and her husband, Judge William Murray, sold the house next door, which they had built in 1909, and moved in with her mother. Pat Haskell, a granddaughter of David Allmendinger, remembers Judge Murray as an imposing and portly gentleman, and a real character who smoked five cigars a day and cussed all the time. Murray was the developer of Murray and Mulholland Streets to the south and east of this property. The house continued to be occupied by descendants of the Allmendinger family until 1991.

NRHD, OWS

Sturgis Collection

Index

page numbers are given after entry

A

B

Index

D

Index

H

Index

N

R

S

T